S0-ADJ-966

Practical Golf Course
Maintenance

Practical Golf Course Maintenance

The Magic of Greenkeeping

Second Edition

Gordon Witteveen

and

Michael Bavier

WILEY

JOHN WILEY & SONS, INC.

This book is printed on acid-free paper. ♾

Copyright © 2005 by John Wiley & Sons, Inc. All rights reserved

Published by John Wiley & Sons, Inc., Hoboken, New Jersey
Published simultaneously in Canada

No part of this publication may be reproduced, stored in a retrieval system, or transmitted in any form
or by any means, electronic, mechanical, photocopying, recording, scanning, or otherwise, except as
permitted under Section 107 or 108 of the 1976 United States Copyright Act, without either the prior
written permission of the Publisher, or authorization through payment of the appropriate per-copy
fee to the Copyright Clearance Center, Inc., 222 Rosewood Drive, Danvers, MA 01923, (978) 750-8400,
fax (978) 750-4470, or on the web at www.copyright.com. Requests to the Publisher for permission should
be addressed to the Permissions Department, John Wiley & Sons, Inc., 111 River Street, Hoboken, NJ 07030,
(201) 748-6011, fax (201) 748-6008, e-mail: permcoordinator@wiley.com.

Limit of Liability/Disclaimer of Warranty: While the publisher and author have used their best efforts in
preparing this book, they make no representations or warranties with respect to the accuracy or
completeness of the contents of this book and specifically disclaim any implied warranties of
merchantability or fitness for a particular purpose. No warranty may be created or extended by sales
representatives or written sales materials. The advice and strategies contained herein may not be suitable for
your situation. You should consult with a professional where appropriate. Neither the publisher nor author
shall be liable for any loss of profit or any other commercial damages, including but not limited to special,
incidental, consequential, or other damages.

For general information on our other products and services or for technical support, please contact our
Customer Care Department within the United States at (800) 762-2974, outside the United States at
(317) 572-3993 or fax (317) 572-4002.

Wiley also publishes its books in a variety of electronic formats. Some content that appears in print may
not be available in electronic books.

Library of Congress Cataloging-in-Publication Data:

Witteveen, Gordon.
Practical golf course maintenance : the magic of greenkeeping / Gordon
Witteveen, Michael Bavier.—2nd ed.
    p. cm.
    Includes index.
    ISBN 0-471-47582-3 (cloth)
    1. Golf courses—Maintenance.   2. Turf management. I. Bavier, Michael.
    II. Title.

GV975.W58 2005
796.352′06′9—dc22

2004009414

Printed in the United States of America
10 9 8 7 6 5 4 3

Contents

Foreword   vii

Preface   ix

Acknowledgments   xiii

1   Cutting Greens   1
2   Cutting Tees   25
3   Fairways   33
4   The Rough   43
5   Sand Bunkers and Their Maintenance   51
6   Water   67
7   Fertilizer   77
8   Topdressing   85
9   Coring, Spiking, and Verticutting   95
10 Spraying   109
11 Flagsticks and Tee Markers   119
12 Drainage   131
13 Seeding, Sodding, and Sprigging   143
14 Traffic and Paths   157
15 Rules of Golf That Affect Maintenance   167
16 Trees   173
17 Landscaping   183
18 Managing People   189
19 Budgeting for Tools and Machinery   199
20 The Turf Care Center   207
21 Greenkeeping Common Sense   217
22 Job Descriptions   225

Index   235
About the Authors   239

Foreword

There are several paths to follow when embarking on a career in golf course management. With a freshly minted turf degree in hand or not, one can brashly proceed with the mindset of inevitably making all the mistakes and learning from them, and not repeat them. That strategy can work, given sufficient time and latitude by forgiving employers. Alternatively, one can shorten the learning curve by walking quietly—listening, watching and absorbing—in the shadow of a mentor who has been there before and made most of the mistakes already.

Wisdom, skill, experience, and confidence are the fruits of a lifetime dedicated to growing good golf course turf. With 80+ years of golf course management experience between them, Gordon Witteveen and Michael Bavier eagerly share their treasure trove of knowledge through their "Magic of Greenkeeping" seminars and this second edition of *Practical Golf Course Maintenance*.

Although technically "retired" after 40 years of active greenkeeping, Gordon stays active and involved in the industry as owner and occasional acting superintendent of Pleasant View Golf Club in Brantford, Ontario. He keeps in touch with the active practitioners of the industry by sharing his experiences and opinions online with superintendents who frequent the TurfNet.com Forum, and also writes a popular monthly column for *TurfNet Monthly*.

Mike Bavier still enjoys one of the longest running tenures of any active superintendent, almost 35 years at the Inverness Golf Club near Chicago—an accomplishment by any standard.

As easy as it would be to rest on their laurels at this point in their lives, both Gordon and Mike enthusiastically plunge ahead and continue to extend their own boundaries, geographically, professionally and intellectually. They happily share their knowledge and enthusiasm with this updated and refreshed second edition.

Peter McCormick,
Skillman, New Jersey

Preface

Since 1998, when *Practical Golf Course Maintenance* was first published, the book has been widely read, not just in North America, but beyond, in faraway places such as South Africa, Australia, and New Zealand, to name but a few countries. Surprisingly, a good number of copies found their way to non-English-speaking countries like China, Thailand, and Slovenia. A Polish superintendent translated parts of the book for the benefit of a half dozen colleagues in that country. Several turf schools are still using the book as a text for their programs. We are delighted with its popularity. As the title indicates, the approach is practical, based on the experience of its superintendent/authors. In the original text we tried to use everyday English without any technical jargon, and we have maintained that approach in the second edition.

With the prodding of Latin American superintendents, *Practical Golf Course Maintenance* was translated into Spanish in 2003 and today remains the only text on the subject available to Spanish-speaking turfgrass managers.

Almost as soon as the book came off the press, the world of greenkeeping took a giant leap forward with the worldwide acceptance of the Internet, which facilitated the exchange of information among superintendents from all over the globe. Superintendents in Norway, Kenya, and Borneo were no longer isolated from the mainstream of greenkeeping. Questions about anyone's problem from anywhere received immediate replies via the Internet. The second edition is partly influenced by what we gained from participating in the online exchange of knowledge.

This edition also reveals our approach to the pesticide issue, which has been with us since Rachel Carson wrote *Silent Spring* and just won't go away. Superintendents have always enjoyed a reputation for being environmentally responsible, but the general public does not necessarily see it that way. Politicians have responded to voter concerns by enacting restrictive laws that limit the tools in our box to control the pests that attack our grass. In an effort to put a friendly face on golf course maintenance, superintendents have embraced the Audubon Program. They have created naturalized areas in the secondary roughs, resulting in many of our nation's golf courses becoming veritable havens for animal and plant life. But the pesticide issue remained. There are now regions and municipalities that have banned the use of pesticides entirely. Although in some cases golf courses have been temporarily exempted,

As a result of improved environmental practices, golf courses have become havens for wildlife. (Photo by Thomas Bastis, California Golf Club, San Francisco.)

it is only a matter of time for these sanctions to be more widely applied. Superintendents will have to learn to grow grass with fewer pesticides or perhaps none at all.

Green speed is a divisive issue among many superintendents. Some like their greens superfast, and others prefer and maintain a much slower speed on their putting surfaces. A weekly diet of televised golf, combined with pressure from low-handicap golfers, has encouraged the "speedniks" to raise the bar by several feet. In the process some have broken the speed limit, lost their grass and often their jobs as well. This second edition reflects our philosophy of moderation concerning the issue of green speed.

In this edition we have cut and slashed information that was dated or no longer applicable. We have tried to be more inclusive and have added information on overseeding, sprigging, and other southern practices for the benefit of readers in the Bermuda Belt. While basic greenkeeping is much the same from one country to the next, there are regional differences affected by climate, and we have tried to address these in this second edition.

The proliferation of information is not limited to the Internet. In the last ten years more books have been published on golf course maintenance than in the previous 100 years. It is now common to find a shelf full of turf books in superintendents' offices, and we are proud that, almost invariably, a copy of *Practical Golf Course Maintenance* is among these volumes. If, as reported, job security is a major concern among contemporary superintendents, we have proven at our respective positions that we were made to last. How we did it is revealed in this second edition. Read it, practice what we preach, and live to a happy retirement.

Acknowledgments

We are thankful for the many comments that we have received from our readers since this book was first published in 1998. In addition, we have had much feedback from the students in the classroom wherever we presented our seminar, "The Magic of Greenkeeping." These two sources affected our approach to this second edition.

The members of TurfNet.com unwittingly assisted with the new edition every time they posted commentary on the Forum. We read and retained much of that information, and it affected our thought processes as we rewrote the book.

Marie Thorne, with Syngenta in Canada, has always been a source of inspiration and encouragement. She helped with the first edition and again with the second.

Robert Randquist, superintendent at the Boca Rio Golf Club in Boca Raton, Florida, was our guiding light when it came to southern maintenance practices. He reviewed several chapters and made an important contribution.

We thank them all.

1

Cutting Greens

Of all the playing areas on the golf course, none is more important than the green. Fully 40% of all golf shots are played on and around the green. Golfers may tolerate mediocre fairways, poor bunkers, and sparse tees, but they expect, and deserve, puttable, near-perfect greens. When a golf ball rolls onto the green toward the hole, nothing must impede it from its true path. The factor that most affects the roll of the ball is the smoothness of the putting surface. Only shaving the green with a sharp mower will ensure that the golf ball rolls truly and smoothly.

All other work that is done to a green, such as topdressing, aerating, fertilizing, spraying, and watering are wasted unless the green is cut to perfection. No matter how healthy the green, no matter its dark green color, no matter its long root system, no matter the absence of disease, if the green is not cut perfectly, golfers will condemn it, and much work will have been wasted. Cutting the green to perfection is the icing on the cake, the glorious culmination of all the hard work that has been done before. That is why cutting greens is so vitally important in maintaining golf courses in top condition.

KEEPING THE MOWERS SHARP

Just as it is impossible to obtain a clean shave with a dull razor, the golf course mowers must be kept sharp at all times. To check whether a mower will cut grass, simply insert a strip of paper in the mowing cylinder and watch the blades shear it off. If the paper is creased and not cleanly cut, more than likely the same will happen to the grass when the mower traverses a green. If in doubt, get down on your hands and knees and examine the grass with a magnifying lens. A poorly cut grass blade will look bruised, with the veins in the leaf blade sticking out like damaged protrusions or tiny hairs. The collective effect of the bruised hairs is the appearance of a light sheen over the entire grass surface. This phenomenon is not limited to greens alone, but may also occur on tees, fairways, and roughs. It is a common problem that can easily be corrected by adjusting the cutting edge of the mower or by sharpening the mower. It is well to remember that dull mowers are a major factor in reducing the speed of greens. This is particularly important on greens in southern locales that are overseeded for winter play.

There are two fundamentally different methods of sharpening mower reels: spin grinding and relief grinding. The first method sharpens all the blades equally in a perfect cylinder with the entire width of the blade touching the cylinder and, subsequently, the bed knife. Relief grinding results when single blades of the mower are ground on an angle and only the front edge of a blade touches the bed knife. Both methods have their adherents, and both camps tend to believe in the superiority of their particular way.

Equally important to the cutting cylinder is the bed knife, which can be sharpened with or without a relief angle, depending on one's school of thought. One thing everyone agrees on is that the front edge or the face of the bed knife must also be kept sharp. When the front tip of the bed knife becomes rounded, it will once again result in bruised grass blades. The grinding of bed knives and cutting cylinders is usually done during the off-season. Once the grass is cut on a regular basis, the cutting cylinders need periodic attention and are occasionally back-lapped with a grinding compound to maintain their edge. The grinding compound is applied lightly with a brush as the reel turns backward. This process tones the cutting edges of both the reel blades and the bed knife and results in a superior quality of cut. Those who prefer spin grinding over relief grinding often do away with back-lapping, claiming that it is messy, bad for the mower bearings, and unnecessary.

THE HEIGHT OF CUT

A cutting unit that traverses across a greensward is supported by a front and a rear roller. These two rollers touch the ground, and the cutting cylinder turns between the rollers at some distance above the ground. This distance, known as the height of cut, is expressed in parts of inches or millimeters, depending on the country in which the course is located. For repair or adjustment of a cutting unit, it is placed upside down on a workbench. A straightedge is placed across the front and rear rollers; the distance between the straightedge and the top or front edge of the bed knife represents the height of cut. Measuring the height of cut is made infinitely easier by using a solid steel bar and a micrometer attachment. Because the height of cut is measured on a workbench, the resulting measurement is known as the *bench setting,* which often differs from the actual, on the green, cutting height. Why is this so? Superintendents discovered long ago that a cutting height of $\frac{3}{16}$ inch produced different results on different makes of mowers. Obviously, mowers made by different manufacturers are constructed differently and perform in their own peculiar ways, which are rarely similar. Recently a nifty gadget was introduced to the market that makes it possible to measure the actual height of cut on the green. It consists of a triangular prism that is placed on the putting surface with the edge touching the soil. The height of the grass mat is projected against incremental graduations, thus revealing the actual in-the-field height of cut. During the same process one can observe the quality of cut.

Heights of Cut on Greens

Imperial	Decimal	Metric
$\frac{1}{4}''$	0.250″	6.35 mm
$\frac{3}{16}''$	0.188″	4.76 mm
$\frac{1}{8}''$	0.125″	3.18 mm
$\frac{1}{16}''$	0.063″	1.59 mm

At most golf courses greens are cut at $\frac{1}{4}''$ or less. Above that height, the speed of the green slows dramatically and the enjoyment of golf, and particularly of putting, is reduced. A cutting height somewhere between and $\frac{3}{16}$ and $\frac{1}{8}''$ inch is acceptable to the vast majority of golfers. The recent introduction of dwarf species of bent and Bermuda grasses for putting greens has mandated the need to cut the grass below $\frac{1}{8}''$. Who would ever have thought it possible that greens could remain alive and healthy at less than a $\frac{1}{10}$ of an inch or 2 millimeters.

MOWERS AND CUTTING PATTERNS

There are basically only two types of greens mowers: riders and walkers. Both have their place and are widely used on golf greens all over the world. The first reel-type mower was patented in England in 1830, and although many changes and improvements have been made since then, the basic principle of having a cutting cylinder with blades shearing off the grass above the bed knife remains the same.

At first walk-behind greens mowers needed to be pushed. Later, engines were added, as well as many other refinements that made it possible to cut at lower heights. In spite of this progress, cutting greens with walkers remained

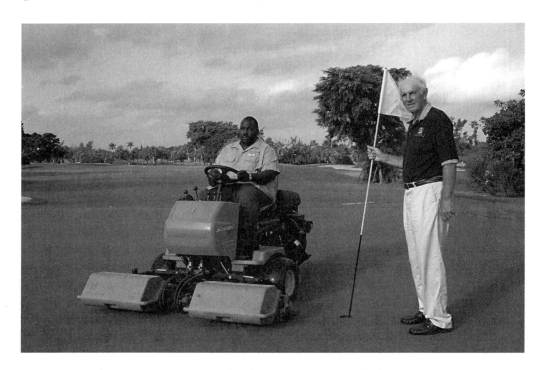

Triplex greens mower at work. Always remove the pin before commencing cutting. (Photo by Michael Dogood, Nassau, Bahamas.)

a slow and laborious process. Not surprisingly, when the first riding triplex greens mower came on the scene in 1963, its introduction was an immediate success. Large numbers of golf courses discarded their walkers and switched over to the riders. Just as quickly it became evident that the riding mowers had certain drawbacks. The heavy machines caused compaction and developed wear patterns. Just as serious were the hydraulic leaks that occurred from time to time and left streaks of ugly dead grass in their wake.

The walk-behind greens mowers have made a comeback and are now widely used on traditional golf courses with small greens. Golf courses with larger greens, 5000 suqre feet and more, find the riders more economical. The quality of cut of both types of units should not be a consideration. In fact, many superintendents use riders and walkers alongside each other. Often, the main body of a green is cut with a rider and a walker is used for the cleanup pass. Occasionally, when sufficient workers are not available, riders are used on weekends and the walkers for the rest of the time.

The distinctive checkerboard cutting pattern on putting greens is a desirable feature, very much appreciated by golfers. Although both riders and walkers are capable of producing these patterns, the use of walkers, because of their narrow tracks, produces a much more eye-catching design.

CUTTING THE GREEN: 10 STEPS
TO A PERFECT PUTTING SURFACE

1. It is customary for the golf course mechanic to check the mower, both in the shop and on the grass, for its ability to perform as expected. At the same time, the engine oil is checked and the gasoline tank topped off. The first function of the greens mower operator is to doublecheck to make sure that everything is in order.

2. Before commencing cutting, inspect the green by walking and scanning the putting surface. Look for stones and debris and fix ball marks in the process. Remove the flagstick and put it aside. Some fast operators believe that they can remove the stick as they pass by, but this is seldom a good idea and quite often leads to accidents.

3. Select the direction of cut, making sure that it is different from that of the previous day. Make the first cut across the hole and then work toward the front of the green, just in case golfers should catch up. With friendly golfers, you may even be able to finish the back of the green while they are putting. The direction of cut is changed every day to help reduce the buildup of grain. The grain on a green is the direction in which the grass leans, much like the nap of a livingroom rug. Change the cut every day, and, ideally, grain will be eliminated or at least reduced.

4. Straight cutting lines are essential. For the first pass, pick a tree on the horizon or some other feature in the landscape and keep looking at it as you mow a strip across the green. A straight line will result. For subsequent passes, it is no longer necessary to look at the horizon. Instead, focus on the straight line that has been completed at the far end of the green.

5. The overlap: Novice cutters should overlap several inches. Experienced cutters may reduce the overlap to a narrow strip. The markings on the baskets can be helpful in determining the degree of overlap. Missing a small strip of grass because of insufficient overlap is a cardinal sin against good greenkeeping. It results in golf balls jumping on the green and losing their direction.

6. The turn: It is important to make long, wide turns. Think of the shape of a light bulb or a teardrop while making the turn. Short, quick turns tear the turf on the apron. If a sand bunker or other obstruction is in the way of completing the turn, maneuver away from the hazard and turn in the adjacent rough. Operators should be cautious when making turns on wet aprons. Mowers may slip and slide on the greasy turf.

7. Check the basket for clippings while the green is being cut. Clippings tell a story: Uneven distribution within the basket means the cutting

Pedestrian unit to cut greens gently and perfectly. (Photo courtesy of Toro Corporation.)

unit is set improperly. Unbalanced quantities between the baskets on a rider may indicate differing heights of cut. If there is a problem, call the mechanic or the superintendent. If you think the green has been cut perfectly and the mowers are as sharp as a Gillette, come back in the evening. With the setting sun over your shoulder, every imperfection on the green is clearly visible and suddenly the perfect green does not look as perfect anymore.

8. Always empty the baskets before they become too full. Baskets laden with wet grass affect the quality of cut. If policy dictates that clippings be spread, learn the sweeping, coordinated motion of the upper body, arms, and hips that result in the perfect dispersal of the grass clippings. The clippings should be spread in the rough behind the green, *never* on the fairway in front nor in wildlife areas at the back. At many golf courses the clippings are collected and composted instead of being spread in the rough.

9. At the completion of the back-and-forth cutting pattern, the outer edge of the green must now be cut. This process is known as the *cleanup pass,* and it requires great diligence on the part of the operator. A cut into the adjacent apron will result in an ugly brown streak. Alternatively, to leave a few inches uncut can result in experiencing the

superintendent's wrath. Instead, slow the mower down to a crawl and concentrate on the edge with all your faculties. The cleanup pass may be omitted from time to time to prevent the buildup of wear patterns along the edge of the green.

10. Although many operators now use earplugs to protect their ears from excessive noise, it is important to listen to the sound of the mower, especially the sound of the reels touching the bed knives. Maladjusted reels can be detected simply by listening to the whir of the reels. When the green has been completely cut, replace the flagstick in the cup or hole liner. Take a whipping pole and brush off the clippings that may have fallen off the mower during cutting near the edge of the green and on the apron. Then stand back for a few seconds and admire your work.

The Sequence of Cutting Greens

A golfer once related how she can tell, when she gets to the golf club in the morning, whether the superintendent has the interests of the golfers in mind. "If the putting green has been cut," our golfer said, "it shows that the superintendent cares about the golfers." We agree, and we strongly recommend that the putting green be among the first greens that are cut in the morning, certainly before the golfers start arriving at the golf shop.

Using riding greens mowers, it is relatively easy to stay ahead of the players. Riding mowers cut faster than most golfers can play. Superintendents should be aware that some golfers may play from the back nine, and the needs of those golfers should be taken into account when the superintendent schedules cutting. When using walker-type greens mowers, three to four operators may be needed to cut all 18 greens, as well as the putting and pitching greens, and keep ahead of the golfers. The cutting sequence is then determined based on the experience of the superintendent, and the sequence will vary from course to course.

When greens are mowed after play has begun, it is best to change the sequence in which they are cut. Many superintendents start with the 18th green and work backward so as to avoid bothering the same foursome more than once during the course of their game.

During the height of the golfing and growing season the greens are frequently cut on a daily basis, but prudent greenkeepers know the beneficial effects of skipping a cut on occasion. This practice can be compared to not shaving one's face for a day after routinely doing so every morning. The skin on the jowls immediately improves after a day of rest. It feels softer and healthier. So it is with a green that has been given a rest from daily mowing.

Taking Care of Weak Greens

Not all greens are created equal. Certain greens may have been constructed from the same material and in the same manner, but there are other factors that cause greens to perform differently, not only during the growing season but also when the grass is dormant. Foremost among these factors is location. Greens exposed to the north tend to be colder and green up more slowly in the spring. The soil on greens that face the south tends to be much warmer, and the growth on such a green is more substantial. Another factor is shade. As a general rule, grasses don't grow well in the shade, and Bermuda grass needs more sun than any other turf. Therefore, greens that are surrounded by trees often struggle for survival. Trees should not be planted near greens. If they have been so established by well-meaning but ill-informed committees, then the trees should be trimmed regularly to reduce shading on the green. The early morning sun is particularly important for the health of the green.

Greens that become weaker during the progress of the golfing season should be treated gingerly. There are several steps that can be taken to prevent the further decline of a weak green:

1. Use only walkers on weak greens. Because they are lighter, they cause less mechanical damage and less compaction.
2. Periodically, roll instead of cutting.
3. Remove the dew on weak greens as early in the morning as possible. Dry greens are less subject to fungal diseases.
4. Do not cut weak greens until the grass is completely dry.
5. During extreme conditions of high temperature and humidity, consider cutting the green in late afternoon or early evening or not at all.
6. Syringe lightly during the hottest part of day.
7. Spread the wear by changing the hole daily, even twice daily if need be. Enlarge the green to allow for more pin placements.
8. Raise the height of cut ever so slightly.
9. Cut with solid rollers instead of grooved rollers. Do not use groomers.
10. Go easy on fertilizer and pesticide applications. Use organics and stay away from cocktail mixes. A mixture of pesticides, wetting agents, and liquid fertilizer is known colloquially as a "cocktail mix."
11. Improve the internal and subsurface drainage of a weak green.

On which days should superintendents choose not to cut their greens? Usually a day or time is selected that is least busy on the course. It may also be a rainy morning, or a cloudy day with no dew on the grass. Other factors enter into the decision as well. Intelligent superintendents who wish to survive the pitfalls of club politics should be aware of the playing schedules of the owners and club officials. That is only common sense, but forgetting this obvious fact

A fiberglass-tip pole is used to wipe the dew off greens and to scatter grass clippings on the aprons.

of life can quickly shorten the career span of an otherwise dedicated but foolhardy professional.

DEW REMOVAL

On mornings when greens are not to be cut and there is dew on the turf, it should be removed for the benefit of the golfers as well as for the health of the grass. Wet turf provides an ideal breeding ground for fungus disease, and drying the grass early in the morning either by means of dew whipping or simply by cutting the green is an essential part of disease prevention.

Methods of Dew Removal

1. Whipping with a fiberglass-tipped pole
2. Using roller squeegies, like those used on tennis courts

3. Dragging a rubber hose or similar device across the green
4. Running the syringe cycle on the irrigation system

We know from experience that disease budgets for courses that religiously practice dew removal are less than those for courses that never remove dew.

THE TRIPLEX RING SYNDROME

When a riding greens mower cuts the same swath day after day along the outer edge of the green, the tires of the mower are on the same track each time. If, in addition, the green is small or has been designed with many exotic curves, the weight of the mower and the wrenching action of the tight turn quickly kill the grass. Ugly dead or brown concentric rings, the dreaded "triplex ring syndrome" (TRS), will result. This is not some mysterious disease related to fairy ring, but pure and simple mechanical damage caused by the misuse of a mower.

TRS Prevention

What can be done to avoid the buildup or the appearance of the triplex ring? Most superintendents, at the first sign of concentric damage, switch back to walk-behind greens mowers. This is not always possible, nor is it wholly necessary. Many superintendents have successfully eliminated the triplex ring by the simple expedient of skipping the cleanup pass every other day. Even for one day on a weekend, the cleanup pass can be conveniently forgotten. It is amazing how quickly the stressed-out grass responds to, and recovers from, a rest from the regimen of daily shearing. It should also be noted that removing the Wiele rollers and the groomers from greens mowers will help eliminate triplex ring damage.

Golfers generally don't notice that the grass has not been cut for the first 3–4 feet near the edge of the green, and if they do, they probably won't mind. Golf balls that are putted from this area are rarely deflected in the initial stages, when they are traveling at their greatest velocity on their way to the cup. It is possible that the green along the outer edge may look shabby as a result of not having been cut. This is especially true during times of heavy dew on the grass. Carrying a whipping pole and brushing the greens along the outside perimeter will solve this shortcoming. Another method involves simply disengaging the reels prior to turning, but not lifting the cutting units. This helps to stop the clippings from falling off the rollers and leaving a mess along the outside of the green.

It is also a good practice to move the cleanup pass in from the edge of the green from time to time, to the extent of 1 or 2 feet. This method results in the tracks of the wheels being straddled and thus helps prevent the buildup of the triplex ring. Perhaps the best method of eliminating the triplex ring is to use walkers for the cleanup pass.

Architects wanting to break the monotony of round and oval greens continue to design fancy-shaped greens with many tight turns, much to the frustration of the superintendent. Superintendents, however, have a friend in Brent Wadsworth, owner of Wadsworth Construction, a company that has built more than 500 golf courses in North America and beyond. Wadsworth refuses to make curves on greens that have a radius of less than 25 feet, no matter what the drawings call for. That makes the development of a triplex ring virtually impossible.

Guidelines to Prevent Triplex Ring Damage

1. Skip the cleanup pass on alternate days.
2. Use walkers for the cleanup pass.
3. Move the cleanup pass away from the outer edge periodically.
4. Disengage the outer reel when using a rider.
5. Enlarge the perimeter of the green by reducing the severity of the curve.

Repairing Damage Due to Triplex Ring Syndrome

In the initial stages, when a triplex ring is just starting to show, it is relatively easy to stop the damage from becoming serious. Simply using a walker on such greens will do the trick. Once the grass has become seriously injured, however, more drastic measures are needed. Aerating with minitines and overseeding (a process that is described in detail in Chapter 9) are probably sufficient to promote the recovery of the turf. In really serious cases, the affected part may actually have to be resodded. In either case, seeding or sodding, the portion of the green that is being treated should be roped off and put out of play until recovery is complete.

HYDRAULIC SPILLS

A most unpleasant occurrence in using a riding triplex greens mower is the occasional bursting of the hydraulic hose. This usually happens when least expected and often goes unnoticed by the operator until it is too late. The results can be disastrous. A careless operator may not notice a hydraulic leak until the machine actually stops functioning. A perfect pattern of brown lines may result on several successive greens. Most often the burn of the grass is limited to a single narrow strip across a green and on a turn on the apron.

There have been many miracle cures advocated by fast-talking salespersons to save the grass from hydraulic burns: activated charcoal, liquid soap, kitty litter, and strips of felt tissue, to name but a few. None of them work satisfactorily. They make the superintendent or the greenkeepers feel better for a little while, because at least they are doing something, but none of these magic cures can bring dead grass back to life. The hydraulic oil from the mower that is squirted onto the green because of a loose-fitting or broken hose is very hot. It is so hot, in fact, that the grass immediately singes and dies upon contact with the oil. It may still look green, and a bit shiny at that, but it will certainly be brown in just a few days. The damage can be mitigated, however, if the area is washed off with a powerful spray of water during the initial stages. Adding a wetting agent at this point may also help, as long as it is also washed off.

Some superintendents now use vegetable oils in their hydraulic systems. These oils are biodegradable and less caustic to the grass. Others use a peat product, immediately after a spill, that absorbs much of the oil and lessens the damage.

Prevention

What can be done to prevent or at least minimize the occurrence of hydraulic burns on grass? It all starts at the "Turf Care Center" (see Chapter 20), the maintenance headquarters, with a good, well-qualified mechanic, the unsung hero in the golf course maintenance industry. A conscientious mechanic will regularly check and repair the hydraulic hoses on all machinery, but especially on the mowers. If a particular hose is worn or breaks, the mechanic will order not one, but two, to replace it. Thus, a stock of spare hoses is built up in the parts room.

The mechanic and an assistant usually work together to put out all machinery from the storage area in the morning, starting the engines and warming up the machines before they are taken out onto the course. In addition, trained operators look for telltale danger signs before taking mowers out. A small drip can be an indicator of a loose fitting. Fixing it, then and there, can prevent a disaster on the greens later.

Mixing a dye into the hydraulic oil makes it somewhat easier to see a leak, and this can help to prevent running the hydraulic tank completely dry. Some superintendents and mechanics have installed elaborate alarm systems that will immediately detect a drop in hydraulic pressure and signal the operator. Such systems are very expensive but can be justified in terms of preventing damage to a precious green, tee, or fairway.

As long as there are cars on our highways, there will be smashups. So it is on golf courses. As long as we use mowers equipped with numerous hydraulic lines, there will be mishaps and damaged turf. It is inevitable. Therefore, prudence dictates that we be prepared for the worst and be able to restore the damaged grass. A detailed plan of action should be handily available so that when a hydraulic spill does occur, immediate remedies can be executed.

Repairing Burnt Grass Caused by Hydraulic Spills

Quick action and clear thinking are necessary to cope with unexpected hydraulic spills. Several key members on the greens staff should be familiar with one or all of the following steps:

1. Remove the excess oil by spreading Turface or kitty litter over the affected area or applying Peat-sorb. Any one of these materials will soak up much of the oil and prevent the burn area from becoming a much wider strip than it needs to be. Applying a solution containing a wetting agent will further dilute the remaining oil. If a wetting agent is not available, use hand or dish soap and dilute with water.

2. Use a narrow aerator with pencil tines or minitines closely spaced, about 1 inch apart, and make a double pass. Hand-forking is an alternative method. Apply seed, making sure that some of it ends up in the tiny aerator holes. The seed that falls on the surface is mostly wasted, but the seed in the aerator holes has found a growth chamber. Below the surface, in a moist and warm environment it will quickly germinate and sprout up. The small tufts of grass, firmly rooted below the surface, will withstand golfer and mower traffic and rapidly join together to make an acceptable turf. In four to six weeks the ugly scar will disappear. Frequent topdressings will speed the process. Unfortunately, this practice is not an option on Bermuda grass greens.

3. If you absolutely must, take a sod cutter and remove the affected area and replace it with new sod. This is a drastic measure that will affect the putting surface much longer than seeding. Try to obtain a sod cutter with a narrow cutting blade. Make sure that the sod is cut thicker than normal, so that the sod won't shift under the golfers' feet or the greens mower. If there is no sod nursery from which to take the sod, consider taking it from the putting green or along the edge from the back of a regular green. The sod should be carefully laid and tamped down just a fraction of an inch below the adjacent surface. After sodding has been completed, the strip must be topdressed and rubbed with the back of an aluminum rake or, better yet, with a Levelawn. This makes for a perfectly smooth surface that will quickly grow in and become part of the regular green. Although a mechanized sod cutter can be used, hand-pushed, narrow-bladed sod cutters are available that are ideally suited for this type of repair.

Remove the damaged turf with a narrow sod cutter.

The problem with the sodding process is that the sod needs regular watering until it becomes firmly rooted. This means that someone has to be available to water it, even on weekends and perhaps during late afternoons and evenings. If the sod were to die, it would be one mistake compounding another, and a crisis difficult to survive, especially for novice superintendents.

4. Repairing turf on damaged tees and fairways is slightly less cumbersome because these surfaces are not as critical as the green. In many cases, when the scar is narrow, the adjacent turf will grow in quickly. It may still be necessary to either seed or sod or even use a divot mix to help promote growth. In any

Replace with sod from the back of the green so it will blend in.

case, it is always better to repair the damage than to let the visual effects of the dead turf linger. Golfers will lose their patience with superintendents who are indecisive or procrastinate.

CLIPPINGS

Clippings can be spread in the rough behind the green or in the rough between two fairways as long as it is done properly. Leaving clumps of clippings in the playing areas interferes with the game and is not acceptable. For that reason many superintendents collect the clippings and compost them on-site or have them hauled away to a waste area.

We have already discussed the significance of constantly checking the grass clippings in the basket(s) of the mower when cutting greens. Important information can be gleaned from uneven distribution inside the basket. This may indicate that the mower is dull or out of adjustment, but there is more to be learned from the clippings.

Grass clippings have an odor all their own. It is very pungent and distinctive when the green is healthy, but when the green is sick, the clippings don't smell very good. Early warnings of a pending fungus disease outbreak can often be detected by simply sticking your nose into a handful of clippings. A foul odor is a sure giveaway that brown patch disease is trying to gain a foothold. Old-time greenkeepers knew this secret long ago and could often be seen on all fours, sniffing a green and trying to learn about pending problems. In the baskets, among the clippings, look for adult insects of the hyperodes weevil or the aetanius bug. Keeping track of the number of bugs found in the clippings may help to determine the need for spraying an insecticide.

Clippings can also reveal the succulence of the turf. Overfertilized greens produce an abundance of fat, juicy snippets of grass. Lean greens make for wiry, thin, stringy leaf blades. If there are fertilizer granules mixed in with the clippings, it probably means that the green should have been cut with the baskets off after applying fertilizer. Even the small-particle, homogenous fertilizers get caught in the reels and end up in the baskets, and that is definitely not the idea. It makes no sense to pick up the expensive nutrients from the greens and spread them in the roughs. Better to remove the baskets and water in the fertilizer.

It is a common practice to empty the baskets after cutting a green. If the baskets need emptying before the green is finished, it probably means that the green is overfertilized. If, however, the baskets still do not need to be emptied after four or five greens are cut, it indicates that the turf is lean and thin and possibly did not need cutting at all. A light rolling with a high-speed greens roller might have been a better method of creating a perfect putting surface.

Greens rollers were first used on lawn bowling greens in Australia. The original models were 6 feet across, much too wide to cope with undulations of putting greens but ideal for flat bowling greens. Their purpose was to speed up the green without cutting it. Lawn bowling greens are frequently maintained at the very edge of survival in order to be hard and fast. Cutting greens maintained under such stressed-out conditions would almost certainly mean instant death to the grass. A light rolling achieves the desired result without removing any of the grass growth.

Australian golf course superintendents, who often manage bowling greens as well, adopted the speed roller for putting greens by the simple expedient of making it narrower. Such rollers quickly became a hit in North America and are now widely accepted all over the world.

THE FIRST CUT OF THE SPRING

Superintendents in northern regions look forward to the first cut of the spring. It is the harbinger of a new season, full of hope and expectation, and many superintendents insist on making the first cut themselves. The thrill of trying new mowers, combined with the fragrance of the freshly cut grass, brings memories of past seasons and lost youth. At the same time, there is a wonderful opportunity to outline the greens.

During the previous season, the greens may have lost some of their shape because cautious operators made them smaller with each successive cutting. In the process, curves and shapes were lost. Spring is the time to cut into the apron and re-outline a green to its original configuration. Small adjustments can be made without getting off the mower, but if the green will be substantially enlarged, it is best to outline the change with a paint gun. It may be necessary to mark the new outline several times before it becomes established.

Cutting the apron to greens height is a drastic measure that should be performed only during the spring when the grass plants have an inner drive to recreate and are able to recover from the severe scalping. At any other time of year such treatment will result in instant death of the grass plants, but in the spring the grass will manage to survive. Many superintendents also like to cut greens themselves from time to time during the season, even at large operations where there is plenty of staff, not only for exercise, but also to get a feel for the course. It is part of the mystique of being a golf course superintendent and having a love affair with one's golf course. Such a relationship needs constant nurturing on the part of the superintendent, and cutting greens from time to time is an important ingredient of that process.

FAST GREENS

Television golf and the stimpmeter have combined to put pressure on superintendents to provide faster greens—greens so fast that, according to some witty tour players, a dime left as ball marker would slide off the green. That is an exaggeration, of course, but with an element of truth. Greens have been cut to the quick, rolled, and left to dry, all in a quest for speed. It is a miracle that the poor grass plants manage to survive, and all too often they do not.

The stimpmeter is a device used to measure the speed of a green in feet and inches. A ball is rolled from a slotted steel bar at a predetermined height, and its progress is measured on the green. The direction is reversed, and the process repeated two to four times. Several measurements are averaged, and a value for a particular green is arrived at. The stimpmeter should be used on a flat portion of the green. That may present a problem, inasmuch as many greens have severe undulations and no flat areas are available to measure the speed.

It is not uncommon for greens to reach speeds of 12 and even 13 feet. The stage is set every spring at the time of the Augusta National, where lightning-fast greens are commonplace. Golfers from all parts of the world watch and then demand that their superintendents emulate not only the conditions but, especially, the speed of the greens. Those weak-willed souls who give in to the golfers and cut their greens to the root hairs usually lose their grass and their jobs at the same time.

Until the advent of the dwarf cultivars, no grass, whether it was Bermuda,

*Double cutting greens for special events to increase putting speed is common practice.
(Photo by Gary Mathis, Brookfield, Connecticut.)*

bent, or *Poa annua,* could survive being cut at $\frac{1}{8}$ inch for any length of time. Yet rookie superintendents kept on trying at their own peril. They accommodated the club champion and the captain, but completely forgot about the needs of the grass. In the horribly hot and dry summer of 1995, when grass across the continent was dying by the acre on the golf courses, many greens could have been saved if they had just been cut a little higher. The introduction of high-density dwarf varieties of both bent and Bermuda grasses changed all that. On these grasses cutting heights below $\frac{1}{8}$ of an inch are commonplace, indeed a necessity, and green speeds of 12 to 13 feet can be maintained for extended periods.

No factor affects the speed of a green as much as the height of cut on the mower. Superintendents should select mower settings that will ensure the survival of the grass and produce a green speed that is acceptable to the majority of the golfers. A dry wind on a sunny afternoon will speed up the greens as much as 6 inches on the stimpmeter, at the same time stressing the grass.

For special events, such as club competitions and tournaments, the green speed can be increased a trifle by the simple expedient of double cutting. This is an old trick that smart superintendents have known about for years. The double cut results in a smoother and faster putting surface. It is not necessary to double cut the entire green, just three or four cuts on either side of the cup will do nicely. Remember, the ball is most likely to deviate from its true path as it slows near the cup. This is all the reason that the turf should be perfect near the hole, so that more putts will drop and golfers will applaud the hard-working superintendent.

Recently a new machine was introduced to the golf course industry that helps speed up the greens without cutting the grass. As discussed earlier, the greens roller was first used on bowling greens in Australia and later adapted for more undulating golf greens. These fast-moving machines can roll a green in a jiffy and can appreciably increase the stimpmeter readings, by as much as 6–8 inches. The greens rollers have been refined, and rollers are now available to replace the cutting units on the triplex greens mowers. An extra dimension is added by making the rollers vibrate and create a fast, smooth putting surface. After a rolling, the grass blades are still there, to breathe and keep the plant alive. The greens roller is a useful tool and can be used occasionally instead of cutting, or on a regular basis in addition to cutting. We know of superintendents double cutting and double rolling the greens daily for extended periods, but such practices are hazardous, particularly when both the temperature and the humidity are on the rise.

SLOW GREENS

Amazingly, there are some golf clubs that don't want any part of fast greens. Such courses take pride in having slow greens. Using the United States Golf Association's (USGA) guidelines, a green that stimps between 5 and 6 feet is considered slow. In terms of height of cut, this translates to $\frac{1}{4}$ inch or 6 millimeters.

The problem with slow greens is that they tend to develop thatch and grain. Superintendents who cut their greens at the $\frac{1}{4}$-inch height should be vigilant about the potential formation of a heavy layer of mat or thatch. On such greens, the groomer attachments on the mowers must be used on a regular basis. Topdressing frequently becomes important as well, to prevent the buildup of thatch.

OVERSEEDED GREENS

Bermuda greens in the transition zone, south of the Mason-Dixie Line in the United States, experience a period of dormancy during the winter months. Golfers do not like to putt on brown grass, and turf managers respect their wishes by overseeding the greens with northern grasses such as rye grass, rough stalk bluegrass, and bent grass, or any combination of these three. During the overseeding period, grass is left to grow at a higher height of cut and greens are watered several times daily to promote seed establishment. Once the seed is actively growing, the height of cut is reduced to acceptable putting levels, but rarely low enough to satisfy all golfers. Overseeded greens have a reputation of being slow and inconsistent, but recent advances in plant breeding have resulted in superior species of grass for the purpose of overseeding. In addition, superintendents have become more adept at establishing and maintaining overseeded greens.

At the conclusion of the winter months the reverse transition from winter to summer grasses is encouraged by methods that favor Bermuda grass and are harmful to northern turf. This involves reducing the height of cut, verticutting, and controlling nutrient intake.

TEMPORARY GREENS

There are times when the regular green cannot or should not be played on. On such occasions, the ingenuity of the superintendent is called upon to create a temporary green. If the temporary green is to be in use for only a few hours or perhaps even a day, it is simply a matter of moving the pin of the regular green and cutting a hole in the fairway. A sign explaining the reason for the temporary green is advisable, and it is best to place the sign on the tee of the hole that is under repair.

Golfers will accept a temporary green much more readily if they know the reason. Another little trick that will put a smile on a golfer's face is to use a larger-than-normal cup on a temporary green. Use an 8-inch hole auger for the initial cut, and then place the regular hole inside it. Even a square hole that can be made with the help of an Australian Turf Doctor, a handy turf repair tool invented by an Aussie greenkeeper, can be used to give an unusual twist to a temporary green.

When a temporary green is planned to be in use for an extended period, more care should be taken in its preparation—golfers deserve a decent putting surface at all times. Prepare the temporary green at least several months in advance of its intended use. Select a level portion of the fairway and mark out the green with a paint gun. It is very important that even this temporary green be of sufficient size, at least 3,000 square feet. Double cut the temporary green about $\frac{1}{8}$ inch lower than the existing fairway. Then verticut the new putting surface in two different directions. Fertilize moderately with a starter fertilizer, and topdress heavily. For such a relatively small green it is best to work the topdressing in with the backside of an aluminum rake or, better still, with a Levelawn, another marvelous Australian invention. If there are old divot marks in the green, these should be repaired with a hole cutter or similar tool. In northern climates the temporary green should also be seeded. In southern regions, a Bermuda turf will automatically adjust to the new cutting height.

At this time it is important that the green be soaked thoroughly. This can best be done with a roller-base sprinkler connected to a fairway outlet. Finally, it is necessary that the temporary green be fenced off with stakes and ropes and be declared as "Ground Under Repair," or GUR for short. It is best to place a sign on the green explaining to the golfers what you are trying to do. The golfers will gladly take a free lift as long as they know its purpose.

Over the next six to eight weeks, institute a regular cutting regimen, lowering the height of cut by $\frac{3}{16}$ of an inch every week until the normal cutting height is reached. In the meantime, topdress and verticut at least two more times; also consider aerating at least once prior to opening up the green to golfers. Temporary greens have to be treated with loving care by the superintendent and greens staff. They should be inspected frequently to ensure their health and condition. If the reason for a temporary green is the rebuilding of an existing green, then it is all the more important that the temporary green is a near-perfect putting surface. There will be less pressure on the superintendent to open the new green prematurely if birdie putts are frequent on the temporary green.

Steps to Establish a Temporary Green

1. Select a suitable location that is reasonably flat and spacious.
2. Outline the green, rope it off, and declare it as GUR.
3. Double cut the existing turf at a slightly lower height and remove clippings.
4. Double aerate and verticut the entire area.
5. Apply seed, starter fertilizer, and topdressing.
6. Keep the green moist and water regularly.
7. Gradually reduce the height of cut at increments of $\frac{3}{16}$ inch weekly.
8. Continue topdressing
9. Fine-tune to putting green quality.

DOUBLE GREENS

Ever since St. Andrews was established along the shores of the North Sea, double greens have been part of golf. In North America, double greens are an occasional oddity that attract attention but also present potential injury liability problems. To prevent the danger of golfers hitting into each other, double greens tend to be of immense size, and it seems to take forever to cut double greens. But double greens are spectacular to look at and to play on, although it often happens that much of the grass is never used. The perceived saving in maintenance is frequently not realized. Therefore, double greens are often abandoned after just a few years and converted to separate greens.

SAND GREENS

There are places in this world where it is just too difficult or too expensive to grow grass greens, such as arid areas and extreme locations. We have found that in the prairie states of the United States and the provinces of western Canada, sand greens were until recently quite common. We also discovered sand greens on the Royal Kathmandu Golf Course in Nepal, although these have since been converted to grass. To create a firm surface on sand greens, old engine oil or diesel fuel is added, and a local rule permits players to smooth the putting line to the hole by dragging a small mat over the intended line of play.

GREENS FOR HOME OWNERS

Every superintendent is asked from time to time to build a putting green in someone's backyard. The temptation to accept the assignment is often irresistible. Ardent and enthusiastic golfers have a way of making otherwise rational superintendents lose their heads. We have built several backyard greens during our long greenkeeping careers, and every single one has been converted to flower beds or a swimming pool, or has just become part of the lawn, characterized by an overabundance of *Poa annua*. During their brief existence, such greens are the pride of their owners, but rarely do they last beyond a few years.

THE EXPENSE OF BUILDING A BACKYARD PUTTING GREEN

1. When home owners dream of a putting green for their backyards, they think in terms of one similar in size to their living room or master bedroom, and that is just too small. The minimum size for a backyard green is 1,500 square feet. Twice as large would be better. Invariably, the existing soil needs to be modified, which means importing several truckloads of sand and topsoil.
2. An automatic irrigation system is a must. It may be possible to modify the existing sprinklers, but undoubtedly several new irrigation heads, new pipe, and a new controller may be needed.
3. Although it is initially less expensive to seed the new green rather than sod it, both operations require expertise and much can go wrong before a desired result is achieved.
4. Maintenance involves buying a new or used mower and cutting the

green four to five times a week. Perhaps it is best to use a push-type mower for a small backyard green. Using such a mower would provide an opportunity for regular exercise and eliminate the need for joining a health club. Maintenance also includes fertilizing, spraying with pesticides, and topdressing the green on a regular basis. Spraying for diseases should be postponed as long as possible. Once the green has been treated with a pesticide, it quickly becomes dependent on regular chemical sprays.

Obtaining a cup and a flagstick is probably the easiest part of the assignment. Making sure that the maintenance work is done on a regular basis is by far the toughest part.

Home owners should analyze their reasons for wanting a backyard putting green. Is it to improve their putting and chipping skills, or is it because they want to live on a golf course? Most golf course superintendents discourage golfers from building backyard putting greens. But if a golfer has completely lost his or her senses and insists on proceeding, then as a last resort, we advise our colleagues to charge double the normal rate for all the work. The hope that this will bring the irrational golfer back to reality. If it doesn't, the client deserves to pay dearly as a penalty for foolishness. Knowing beforehand that the backyard green will probably not last very long should make a home owner realize that it is best to build such greens modestly.

Recently, the manufacturers of artificial turf have improved the quality of their materials. There now are available ready-made contoured greens that are completely made from artificial materials. Such greens are used as target greens on driving ranges and are ideally suited for backyard use. Like artificial Christmas trees, they look just like the real thing and are much less expensive to boot.

BALL MARKS

The introduction and the acceptance of nonmetal or soft spikes has improved the day-to-day condition of golf greens immeasurably. Gone are the days of spike-marked greens and putts deflected on the way to the hole. But ball or pitch marks remain and continue to scar and mar otherwise perfect greens. Ball marks are caused by high-flying golf balls leaving ugly indentations in a soft green. Ball marks are rarely a problem on firm greens, and on that premise we can assume that badly ball-marked greens are often the result of overwatering. We cannot stop the rains that produce soft greens, but we can turn off the sprinklers and help prevent the problem.

Ball marks left unrepaired become the responsibility of the superintendent and the greens crew. On a daily basis, the task of repairing them falls to the greens cutter and/or the hole changer. Some superintendents assign special staff to fix ball marks with seed and divot mix. In severe cases periodic top-dressing alleviates the problem. Of course, we can also appeal to the golfers to repair the damage resulting from their actions. All golf courses, without exception, encourage players to repair ball marks. In fact, the practice is a primary ingredient of the codes of conduct and ethics everywhere.

SUMMARY

We must assume that the great majority of golfers will want to continue putting on grass greens and that these greens must be smooth and reasonably fast. A superintendent's greatest accomplishment will be to provide such greens. In the process, the superintendent walks a fine line between ultimate success and abject failure in balancing the needs of the grass with those of the golfers.

2

Cutting Tees

Golfers receive their first impression of a course on the tee, usually the first tee, unless they are playing in a shotgun tournament or are starting on the back nine. Although all tees are important, none is more important than the first tee. We want our golfers to feel comfortable on the first tee. Everything possible should be done to allay fear and anxiety, so that the golfer will be relaxed and able to execute a near perfect drive from the first tee. Such a marvelous beginning sets the tone for the rest of the game.

Golf course superintendents contribute much to a golfer's happiness or, at times, to his or her despair. What do golfers expect from the superintendent on the tees, particularly on the first tee, that will put them in a positive frame of mind?

1. The surface of the tee must be perfectly flat. The tee may tilt slightly forward, backward, or sideways, depending on the architect's specifications, but the surface must be flat and even. No bumps or hollows are permitted; no sudden grade changes allowed. The reason is obvious: The golfer needs a level stance to make a perfect shot.

On elevated tees, the surface may tilt slightly forward, so that golfers can see more of the fairway when the blocks are at the rear. On fairways that slope uphill, the tee should also have a built-in incline. The advice of an architect or a golf course builder should be sought before determining the incline of the teeing surface, but regardless, the tee surface itself should always be flat and remain that way.

2. The first tee must provide some degree of privacy. Most golfers are apprehensive about driving from the first tee. Having to hit one's drive in front of a critical gallery can be nerve-racking. Without creating shady conditions that are detrimental to the growth of healthy grass, superintendents should

NWTC Library
2740 W. Mason St.
Green Bay, WI 54307

work with architects to provide some privacy. Once away from the clubhouse, tees should be as open as possible and trees and shrubs should be kept away from the tees.

3. Tees should not be cramped, but spacious and sufficiently large to accommodate 200 to 300 golfers a day. It is to be hoped that some of that number will use the forward or ladies' tees, and perhaps an equal number will play from the championship tees. The main tee, from which the majority of players will hit their drives, should be at least the same size as the corresponding green. On par 3 holes, the tee should be twice the size of the green. A rule of thumb dictates that 100 square feet of teeing area is needed for every 1,000 rounds of golf on par 4 and par 5 holes. On par 3 holes, that area should be doubled for every 1,000 rounds. Some believe that the tees should be the same size as the green on par 4 and par 5 holes, and double the size of the green on par 3 holes. Whatever rule is applied, tees are rarely too big.

The tee on the first hole should be larger than most others. Many golfers coming to the first tee need to warm up. Frequently, they do so by hacking away at the turf on the first tee. Provide plenty of space, and the tee can be repaired on a regular basis and recover quickly.

4. The slopes surrounding the tees should be gentle, so that golfers can ascend to the deck without having to climb a steep grade and be out of breath when they must drive the ball. Although steps and stairs are objectionable around tees for a variety of reasons (expensive to maintain and aesthetically unappealing), in some cases the location of a particular tee makes it necessary to provide a way for a golfer to get up to the tee. It is then up to the superintendent to concoct something that is functional and not too ugly.

5. A tee should be firm, for better footing, but not so hard as to make it impossible to get a wooden tee into the ground. The tee should also be free of ugly divot scars, especially the first tee, for that all-important first impression. The grass on tees is usually cut somewhat longer than on greens, but it should be sufficiently short to ensure that there is never any grass between the clubhead and the ball at the time of address.

CUTTING TEES

Because most tees are elevated, they are inherently difficult to cut. Steep slopes make it hard for operators to maintain control of their mowers as they make tight turns. Nevertheless, it is important to cut a tee perfectly; otherwise, its appearance will be destroyed by a shoddy job of mowing. Before beginning to cut, walk over the tee and look for broken wooden tees and debris such as branches and twigs. Everything must be picked up and discarded before cutting the tee.

It is important to change the direction of cut on the tee, just as on the green, in order to prevent the buildup of thatch and grain. Usually, on the day before the weekend, the tees are cut lengthwise. The striping that points to the center of the fairway assists the golfer subconsciously to drive the ball in that beneficial direction.

Many superintendents use riding greens mowers on the tees, but on smaller tees walk-behind mowers are preferred. Because tees are usually not cut on a daily basis, the triplex ring is not a serious problem. When it does develop, omitting the cleanup pass will quickly remedy the situation.

Tees are normally cut every second day, or three times per week at a minimum. It is a mistake not to cut tees over a long weekend. On the third day of a long weekend the grass on the tee will look quite shabby, and by the time the tee is cut on the morning of the fourth day, the grass is much too long and will suffer from the shock of having so much of its growth removed all at once. Tees that are growing actively and are not cut on a timely basis become spongy, an objectionable condition from a golfer's point of view.

We have already mentioned the slopes that make cutting tees a difficult operation. There are other obstacles on and around tees, such as benches, ball washers, garbage cans, and divot boxes, that must be avoided while cutting tees. In addition, there are tee blocks that have to be put aside, while the tee is being cut, and returned precisely to their former places. For all these reasons, cutting tees requires not only great dexterity but also much savvy and experience. Cutting tees is a job for veteran golf course workers, and for rookies only as a last resort.

Ever since the U.S. Open was played at Pebble Beach in 1992 on rectangularly cut tees, golfers have been demanding that superintendents follow suit and cut the tees with right angles so that they can be lined up perfectly with the fairways. This is not possible with banana-shaped tees or free-form tees. To cut a tee rectangularly is very difficult and can be done only with mowers that are equipped with on-and-off devices for individual reels. Cutting tees in such a manner is a luxury that not every club can afford.

Golf courses with modest budgets may decide that cutting tees with greens mowers is too expensive for their liking, and choose less sophisticated mowers. Some will use utility reel-type mowers, trim mowers, or even rotary mowers to cut their tees. In any case the height of cut will be higher, and golfers on such courses will need to use longer wooden tees on which to place a golf ball.

Many otherwise near-perfect tees are spoiled because the surrounds have not been trimmed adequately. Long grass at the front of a tee may impede a low ball as it is driven from the tee. At the back of a tee, long grass may make it impossible for the club to be taken back at the time of address. Superintendents should be vigilant about such adverse conditions and make sure that the surrounds of tees are trimmed regularly, especially on tees in out-of-the-way places. The latter tend to be forgotten because they are not inspected with regularity.

When all is said and done, golfers of all calibers will agree on one thing only, and that is that tees need to be perfectly flat in order to execute a perfect shot. Golfers will accept divot-scarred tees, worn tees, hard tees, or soft tees, but

*The edges of tees in desert settings are trimmed from time to time
to keep the grass from spreading into the sand.*

never tees with too many undulations. Superintendents must do everything in their power and employ all their skills as greenkeepers to make sure that tees are kept flat and firm and have an adequate cover of grass at all times.

Tees are rarely constructed with the same degree of diligence that is devoted to the creation of greens. Tees seldom have a network of tile or a bed of gravel in their base, and as a result, the drainage on most tees is not nearly as good as it is on greens. In addition, the soil mix used for greens tends to be selected after much study, whereas for tees it is frequently just a matter of pushing the topsoil back onto the finished grade. Tees therefore will lose their shape and their grade.

THE HEIGHT OF CUT ON TEES

The demands of the game dictate that a ball on a wooden peg is sufficiently elevated above the grass, so that it can be cleanly struck with a driving club.

The large heads of contemporary driving clubs have made it all the more important that the grass be closely cropped. The grass mat on today's tees is of the same quality as the greens of yesteryear. In fact, some quality tees are cut at the same height as the greens, and it is not unusual to find a putting cup at the back of the tee for golfers to practice their putting strokes while they wait their turn to tee off.

Thus, it is not surprising then that on some tees the height of cut can be as low as $\frac{1}{8}$ inch, but far more often it will be $\frac{1}{4}$ inch, which is comparable to that of slow greens. When we get away from bent and Bermuda grasses into fescues, bluegrasses, ryes, and even kikuyu turf, the height of cut will fluctuate nearly $\frac{1}{2}$ inch. A cut any higher than that will make for many unhappy golfers.

FORWARD TEES

Playing mixed golf makes one realize very soon that female golfers who use the forward tees, also known as ladies' tees or senior tees, are often at a serious disadvantage when it comes to the placement of the tee in relation to the fairway. Superintendents must take part of the blame. They have been as guilty as architects in constructing unduly small, poorly directed tees and unsually high tees that are an eyesore and a blemish on the landscape. Forward tees are often an afterthought. They are frequently inadequately built and cannot be maintained properly. Superintendents owe it to their profession and to all women golfers to provide sufficient tee-off space of the same quality as provided for men.

PRACTICE RANGE TEES

No tee takes more abuse and no tee is more difficult to maintain than the practice range tee. The primary cause is that many practice tees are far too small for the daily traffic. Another reason is that there is not enough time for the grass to recover before it must be used again. For these reasons superintendents often use a combination of artificial grass and real grass. By switching between the two, the life of the grass tee can be extended. If you closely watch golfers practice, you will see that some dig up the turf systematically. Divot by divot they denude a measurable area in a matter of minutes. Fortunately, there are many other golfers who treat the turf gently and kindly. In any case, the practice range tee needs constant attention. The divots must be swept or blown off daily and the scars refilled with seed, fertilizer, and topsoil. Some superintendents battle with bentgrass on the driving range tee; many others have switched over to rye grass that grows faster and fills in more quickly. In either case, the turf must be encouraged with extra fertilizer and water. Just as on all other tees, the grass should be cut on a regular basis.

WHAT SUPERINTENDENTS CAN DO TO IMPROVE TEES

1. Improve the drainage. Not all tees are equal; some drain well and others dry up very slowly. The latter must be tiled. This is routine maintenance, and superintendents should not use the club's committee structure as a reason for inaction. When it has been determined that tiling a particular tee is necessary, prepare the plans and execute them during the shoulder or the off-season. In northern climates, improving the drainage will also reduce the deleterious effects of soil heaving as a result of deep ground freezing.
2. Regrade the tops of the tees so that they are perfectly level. It is best to remove all the sod before starting the grading operation. Chunks of sod will hamper the grading work. Use one of several new graders that are now employed by golf course construction companies. Some of these are laser operated, and their use will guarantee a perfectly flat surface. It is vitally important to maintain the edge between the flat level top and the side slopes. If the edge is lost during excessive grading, the tee top will be rounded, a result that is most undesirable.
3. Enlarging an existing tee can be tricky, because it is almost impossible to match and marry the old and the new tee perfectly. The extended portion of the tee will probably settle somewhat, and the joint will become clearly visible. In most cases it is better to regrade the entire surface and turf it with a homogenous stand of quality grass.
4. Once a perfectly flat top has been established, it is necessary to keep it that way. Applying topdressing improperly will distort the flat surface. We have also seen tee surfaces that have been ruined by the improper application of divot mixes. How is this possible? It is caused by applying divot mix by the shovelful and working it in haphazardly. Greenkeeping tools such as drag mats, the backs of aluminum rakes, and Levelawns should be used at all times on the surface and only carefully near the edge. Brushes will adequately work soil mixes into the grass mat but often leave waves and undulations, results that should be avoided on perfectly level tees.
5. The location of sprinkler heads can be a nuisance on tees. All sprinklers need repair and maintenance from time to time and this may involve digging a deep hole in the middle of a tee. Consider the consequences should this happen during an important event! Therefore, if at all possible, sprinklers should be located off to the side of the tees. On large, wide tees this may not be possible, nor is it nearly as critical.

TEE RENOVATION AND BUILDING NEW TEES

1. Site selection is best left to a golf course architect, who should be encouraged to make the forward or ladies' tees part of the overall master plan. Naturally, the superintendent may have some input in the decision inasmuch as he or she is familiar with the property, the drainage, and the irrigation lines.
2. It is vitally important that the new tee is properly aligned with the center of the landing area.
3. Construction can be done either in-house or by a reputable golf course contractor. No tee should be smaller than 20 by 30 feet. Small tees are difficult to cut and for sprayers and aerators to get around. The importance of good drainage and high-quality topsoil has already been stated.
4. Seed, sod, or sprig the new tee. See Chapter 13.
5. The tendency to plant hedges or shrubs on the sides of the tees should be resisted. Inevitably, such growth reduces the amount of usable space on the tees. Similarly, stairs leading to the teeing deck, by their very nature, restrict traffic and cause ugly wear patterns. No amount of expert greenkeeping can avoid the development of bare areas near the top of the stairs. For that reason alone the slopes around tees should be gentle enough that no stairs are necessary.
6. Tees and trees are not compatible. It may be desirable for golfers to enjoy the shade of a tree while waiting to tee off, but the grass on the tee does not tolerate shade or the competition from tree roots for nutrients and water. Every effort should be made for tees to be in the open, free from the harmful effects of nearby trees.

CONCLUSIONS

Once superintendents understand the importance of the need for perfectly flat tees, and assume responsibility for creating and maintaining such tees, they will also make some of these recommended procedures part of the maintenance regimen. Superintendents are often at the mercy of the architect who has created the course. During the career span of an ambitious superintendent, however, there are many opportunities to improve the architect's shortfalls or highlight the brilliant features of the design. Foremost among these should be work on the tees. A golf course with many tees that provide panoramic views from flat, firm surfaces will always be a favorite with golfers.

3

Fairways

Nowhere has the improvement in turf quality and playability been more pronounced than on the fairways. Just a few decades ago, fairways were cut with tractor-drawn gang mowers, much the same mowers that had once been pulled with leather-shod horses prior to World War II. Nothing changed for the longest time, until the 1950s and '60s, when large tractors equipped with multiple hydraulic cutting units made their appearance. These behemoths struggled with our fairways, twisting and turning and many times tearing the tender turf in the process. Although these cumbersome mowers cut a wide swath in short order, their excessive weight caused serious compaction and subsequent turf damage.

Golf itself was undergoing a change of sorts. No longer a game of wide-open spaces, its target areas were defined by well-placed bunkers, trees, and water hazards. Fairways became contoured and smaller in total area. Superintendents needed lightweight mowers, and some experimented with the riding greens mowers. At first these handy units were tried on aprons or collars as well as on tees. The riders were ideally suited for this new application. They proved to be fast, relatively maintenance-free, and, above all, user-friendly. The next step was to extend the aprons on the par 3 holes. The results were spectacular; the closely cut grass with the clippings removed looked awesome and was a delight to play from. Golfers loved it!

It was not surprising, then, that enterprising superintendents began cutting entire fairways with triplex greens mowers. These gentle machines cut the grass beautifully and produced a playing surface of outstanding quality. Initially the intent was to remedy a difficult mowing problem on a single fairway, but it quickly became apparent that all fairways would benefit from the new practice. Outstanding displays of striping were created in the process—at times so breathtaking that country club golfers applauded the work of their super-

Striping fairways attracts the attention of golfers and makes it easy to focus on the target.

intendents and raved about the new fairways to their friends and relations. At first, the professionals on tour were reluctant to accept the new cutting patterns, and for a while tours prescribed "plain" fairways, without stripes. Eventually tour officials relented, and with some prodding from television producers, superintendents were given a free hand to use their imagination. Interestingly, some traditional courses have maintained their fairways the old-fashioned way by cutting half the fairway in one direction and the other half the opposite way.

There was an unexpected and beneficial side effect of cutting fairways with riding triplex greens mowers and removing the clippings. Superintendents in northern regions who had been struggling with *Poa annua* infestation in their bent grass turf noticed that the bent grass thrived, once the switch was made to lightweight mowers. After only a single season of regular cutting with the riding greens mowers, bent grass could be seen spreading and outgrowing the *Poa annua*. This was most remarkable, and a huge bonus for superintendents who wanted to promote bent grass at the expense of *Poa annua* without resorting to costly and unpredictable herbicides.

Little scientific research has been done at our colleges and universities to explain this phenomenon, and we know of no good reason that the bent grass should be able to outcompete the *Poa annua* as a result of lightweight mowing. We suspect, however, that it is related to compaction in the surface layer of the soil. Bent grass grows best on loose soils, and *Poa annua* is one of only a few grasses that will survive on tight soils. Lightweight mowers, by their very nature, cause less compaction than the heavy tractors of years past, and hence the bent grass has a better chance to prosper.

Superintendents who were in the vanguard during the early 1980s and switched to the new cutting methods deserve a great deal of credit for their foresight and determination. At first, those individuals were ridiculed and berated by their colleagues for catering to the whims of finicky golfers. They received little support from college professors who really did not know what was going on and thought the new method was a passing fad. The industry was also slow to recognize the potential benefits. Eventually, the manufacturers of reel-type mowers saw the light and produced a five-gang mower that gained wide acceptance in the industry. Seven-unit fairway mowers with baskets for the clippings were quick to follow, but the triplex mower is known to provide a superior quality of cut and is still widely used. New courses that were seeded to bent grass have been able to maintain homogenous cultures with very little *Poa annua* invasion. With the much improved cutting units, fairways can now be cut in a very short time and satisfy the most discriminating golfers.

On southern courses, Bermuda fairways have long provided extraordinary playing conditions for skilled golfers. The turf is cut very closely, at less than $\frac{1}{2}$ inch, and provides tight lies that enable golfers to apply spin to the ball. Another benefit is that the closely cut fairways allow plenty of roll for well-struck shots. Kikuyu and Zoysia, both warm-season grasses, provide quality turf but at a much greater height, which allows golfers to scoop their shots without imparting spin. In the northern climatic zone, bluegrass cultivars are often used instead of the fragile bent grass, but, again, these cultivars require a higher cutting height. When neither bent grass nor Bermuda grass fills the bill, perennial rye grass provides yet another alternative. Rye grass is a tough, fast-growing species that is wear- and drought-tolerant. It is often used in conjunction with other species or alone as in overseeded winter turf. Some of the most scenic golf courses are frequently poorly maintained and, conversely, a boring layout may at times be exquisitely manicured. Such is golf, and we must accept and enjoy it wherever we find it, from the sand greens on the prairie plains to the emerald jewels sparkling along the California coast.

CUTTING FAIRWAYS

The objective is to provide the golfers with a consistent playing surface, and consistency can be provided only when the grass is mowed regularly and expeditiously. The height of cut must be sufficiently low to ensure that there is no grass between the ball and the clubhead at the time of impact. The ball should sit up perfectly on closely groomed turf. Low-handicap golfers and professionals prefer tight lies with very little grass between the ball and the earth. From such lies they make the golf ball spin when it lands on the green. Higher-handicap golfers tend to be happier with more turf under the ball so that they may scoop the ball with a fairway wood or a low iron. To achieve these conditions for all golfers alike is, of course, impossible, and we must compromise somewhat, also taking into account the needs of the grass.

The following factors should govern the decisions that prudent superintendents must make when cutting fairways:

1. The height of cut on fairways should rarely be more than $\frac{1}{2}$ inch. Golfers the world over demand closely cropped turf on the fairways. They want tight lies and lots of roll. It is only when a certain species of grass does not tolerate such a short cut that the cutting height is actually raised. Such is the case on bluegrass fairways in the northern zone. Not every golf course wants or needs close-cut fairways. Various bluegrass mixes make an excellent turf that is quite playable for even the most discriminating golfers. The cool-season fescues and ryes are also often cut at below 1 inch. Fairways that are overseeded with rye and *Poa trivialis* in the southern states during the winter season are also cut at the $\frac{1}{2}$-inch height. Superintendents who, for whatever reasons, wish to grow 1-inch grass on their fairways should expect to struggle with their bosses and their committee people, as well as their golfers.

Using triplex greens mowers to cut fairways creates startling striping effects. (Photo by Anthony Girardi, Rockrimmon Country Club, Stamford, Connecticut.)

At many golf courses fairways are cut at less than $\frac{1}{2}$ inch. Both bents and Bermudas will tolerate the lower height without any ill effects. Fairways that are cut really short approach a turf quality similar to that of the greens.

2. The frequency of cut is mostly determined by the rate of growth of the turf. The faster the grass is growing, the more often it needs to be cut. When the grass is fertilized regularly and growing actively, it may need to be cut every other day. Many superintendents cut fairways Mondays, Wednesdays, and Fridays. At times, the grass is growing so prodigiously that three times per week is just not enough. Arrangements then have to be made to cut the fairways on weekend mornings or to add an extra day to the weekly schedule. The recent introduction of growth retardants has significantly reduced the rate of growth on fairways and the need to cut so often. Clipping disposal has become much less of a problem on fairways treated with growth retardants for the simple reason that substantially fewer clippings are removed.

3. Pattern cutting on fairways is a matter of personal choice, but if it is not practiced with some degree of imagination, television-fed golfers will soon find a superintendent who can provide picture-perfectly-cut

grass. Straight cutting lines on fairways are as important as they are on greens and tees. The age-old method of cutting toward a tree on the horizon works every time. Of course, there are courses without trees and in such cases another feature, such as a promontory, will do just fine. Instead of cutting a straight line, superintendents have been known to follow the contour of a water hazard. This makes for an interesting deviation from the more commonly used checkerboard pattern.

4. With target golf and lightweight mowing machines came contouring of the fairway edge. The contrast between the short, light green fairway and the much darker and longer rough was startling. Sometimes there is an intermediate cut, or step cut, to make the shapes and the shading even more interesting and pronounced. Golfers like the intermediate cut, and tournaments often specify that it be implemented. It reduces the severity of the penalty between a heavenly lie on the fairway and a difficult shot from an ankle-deep rough.

   To create the long sweeping curves, it is best for superintendents to seek the help of a recognized golf course architect. It takes a special talent, as well as specialized knowledge, to make the curves suit the needs of the game of golf. Architects are authorities on where fairways should be narrow or wide, where they should bell out or crimp in. When no architect is available, use a golf cart to outline a fairway. Drive the cart at a steady pace and at the same time activate a spray gun, thus marking the fairway with a narrow white line. Driving a cart in this manner results in sweeping lines instead of the busy, short curves that are often the result when the paint is applied while walking. Because paint on grass will disappear quickly, superintendents should mark the line with stakes until the new cut becomes established. Some will go to great lengths to retain the new curves, cutting a strip of sod along the intended line and replacing it with bent grass, thus ensuring that the line will be clearly visible for many years to come.

5. *Collars, aprons,* and *frogs' hair* are all terms to describe the short turf that surrounds the greens and is, in reality, an extension of the fairway, except that this area is usually cut at an even lower height than the fairways. At some courses the collar may just be one cut around the outside of a green, usually at a height slightly higher than the green and somewhat lower than the fairway. At other courses the collar, which now becomes an apron, is extended somewhat, especially at the front where it is cut in such a fashion that it blends in with the fairways. Yet another method involves using a walk-behind greens mower for the collar and the transition zone between the fairway and the green. Turf maintained in this fashion encourages golfers to putt from these areas. Superintendents all have their own particular preferences and are usually assisted by their green committee in determining what's best for the membership.

A fairway mower makes repeated passes to accentuate striping.

6. Cutters should be wary of sprinkler heads that they are apt to encounter when cutting the grass. Rarely are the sprinklers ideally leveled so that the cutter can drive over the top without worrying about cutting a sprinkler instead of the grass. It is best to slow down on the throttle and ever-so-gently glide over the sprinkler. If it is obvious that the sprinkler head is higher than the grass, there is no choice but to cut around the obstacle.

When a mower swallows a sprinkler, all sorts of horrible things are apt to happen. At best, the mower will just take a bite from the collar of the sprinkler—no big deal, just an ugly scar. At worst, the sprinkler will be torn from its subterranean mountings, which is immediately followed by a geyser of water nearing Yellowstone proportions. Operators had better be prepared for this sudden catastrophe, because it will draw all kinds of unwanted attention, not the least of which is the wrath of the superintendent.

Good greenkeeping calls for level sprinkler heads that are neatly trimmed, not just on the fairways but especially on the tees and on the collars around the greens. If the sprinklers have been pushed out of kilter by vehicles or because of frost, they should be readjusted on a regular basis. There is no excuse for this condition to persist on any golf course.

7. When clippings are picked up as part of the fairway cutting process, they must be removed in some manner that is economical and expeditious. Some superintendents have arrangements that include a large dumpster to be emptied at a local waste disposal site. This method tends to be costly and can be malodorous during the warm summer months when the dumpster cannot be picked up as often as needed. Another method involves composting the clippings and, in the process, mixing fresh soil with the grass snippets. A large area is required for this method, but the resulting mixture of humus-rich topsoil can be put to good use on the golf course.

If the rough is spacious, the clippings may be spread there without having any adverse effect on the play of the game. Keep in mind that the clippings disposed of in the roughs get chopped up by the mowers on a regular basis. Of all the ways to get rid of clippings, spreading them in the adjacent rough is probably the most economical and environmentally friendly. Care must be taken that the clippings are spread properly. Operators who just dump the grass will cause grief to the golfers whose balls roll into these piles and make for unplayable lies. If the clippings are left for any length of time, the grass underneath will smother and die and become an eyesore. Merely dumping clippings in naturalized areas is sloppy maintenance.

DEW REMOVAL AND DRAGGING

The formation of dew on grass during the early morning hours makes for all kind of unpleasantness:

- Dew on grass provides an ideal environment for the development of fungus disease. It is easy to spot the mycelia of Dollar Spot and Pythium as they spread on the wet turf.
- Heavy dews impede the quality of cut of the fairway mowers. It's always best to mow dry grass as opposed to wet turf.
- Golfers hate dew-covered fairways because they slow the roll of the golf ball and many times cause wet feet.

For those reasons alone many superintendents have resorted to dew removal in the morning before the golfers arrive and before the cutters mow the fairways. A heavy rubber hose is strung between two maintenance carts and dragged across the turf. The dew is dispersed and filters down among grass blades and into the soil. Instead of a rubber hose, a thick polypropylene rope

Grass clippings left uncollected are an impediment to golf. Clippings can be scattered by dragging a mat or collected in catcher baskets.

embedded with a lead cable can be used. Yet a third method is to drag a heavy net behind a truckster. It is best to drag from the green to the tee, in the opposite way to which the grass leans. Don't be afraid to include the green and even the tee in the dragging process. It takes only a few extra minutes. Experienced workers can drag all 18 fairways in just over an hour.

When worm casts are a problem, dragging will break up the casts and turn the messy little piles into beneficial topdressing. On some courses clippings are not collected, and on wet fairways clumps of clippings left behind can also be scattered by dragging. The greatest benefit of dragging is to dry the grass for golfers and for the cutters, and in the process diminish the spread of fungus diseases.

UNEVEN FAIRWAYS

On older courses it is not uncommon to find irregular depressions on the fairways. Such areas are difficult to cut smoothly, and their uneven growth spoils the appearance of otherwise perfect fairways. Low areas should be raised to blend in with the surrounding terrain. This work is best done during the shoulder season when nature provides ideal conditions for growth. Do not wait for committee approval. Instead take the initiative and improve the appearance and the playability of the golf course.

SUMMARY

Fairways are prime play landing areas, and as such ought to be in excellent condition at all times. Superintendents should remember that the smoothness of a fairway is proportional to the number of times it is cut. Fairways that are cut daily will become shiny sleek, and balls that land on such fairways will roll many extra yards. The importance of dew removal as a method of disease prevention cannot be overemphasized. Anyone who has witnessed the ugly mycelium on damp grass in the morning will know precisely what we mean and will be motivated to make dew removal part of the fairway maintenance program. A well-cut fairway, exquisitely striped, is a magnificent piece of turf that even the most discriminating golfers will find irresistible to play from.

4

The Rough

When North American superintendents speak of the rough, they mean the grassed areas immediately in front of the tee, adjacent to the fairways, and on both sides of, as well as behind, the green. The rough in these areas is, as a rule, maintained at just under 2 inches, fertilized and watered regularly, and generally of superior quality to most home lawns. On golf courses anywhere else in the world, the rough is as it ought to be: unkempt grass, gorse, heather, shrubs, and even small trees.

The rough on our courses in North America is very much like the fairways of a half-century ago. It is trimmed regularly, often twice a week during the growing season, and fertilized so that it will be thick. The weeds in the rough are sprayed as needed, and occasionally the turf is treated for fungus disease. It is apparent that the rough receives a great deal of care. Our golfers in America are the most pampered players in the world. They play on the slickest greens, the flattest tees, and the smoothest fairways, but nowhere are they more spoiled than in the rough. Golfers on our courses rarely lose a ball unless it is hit into the water or out-of-bounds. Anywhere else, golf balls can usually be found with ease.

TOTAL ROUGH AREA

In terms of the total area of the golf course, the rough occupies the largest acreage. A typical 18-hole course is built on approximately 150 acres. Following is a breakdown of the land area devoted to each playing area:

Greens:	2–3 acres	2%	Water:	0–10 acres	0%–6.7%
Tees:	3–4 acres	3%	Trees:	10–20 acres	10%

Fairways: 30–40 acres   23%   Rough: 80–100 acres   60%
Sand: 1 acre   0.7%

Obviously, these figures vary somewhat from course to course. In any case, maintaining the rough when it is growing actively is a mammoth job, requiring more workers with machines than any other activity in the maintenance department. When the rough cutters go out in the morning, they are like a swarm of locusts, devouring the long grass in front as they move and leaving behind a sward of neatly trimmed grass that pleases even the most particular golfer.

Rough needs to be cut regularly for the sake of the speed of the game. It needs to be cut uniformly so that playing conditions do not vary throughout the course. To cut all the rough, superintendents use a combination of some of the following pieces of equipment:

- Several rotary-type mowers of varying widths, either self-propelled or tractor- drawn
- A set of tractor-drawn gang mowers
- One or more riding triplex reel-type mowers, also known as trim mowers
- Several hand rotary mowers as well as a number of string trimmers.

It is not unusual on an 18-hole course to have as many as a half dozen people cutting the rough, especially in the springtime when the grass is actively growing. To coordinate the efforts of all these workers takes the skill of a well-organized superintendent.

It stands to reason that the largest area should be cut by the fastest and the largest machine. In most cases this is a rotary with multiple decks, or a set of tractor-drawn gang mowers. The smaller rotaries are used to cut around and between trees. The riding triplex, reel-type mowers are ideal for steep banks around tees and bunkers and, finally, the hand trimmers and rotaries pick up the grass that all the other mowers miss. Cutting the rough is a team effort, and the results are best when all well-trained participants know their parts and work together. In that manner, the work gets done quickly and the entire course is constantly kept trimmed.

The danger with the rough is that the greens crew can fall behind while the grass grows faster than it is cut. This happens in the spring when there is a sudden surge of growth. The worst scenario imaginable is a warm rain on a Thursday in May, followed by a long weekend. In just hours, the grass will burst from its roots and provide a thick green carpet that grows faster than the mowers can cut. Such circumstances will cause the golfers to experience inconsistencies in the playing conditions: In some areas the rough will be freshly cut and of perfect playing height; in other places the grass will be much too long and golfers will waste time looking for balls. Therefore, turf managers should

*A step cut between fairway and rough height is an attractive
feature of contemporary maintenance.*

be prepared for long weekends or any weekends in the spring that coincide
with periods of rapid growth. The greens crew should be willing to work overtime, or the rough will get out of hand and the superintendent is likely to receive phone calls and e-mails from angry golfers.

Riding mowers on steep slopes present a special problem. If such areas must
be cut at all, it should be attempted only when the turf is dry, and then by only
the most experienced and fearless operators. The machines need to be in the
best of mechanical condition, each equipped with a rollover bar and a seat belt
for the operator. Recently cutters have been manufactured with hydraulically
adjustable seats, so that the operator is seated horizontally while the mower
cuts a steep slope. Such slopes are very dangerous, and if at all practical, are
best naturalized.

Mower operators who watch televised golf on the weekends may notice the
beautiful striping exhibited at tournament sites and may try to imitate these
works of art at their places of work. Such workers ought to be commended for
the interest they take in their work, and golfers will also be impressed with and
appreciative of their creations. In this context, a new verb has developed in

*Workers using string trimmers need protection such as a rubber apron,
face shield, work gloves, and safety boots.*

greenkeeping jargon, *striping,* which refers to creating alternate light and dark green stripes. Striping can be enhanced by installing solid rollers on the cutting units.

Superintendents at many courses now cut a strip varying in width from 5 to 10 feet from the tee to where the fairway starts. This path is for the golfers who walk, so they won't get their feet wet, and is therefore known as a dew walk. It is maintained like the fairway and watered and fertilized in a like manner. From time to time this path may have to be moved sideways so that the turf will not wear out and die. The practice of cutting a dew walk has spread rapidly as a result of televised golf and has gained wide acceptance among golfers.

SMALL ROUGH MOWERS

No matter how diligently the large-machine operators perform, there is always some long grass left behind that can be cut only with small rotary mowers or with string trimmers. If it is left unattended, the course takes on an unkempt appearance. At every golf course, there is a routine of trimming around trees and other hard-to-get-at places. Such work is best done immediately following operation of the larger rough-cutting units. In that manner, the entire area looks uniformly maintained.

Steep, grassy banks are especially difficult to keep trimmed. The wheel-less "Flymo" performs admirably in such areas, but it is an arduous task to handle such a mower on a continuous basis. String trimmers also need expert handlers, otherwise the end result will be a series of scalps and misses that will continue to look ugly long after the work has been done.

A rotary crew of several persons needs a leader for best results. The leader will look after gassing the machines, making small repairs and adjustments, and most important, making decisions about what area needs to be cut next. Aspiring assistants often get their first experience at personnel management as rotary crew leaders. We emphasize that such a leader should be a working leader and not someone who stands around idly while others sweat.

Small trees of 3-inch caliper or less can easily be debarked by careless rotary mower operators. The danger is even greater when string trimmers are used. The small trees can be protected by surrounding the stems with short pieces of flexible drainage tile. Many superintendents, in an effort to save time and labor as well as the health of the small trees, spray around the bases of trees with glyphosate or "Roundup." This widely used grass killer affects only the grass and not the bark of the tree or the roots. One or two applications around the bases of trees during the course of a season will eliminate the need for mowing.

NATURALIZED ROUGH AREAS

Recently fescue rough has come in vogue on golf courses, and golf course architects now often specify seeding some of the secondary rough with homogenous stands of fescue grass. Such turf is rarely cut at all and can look quite spectacular, especially when the wind blows and moves the stems and seedheads like waves on water. This action brings an element of tranquility to a golf course that may have been absent before.

Superintendents who think that fescue rough is maintenance-free are sadly mistaken. Very quickly the sparse turf is invaded by all manner of weeds that make the naturalized rough unsightly. Such weeds must be removed, and because weed spraying in fescue rough is not always advisable, milkweeds, burdocks, goldenrod, and thistles are often pulled out by hand, an arduous job, to say the least. Others have employed the age-old scythe of a bygone era to cut the objectionable weeds.

To preserve the naturalized look of the fescue rough, it must be cut from time to time and excessive amounts of clippings should be removed. The fescue can be trimmed with a tractor-driven rotary mower or farm-type sickle bar

Naturalized areas on a golf course need to be protected from hazardous materials for the benefit of wildlife.

mower at a height of at least 6 inches. From time to time a herbicide is needed to control the weeds, and many superintendents concur that naturalized areas are often more expensive to maintain than the primary roughs. It appears that beauty has a price.

When the naturalized areas encroach on the playing areas, it results in golfers losing balls and slowing down the pace of play. Superintendents should be alert and look for excessive concentrated foot traffic in the long grass, which is an indication that many golfers are looking for lost balls. Such areas should be trimmed shorter to speed up play. Naturalized areas that are out of play add an element of beauty to golf, but if allowed to expand and to interfere with the regular flow of the game, such beauty can quickly become a trodden-down ugly hazard.

Although many superintendents have sanitized their naturalized areas by removing weeds, others have added wildflowers such as black-eyed Susans, columbines, cornflowers, and others in accordance with the hardiness zone. To establish wildflowers requires a fertile soil, moisture and an occasional mulching to preserve that moisture. To regenerate the plants, the vegetation is often burned, much the way it happens in nature when lightning strikes. Maintaining wildflowers requires as much attention as for any other plant material.

It is not necessary to overseed with fescue grass or to plant wildflowers in order to create naturalized areas. When out-of-play areas are left to their own devices and are no longer cut, they will automatically revert to their native state. We have seen this happen time and again, but the superintendent must be patient when adopting this method. It may take several seasons for the desirable species to become established and predominant, and during that time some selective trimming may be necessary to achieve the desired results.

Some superintendents have combined their naturalized areas with tree nurseries. This idea has merit, as long as it is understood that small trees need encouragement in their initial stages, such as by being protected from rodents and rabbits, and that they must compete for nutrients with the thick grass that surrounds them. In the end, only the healthiest trees will survive in this natural environment. As the trees get bigger, they can be transplanted for use on the course or near the clubhouse; others may eventually become part of a forest. There is always a danger that trees will take over the fescue areas. To avoid this situation, sapling trees can be pulled out before they become established.

SUMMARY

There are times when superintendents have wonderful opportunities to leave living legacies. Letting the grass grow in out-of-play areas and planting trees and wildflowers are examples. Such havens of tranquility, where birds make nests and rabbits scurry, are proof of the superintendent's role as an environmentalist.

A rough may mean different things to different people, and golfers and superintendents rarely agree on what the rough should be like. To the golfer the rough is meant to exact punishment for errant shots. For the superintendent the rough provides an opportunity to frame the golf course in a natural way. A rough is never static. It changes with the seasons, it changes over the years with the encroachment of natural growth, and it also changes as a result of humans' interference with nature. Whatever form or shape a rough takes, it usually provides character and contrast on a golf course. If a rough provides a challenge as well, then most players will also be happy.

5

Sand Bunkers and Their Maintenance

Only a few shots are played from bunkers during a typical round of golf, but nowhere are golfers more critical of course conditioning than when it comes to the sand in the bunkers. When golfers fail to execute a perfect shot from a sand bunker, it is rarely seen as the fault of the person swinging the club. The blame invariably lies with the sand in the bunker. It is either too soft or too fluffy, too hard or too dry, too coarse or too fine, or, even more politically correct, the sand lacks consistency. Sand and bunkers are a very emotional issue, and otherwise rational persons can become quite unreasonable when discussing sand and bunkers.

THE NEED FOR SAND BUNKERS

Bunkers are an essential part of golf for the following reasons:

- They add challenge to the game.
- They frame and define golf holes.
- They provide contrast and accent.
- At times, both sand and grass bunkers serve to catch wayward shots.

Trees or water can take the place of bunkers effectively, but when a property lacks either or both, then sand bunkers are often the only desirable alternative. Golf course architects use their creative talents to shape mounds alongside fairways and then accentuate these features by including hollows and flashes filled with sand. In that manner, they try to duplicate what the sheep and the winds did naturally in Scotland many years ago.

It has been alleged that the location of fairway bunkers on golf courses in

*Too much sand perhaps? Golfers will have difficulty finding
their way to the next tee after putting out.*

olden times was often determined by the abundance of divots in certain locations. Rather than repair the divots constantly, greenkeepers would simply hollow out a bunker.

Near the green, the bunkers are placed with much forethought in order to add difficulty and challenge for the golfers in reaching the putting surface. For many a golfer, to be buried in a bunker is a scary thought and often leads to a poor score. Being able to escape from bunkers or to avoid them altogether is part of what makes golf such an interesting and addictive game. Meanwhile, golf course superintendents have to deal with the realities of maintaining sand bunkers, which is often a much more difficult task than just growing grass.

THE SAND IN BUNKERS

An acceptable bunker sand is hard to find and rarely available locally. White silica sand is the favorite with many superintendents and golfers alike. The sand particles are uniform in size and angular, rather than rounded, which makes for a firm surface. Its brilliant white color makes the bunkers stand out

Spectacular sand bunkers originally created during practice bombing runs with airplanes, and later modified by golf course architect Arthur Hills at the Dunes Golf Course near Brooksville, Florida.

on the golf course. Especially when the sand is still new, it can be dazzling and almost blinding to the golfers who have the misfortune of finding themselves in such bunkers. Precisely for that reason, some architects and superintendents prefer a more subdued color that will blend in better with the existing hues of the surrounding landscape.

Before superintendents switch sand, they should analyze precisely why a change of sand is necessary. It may well be that the poor condition of the bunkers is not the fault of the sand, but a lack of drainage or the design of the bunkers. Whatever the reason, the bunkers may need to be rebuilt before any new sand is ordered. Once new sand is deposited in a bunker, it should be compacted with a mechanical tamper before the bunker is put into play. Wetting the new sand also helps stabilization. Because it takes time for sand to settle, it is best not to add fresh sand immediately prior to a tournament.

The particle size of sand is extremely important. Fine sand blows away in the wind. Coarse sand leaves scratch marks on golfers' clubs and dulls the greens mowers. Sand that is characterized by round-faced particles tends to roll underfoot and is difficult to play from. When the sand particles are angular, they will compact more easily and provide stable footing. At the same time, such sand may easily become too hard. The perfect sand is neither fine nor coarse, nor is it too round or slippery. The perfect sand is hard to find, but once a source has been discovered it is prudent to keep a pile in storage. To express the perfect sand in terms of particle size diameter leaves many factors out of the equation, but it is generally agreed that a major portion of the granules should be between 0.25 and 1.00 millimeters in size. A superintendent charged with choosing a certain type of sand for use is well advised to check with neighboring courses in a wide area and do a thorough study of the materials available. The final decision is best left to an expert, which in most cases is a capable superintendent. Such a professional will not hesitate to seek outside advice for the benefit of the golfers.

Golfers have asserted that they prefer firmer sand in fairway bunkers than in greenside bunkers, the reason being that they may wish to play a wood club from fairway sand, but from greenside sand they will invariably prefer to play a wedge. It certainly is a challenge for the contemporary superintendent to provide appropriate bunker conditioning at these different locations.

BUNKER DRAINAGE

The very shapes of bunkers ensure that they become recipients and collectors of water, and all too often no adequate provisions are made for the water to drain from the bunkers. Elaborate gridiron tiling systems under greens are commonplace, but many otherwise knowledgeable superintendents still have not accepted the necessity of equally extensive drainage systems for bunkers. One single tile line through the center of a bunker is insufficient under most conditions. A herringbone system of 4-inch-diameter tile, with the lateral lines no less than 10 feet apart, is essential to take away storm water and rainwater. The header of the herringbone should empty into a catch basin just outside the bunker, and from there be connected to a drainage main or taken into the rough. The catch basin serves as a means of cleaning out the tile, because it is possible that the lines may fill up with sand. Using a hose with pressured water will enable the greens crew to flush out the tiles.

Many superintendents have experimented with stockings made from filter cloth around the drainage tiles. It is thought that the stockings prevent the sand from entering the tile and clogging it. Others are equally adamant that the stockings block the movement of water, or at least slow it down. We believe that the tile should be embedded in rounded and smooth pea gravel for best results. On new bunkers, the trench should be 5–6 inches wide and partially filled with pea gravel. The top of the tile should be at least 8 inches below the bottom of the bunker. This helps to prevent frost from bringing the tile to the surface. Throughout the installation, levels should be taken to make certain that there is adequate fall. The pea gravel in the bottom of the trench can be used to make small adjustments in the grade to ensure proper flow. When

White sand bunkers define the target.

the base is satisfactory, install either perforated, flexible plastic tile or rigid construction-type tile with holes in the walls. Either type should be of 4-inch diameter. Cover the tile with more pea gravel, but make sure that both the tile and pea gravel are below the base of the bunker. It is important that the pea gravel does not get mixed up with the sand. Sometimes a choker layer of coarse sand is established between the base and the sand from which golfers play. Golfers become justifiably irate when their expensive sand wedges are scratched or dented by stones. There is understandable concern that no matter how careful the installation, some of the pea gravel will get mixed up with the sand. For that reason alone, one should consider backfilling over the tile with a coarse sand.

FILTER CLOTHS

It is a common occurrence for the material in the subbase of a bunker to get mixed up with the sand above. It is guaranteed to happen when the bunkers are characterized by steep flashes. Such flashes often look spectacular and make the bunkers visible from afar, but they are a maintenance headache for the greens crew. Any sudden downpour, summer storm, or prolonged rainfall is guaranteed to wash the sand from the steep faces. Once the sand starts to run, the base underneath also erodes and mixes with the sand. Shoveling the sand back up the face often results in the sand and the base material becoming mixed. If the base material should happen to be mainly clay, the resulting mixture will be as hard as cement once it dries. To prevent this from happening, a thick pervious mat can be installed on the flashes between the sand and the subbase. This method permits the water to flow down through the mat without disturbing either the sand or the base material. Such liners are often extended to cover the entire bunker floor and tucked in under the surrounding sod.

Although a depth of 3–4 inches of sand is adequate for new bunkers, extra sand is needed on top of the filter cloth. When using filter cloth in the bases of bunkers, superintendents need to be wary about golfers getting their sand wedges stuck in the material. This happens when the sand cover starts to shift and becomes inadequate. Motorized bunker rakes have a tendency to dig in along the sides of bunkers and have been known to tear into the filter cloth with disastrous results. For all these reasons, superintendents should be cautious about installing filter cloth in the bases of bunkers in the first place.

In northern climates ground frost may cause severe heaving in the subbase. Such natural action may free stones from the subbase and pop them to the surface. This is an unwelcome surprise in the spring. Stones must not be allowed to remain as part of the playing medium, inasmuch as golfers, under the rules of the game, are not allowed to remove them. Superintendents have an obligation to keep the bunkers clean of objectionable materials. If such impediments cannot be removed manually, superintendents should make use of the mechanized sand sifters that are also employed to keep beaches clean.

REASONS WHY SAND BUNKERS SHOULD BE RENOVATED

- The sand has become contaminated with clay, silt, or stones.
- The sand lacks uniformity from one bunker to another.
- The particle size of the sand is either too small or too large.
- Golfers desire white instead of gray sand.
- The bunker drains poorly or not at all.
- The original shape of the bunker has been lost under the management of several superintendents over a period of years.
- New construction technology may improve a malfunctioning old bunker.

Whatever reason(s) may drive the renovation process, it is best to employ a reputable golf course architect at a very early stage. Once the plans have been approved and the money allocated, a competent golf course construction com-

Depositing new sand in a bunker via a conveyor belt from a truck with balloon tires saves labor and reduces damage to surrounding turf.

pany should be engaged to carry out the work. At all times the superintendent should play an important part in the decision-making process. After all, when the work is completed and both the architect and the contractor have departed, the superintendent is left to look after the new bunkers for many years to come.

POT BUNKERS

The most interesting bunkers of all on any golf course are without a doubt the pot bunkers. When properly constructed, pot bunkers capture far more balls than their size would lead one to believe. They may encompass just a few square yards in total area, but all the surrounding land slopes toward the crater and golf balls easily become entangled in their clutches and are released only with reluctance. We have all seen and commiserated with golfers trying to extricate themselves from pot bunkers, only to fail time and time again. How agonizing it must be to fail so miserably and finally just throw the ball onto the green in disgust! Greenkeepers are only too familiar with the anguish of golfers because they observe it so often and on occasion experience it themselves when they play the game with their friends or colleagues.

The face of a pot bunker is frequently constructed like a sod wall, with layers of sod piled on top of each other and held in place with metal bars and wires. Such sides are hand-trimmed with Weed Eaters and at times even with scissors. An unfortunate golfer who finds his or her ball up against the face may have to play sideways, or even backward, to get out of the bunker.

Pot bunkers are invariably so small that they cannot be maintained by mechanical rakes but must be looked after manually. Because of their size, they quickly become foot-marked and need constant care by the greens crew. The sandy bottom of a pot bunker should be shaped like a bowl so that golf balls will roll away from the edges. Pot bunkers are very maintenance-intensive.

THE REVETTED BUNKERS OF ST. ANDREWS

Walter Woods, the legendary links supervisor at St. Andrews, in a letter, contributed this information about bunkers in his native country:

No one knows when bunkers came into play, and like many things in the old days, just evolved by trial and error. We do know that golf originated on the East Coast of Scotland on the sandy windswept coast from Aberdeen right down to St. Andrews and round to Edinburgh. This is where golf as we know it began, and the golfers would play on roughly-mown fairways through hollows and mounds from tee to green. Most of this land supported nothing else but rabbits and sheep and the golfers soon discovered that some areas in the lee of the hollow protected the sheep from the wind, and soon the whole depression was so severely worn that it was better to turf the banks and make the sand uniform to make it a fair hazard for everyone. As the years passed, more bunkers came into play, particularly at the greenside, for it was discovered that they did create more interest and demand more accuracy.

Owing to the introduction of the rubber gutta percha golf ball, which made golf easier and more predictable and most importantly, less expensive, golf soon became popular first of all in England, then Europe and Asia, followed by North America. Scottish professionals were in demand to become golf course architects, having a head start in golf course design. Bunkers provided one area where strategy could be provided and used to create interest into the concept of parkland golf courses.

Architects all over the world soon realized that bunkers could improve the visual effect to what could be flat boring ground into mounded interesting land which was more appealing to the eye. American architects

Revetted bunker at St. Andrews Golf Course, Scotland.
(Photo by Walter Woods, St. Andrews, Scotland.)

took advantage of this and were soon constructing large bold bunkers filled with white silica sand that provided a more modern approach to golf course design.

Building Bunkers in Scotland

St. Andrews was the forerunner of bunker building and the easiest way was to copy the stonemasons on how they built walls. Starting at the bottom, a solid foundation is made to the shape of the inside of the bunker. Then a layer of turf is laid onto the compacted sand. This is continued upward by laying the next layer slightly back from the previous layer, which dictates the angle and prevents the face from being vertical. The more one sets the next layer of turf back from the previous layer, the greater angles one makes. At all times one must backfill with sand and keep the turf and the sand compacted. Once the revetted turf is up to the desired height, it is topped with a collar of turf. Revetted faces last for about 3–4 years but can be made to last longer if good maintenance is applied with brushing and watering with a fine hose and adding a wetting agent. Apprentice greenkeepers are taught this skill at an early age and just like golf, this has been introduced all over the world.

When part of the turf wall is worn, usually by golfers walking or climbing out, it can be patched by creating a foundation at the worn part and then building upward and fitting the side into the existing turf. Revetting bunker faces is labor-intensive and can only be of value where mounds can provide no alternative. Links land is one area where revetted faces can be beneficial, mainly to prevent sand from blowing away. If a large amount of revetted bunker faces are required, it will be necessary to have a large turf nursery. The thicker the turf, the quicker the face can be built and the thick, fibrous roots also look more attractive, providing the block effect.

When the bunker is selected that has to be built, an awareness of the surrounding features and flow of slopes and landscape will be required so that the bunker face is set to blend into these surroundings. On many occasions, on fairway or greenside, the bunker face can be shown to provide strategy and balance to the golf hole. Sand selection is also important. The sand should be compatible with the root zone material used to construct the greens. It should also be able to compact sufficiently and yet allow the top two inches to be slightly softer. When the bunker is raked it should appear to be saucer-shaped with the sand drawn to the edges. The steeper the face, the longer the slope of sand should be to allow the ball to roll backward, away from the face or edge.

The selection of rakes to maintain the bunker is important. Old-fashioned wooden hay rakes are often chosen due to the fact that the wooden teeth provide evenly spaced grooves and the width of the rake can achieve the work fast and efficiently. Some golf clubs provide small bunker repair rakes which are often thrown about with no regard for the play that follows. Where to place the rake is often discussed. Some say outside the bunker and others say inside. Logically speaking, it would be better to place the rake inside and away from the line of play, to prevent golf balls from being deflected.

REVETTING BUNKERS IN NORTH AMERICA

The practice of revetting bunkers has been copied in North America. Sometimes just a few bunkers are done in this manner to give a particular course a Scottish flavor. At the Devil's Paintbrush in Ontario all the bunkers were constructed with revetted facer walls and have been in place for several years. Such steep walls may become a nesting ground for birds that dig holes and nest in the walls. The walls occasionally collapse and need to be rebuilt every three to five years.

GRASS BUNKERS

As the name implies, the sand in grass bunkers has given way to grass. Nevertheless, such bunkers are still very much a hazard because they present the golfers with a variety of up- and downhill lies, as well as frequently longer-than-normal rough-height grass. Just like regular bunkers, grass bunkers need to be well drained and must be constructed with a catch basin in the lowest spot.

WASTE BUNKERS

Recently, architects have introduced large areas of unraked sand intermixed with clumps of grass and even shrubbery and small trees. Such areas are at times used to define a dogleg, and their purposeful neglect is in sharp contrast with the neatly manicured adjacent fairway turf. Waste bunkers are not hazards as defined by the rules of golf, and golfers are allowed to ground their golf clubs in a waste bunker. Nor are waste bunkers raked on a regular basis, and difficult lies are commonplace in such bunkers. It is a fallacy to believe that waste bunkers are maintenance-free. The vegetation inside the waste bunkers needs to be maintained. Trees and bushes need to be trimmed. The ornamental grasses that are frequently planted in waste bunkers need to be tended, and the sand needs to be smoothed at intervals. If weeds become a problem, they must be sprayed. Because waste bunkers are generally quite flat and often lower than the surrounding lands, drainage must be provided for. Tile line similar to that used in regular bunkers should be installed at the time of construction.

RAKING THE BUNKER

The daily routine of golf course maintenance includes raking the bunkers. Prior to the invention of the mechanical bunker rake, caring for bunkers could be a monotonous chore taking the efforts of several workers for a whole day on an 18-hole course. A smart-thinking superintendent from Georgia was the first to invent a motorized bunker rake. Never mind that the contraption looked like a moon buggy. It was a prototype and soon copied by all the major manufacturers. Raking bunkers was changed forever. Architects were no longer restricted by the workload of the greens crew and immediately set out to create large and impressive fields of sand that accentuated the playing areas and made for target golf at its best.

Raking bunkers is a chore usually reserved for junior members of the greens crew. This does not mean that superintendents consider the job of trap-raking bunkers any less important than other assignments. To the contrary, raking

White bunker sand contrasts sharply with adjacent waste bunker.

bunkers must be done with the same degree of perfection that is applied to all other tasks. To rake bunkers quickly and efficiently requires a young, agile person who can get on and off the machine in a jiffy. This person can do the work between foursomes and get out of the way quickly when he or she must. A "trapper" is alert to the surroundings. This worker sees golfers coming behind his or her back and gets the work done without being in the way.

If golfers complied with the ethics of the game and raked the bunkers every time they played from the sand, maintenance costs could be reduced sharply, but we live in an imperfect world. Golfers are usually so absorbed in their game that they either forget to rake the sand or do a willy-nilly job of it. A perfectly raked bunker in the morning quickly starts to resemble a miniature battlefield after just a few golfers have played from it. Superintendents who know the shortcomings of their players should consider sending out staff in the afternoon to touch up the bunkers by hand-raking, after they have been machine-raked in the morning. At the same time, golfers should be encouraged to rake bunkers with two hands on the rake so as to achieve a more acceptable result.

On older golf courses with traditional bunkers there may not be enough space for the bunker machines to maneuver, and in such cases hand-raking is the only alternative. The bunkers at Oakmont of USGA fame in Pittsburgh

Hand-raking the sand in bunkers produces superior results, according to Anthony Girardi, superintendent at the Rockrimmon Country Club in Stamford, Connecticut. (Photo by Anthony Girardi.)

were hand-raked with hay rakes for many years. These antique instruments left characteristically deep grooves that many golfers despised and others thought lent charm to this famous course.

STEPS TO RAKE A BUNKER PERFECTLY

1. Inspect the bunker, remove debris, and place the hand rakes on the grass outside.
2. Rake the bunker slowly at half throttle through the center, and make a gentle turn at the end.
3. Stay away from the bunker's edge by at least a foot. Touching the grass or the soil with the rake will contaminate the sand.
4. When the entire bunker has been raked, exit carefully, making sure not to drag any sand onto the surrounds.
5. Hand-rake the edges upward, and make sure that any marks left at the exit are obliterated. Any ruts in the bunker should also be hand-raked out.

6. Replace the hand rakes inside the bunkers, but not before checking for broken handles and tines.

There has been an ongoing debate about placing the rakes either inside the bunkers on the sand or outside the bunkers on the grass. Rules officials have had a difficult time making up their minds about where the rakes belong. Now it seems that the majority of courses place the rakes on the sand where they can easily be seen by golfers. There can be a problem with trees near bunkers, especially fruit trees. When the fruit ripens, it falls into the bunker, and golfers, obeying the rules of the game, are not allowed to move the loose impediments in the hazard. No matter if the superintendent removes the fruit several times a day, it keeps on falling, and some golfers will be affected by this bit of unjust adversity. Leaves in the fall season can have the same effect, and committees and architects should consider keeping trees away from sand bunkers.

EDGING THE BUNKER

On finely manicured golf courses, the bunkers are characterized by a sharp, distinctive edge. That is no accident, but the result of meticulous work by knowledgeable greenkeepers. If left unattended, the grass surrounding the bunkers would quickly grow into the sand and the bunker would lose its shape and definition. Golfers would have difficulty determining whether their balls were inside or outside the bunker, and because different rules apply, there could be problems with interpretations and with fellow players.

For the longest time, superintendents and their staff hand-edged bunkers several times during the golfing season. Then came power edgers with oscillating blades and, more recently, power trimmers with reciprocating teeth. The work can now be done quickly, and a sharply defined edge is created with little effort. The problem is that the location of the bunker line cannot always be determined with certainty. Unless edging is done regularly, it is possible for the bunker's edge to be lost. Bunkers quickly lose their original shape, and the architect's design may be lost forever unless construction drawings are kept on file. Before any serious edging is contemplated, the superintendent should outline the bunker with a paint gun on the basis of the construction drawings. If these drawings are not available, the superintendent should use his or her best judgment or, failing that, bring in outside help. After the bunker has been edged, the chunks of sod and strings of rhizomes must be removed from the bunker and the sand should be raked back up to the grass level. If the sand is raked flat with the bottom of the bunker, a sharp edge in the form of a deep cut will result, which may occasionally produce unplayable lies. Bunkers do not need to be edged mechanically—there is another way. It is quicker and in many ways more efficient, but it does not leave a sharp edge. We are referring to a process that involves spraying the edge of a bunker with glyphosate or

Edging the bunker with a mechanical trimmer.

Roundup, a grass killer that effectively stops the grass from growing into the sand. There is another important benefit: By eliminating the edger we are also eliminating the opportunity for surrounding soil to mix with the bunker sand. That is an important consideration because once the sand loses its purity, it loses its playability at the same time. The Roundup must be applied carefully in a narrow band; otherwise, it is unsightly. It has been suggested that this method of trimming bunkers produces a less artificial look and is thus more appealing from an aesthetic point of view.

SUMMARY

Although we think of greenkeeping primarily as an endeavor to trim the grass, maintaining the bunkers is equally important. It is not surprising, then, that the measure of a greenkeeper's competency is often determined by the way the bunkers are maintained. There lies an opportunity: Rake and maintain the bunkers to perfection, and be a hero with the golfers!

A regular routine of raking and edging the bunkers, trimming the surrounds, and making sure that the hand rakes are in good repair and that there is a sufficient number in each bunker—all these factors help create a favorable impression of the golf course to regular golfers and visitors alike.

6

Water

GREEN GRASS AND WATER

There will be no grass without water. In those few words lies a simple truth about greenkeeping: Green grass and water are closely related. Novice green-keepers learn early in their careers that they must have water to grow grass, and in the days of rubber hoses, that lesson was brought home through hard work and long hours. Anyone who has done a night shift on the watering crew knows about groping in the dark for pipe fittings, lugging water-filled hoses, and taking a nap in the pump house between sprinkler changes. Not only did the job take a strong back, but a fearless mind as well. There were always fright-ening shadows in the dark and inexplicable sounds that sent shivers up the spine of the most stouthearted waterman. The first glow of dawn was a wel-come sight, and the company of fellow greensworkers arriving for the day shift was warmly appreciated.

It can readily be understood from the foregoing that the advent of auto-matic sprinklers was welcomed by those charged with the responsibility of maintaining fine turf. Suddenly the superintendent was back in charge of the watering operation and no longer at the mercy of watermen who performed their work under the cover of darkness. The advent of automatic sprinklers was accompanied by a whole new philosophy toward watering. Manual watering, by necessity, had encouraged drenching an area until it was thoroughly soaked, and then not watering it again until it had dried out. This method of watering was supposed to encourage root growth because plants had to extend their roots between waterings to obtain the precious liquid needed for their metabo-lism. Once watering became automated, it also became possible to water the entire course—tees, greens, and fairways—nightly. Only a light watering, per-haps one single turn of the sprinkler, but water just the same. Inevitably, nightly watering led to overwatering, and sloppy wet turf was commonplace at some courses. Superintendents had to learn how to water all over again and how to manage their watering systems for the benefit of the grass and the golfers.

WHEN WET IS TOO WET

A good example of wet turf occurs when a fairway sprinkler is left on all night because it would not shut off when it was supposed to. Imagine an irrigation head spewing 50 gallons per minute or more over a circle with an 80-foot radius for six hours. That amounts to the equivalent of a 2-inch rainfall, and the mishap will result in a wet spot for at least a day. A greenside sprinkler, with much less output and smaller coverage, can still cause excessive wetness on the green and will more than likely result in plugged balls or mucky ball marks.

When excessive wetness is caused by a malfunctioning sprinkler, the affected area can be roped off and taken out of play. When rain is the culprit, power cart traffic may have to be restricted, or even worse, the golf course may have to be closed. Soil scientists will testify that supersaturated soils should not be walked or driven on. If that does happen, the soil structure will lose its natural composition and become quite squishy, much like a mud cake in a child's hand. Such soil, when it finally does dry, may have lost structure and reduced pore space and can be a detriment to healthy root growth for plants. Therefore, the excess water must either be allowed to drain naturally or be removed mechanically, so that oxygen can once again enter the root zone. The poor grass plant that almost choked to death when it could not breathe, is thus saved in the nick of time by a vigilant superintendent. Freestanding water in the heat of summer on turf becomes quite warm and may actually scald the turf. Superintendents should be aware of this phenomenon and make every effort to empty puddles. Sometimes this can be done by opening existing drains; mostly it means pumping the water away.

WHEN DYING GRASS NEEDS WATER

Of all the skills that aspiring superintendents must learn, none is more difficult than recognizing the latter stages of dying turf. Otherwise competent assistants often draw a blank or go color-blind when it comes to ringing the alarm bells for wilting grass. It can all happen so quickly. The greens look perfect in the morning, freshly cut with a distinctive checkerboard appearance. The wind freshens as the morning progresses, and by noon there is a stiff breeze. As the temperature rises the humidity is lowered, and by midafternoon the grass plants are losing more water through the leaves than they can take up through the roots. The plants quickly lose their turgidity and characteristically turn a purplish blue. Footprints from golfers on turf at this stage show as depressed grass that won't spring back up. A keen eye will recognize all the symptoms. Inexperienced operators who fertilize, topdress, or verticut when such conditions prevail, may ensure death for the grass plants.

SYRINGING

Wilting grass can be brought back to health by the simple expedient of syringing—a very light application of water, administered either by hose and nozzle or by the syringe cycle of the automatic watering system. Either way, the idea is to apply a small amount of water to the drying grass plant. The water will improve the moisture level in the plant, and it will survive. It is a proven method that works every time. Applying too much water can be detrimental; it will once again result in a soggy upper layer of the root zone, with all the bad side effects mentioned earlier.

It is not only the greens that may require syringing. More often than not the collars or aprons start wilting even before the greens do, and these sensitive strips have to be wetted during the course of a drying day. The reason that aprons show signs of wilt before the greens do is that the turf on aprons is often more thatchy or spongy than the grass on the greens. If aprons are lost repeatedly, they should probably be replaced with superior turf. One should also keep in mind that aprons are subjected to mowers turning and sand blasts from nearby bunkers. The first factor leads to compaction, and the second to drying out. In both cases, the apron or collar needs repair or extra maintenance.

High knolls on fairways may also require some cooling on hot days during the summer. Superintendents who know their course, after many years of experience, know the weak areas that will show stress the quickest. Such areas are singled out and often receive extra water at the crack of dawn in anticipation of a stressful day. That is smart greenkeeping and results in success where others fail.

WHEN TO WATER

Every golf course has certain indicator areas, such as the back of a green or a high tee, that are the first to show signs of drought stress. Another sure sign of the need to water occurs when the tops of the French drains start to turn blue. Experienced superintendents know these signs, and know where to look for them. Their appearance rings a bell and triggers a reaction: It is time to start an irrigation cycle. We recommend watering just a little less than seems to be needed and then playing catch-up in the morning with the help of daylight. This method prevents overwatering and, in fact, keeps the golf course as a whole on the dry side and very playable.

There is a lot of fancy instrumentation available that will help a superintendent decide when to water, but there is no substitute for experience and sound judgment. Not every blade of grass on a golf course needs to be lush and green. It is quite acceptable for some areas along the fringes of fairways to be browning off and for greens to be firm. Greens that are pockmarked with ball marks are not necessarily the result of golfers failing to repair their ball marks, but more often the direct result of overwatering. The same applies to fairways that are soggy underfoot and permit no roll of the ball.

LOCALIZED DRY SPOTS

The trend toward high-sand-content greens had its beginning in California where it was believed that a so-called dirty sand (containing small amounts of other soils, such as peat, clay, etc.) would make the ideal matrix for growing grass on putting greens. Dirty sand occurred naturally in many places and was an easy shortcut for the establishment of golf greens. When dirty sand was not available, superintendents used washed sand and added peat or similar organics to duplicate the dirty sand. Whereas initially sand had been one of three components of the ideal greens growing mix, it now quickly became the major, in some cases the only, component of the growing medium. Sand has several advantages as a soil:

- It drains well and rarely gets overwet.
- Sand is difficult to compact and needs little aeration.
- Sand greens hold golf shots well, even when dry.

Sand is now commonly used as the only material used for growing grass on a green. A light sprinkling of sand is easy to apply and even easier to work into the turf. But all that sand has one ugly side effect: localized dry spots. Over time, almost all greens that have been topdressed with sand, or built from a homogenous sand mix, develop brown areas of wilted grass ranging in size from grapefruit to umbrella tops. The soil under these dry spots is so dry that it cannot absorb water, no matter how long the sprinklers are left on. This hydrophobic condition is believed to be caused by a fungus that lives in the sand, and its mycelium, or fungal root system, shuts off the pore spaces and prevents water from entering the soil. Superintendents should also be aware that when the organic matter content in soil mix rises above 3%, pore spaces between the soil particles are shut off, which curtails the movement of water and nutrients.

Wetting agents were introduced to break down the viscosity of water and improve water movement. Wetting agents make water droplets smaller and actually make water wetter, so that the water can penetrate into even the smallest of pore spaces and provide relief to thirsty plant roots. Greens treated with wetting agents are characteristically without dew in the morning, at least for the first few days after application. Wetting agents have much the same effect on grass and soil as rinsing agents have in dishwashers. Both break down the water into a thinner liquid. In a dishwasher this results in no spots on the glasses, and in the soil it means that grass roots can drink more easily. In fact, rinsing agents and wetting agents are very similar compounds chemically.

Aerating the localized dry spots (LDS) alleviates the problem for a while. Drenching with a wetting agent also helps, and there are many surfactants to choose from. Many combine iron, liquid nitrogen, and biostimulants to control LDS. Rarely is the problem cured completely, except after a prolonged rain followed by a cool period. Remarkably, the old-style push-up green rarely suffers from LDS, an indication that progress has a price.

THE PERCHED WATER TABLE

The late Dr. Bill Daniel of Purdue University is thought to have been the inventor and certainly the promoter of the perched water table in green construction. Daniel visualized a top layer of sand atop a layer of gravel and a bed of tile. Water in the sand layer would reach field capacity and then flush through the gravel into the drainage tile. Greens built in that fashion could not be overwatered, and drained perfectly. In his lifetime, Daniel witnessed many greens and sports fields being built according to his specifications. By the time of his death, even some of these showed signs of localized dry spots.

THE WATERING SYSTEM

Once it is understood how critical water is for the survival of the grass, it is easy to comprehend that the watering system is the lifeline on any golf course. That intricate system of underground pipes, tubes, and conduits must be in perfect working order for water to be applied when and where needed, all the time. When the system fails for any reason, its repair becomes a priority of the highest order. Fixing pipe leaks, repairing sprinklers and/or hydraulic and electrical lines, has become a highly specialized technical occupation. Most golf courses now employ someone to take charge of the watering system. That person needs to understand fully the operation of the pump house and must have the combined skills of an electrician and a plumber. The irrigation technician should not mind working in mud and water, often in the line of fire of flying golf balls.

In spite of the popularity of computer-controlled irrigation systems, hand watering remains a common practice at many courses.

What an Irrigation Technician Should Know

- How and when to shut the pump off—rudimentary perhaps, but of the greatest importance to avoid overwatering
- How to make pipe, electrical, and hydraulic repairs
- The principles of friction loss and the purpose of thrust blocks
- Sprinkler operation and water distribution patterns
- The operation of the pump house
- In northern climates, how to winterize the watering system
- The principles of water hammer and water and air pressure fluctuations

Leaks and Repairs

The first step in repairing a breakage in the watering system is to determine the nature of the break. Is it the pipe, the swing joint, or the sprinkler that is leaking? Once the cause has been discovered, close the valve(s) that control the affected area. By opening a trash valve or removing the innards of a low-lying sprinkler, the residual water pressure can be lowered. The rest of the water can then be pumped out.

Excavation

Place a piece of plywood near the area to be excavated. Cut the sod and remove it carefully with a long-handled sod knife. Dig a square or rectangular hole to the pipe, being careful not to cut the hydraulic tubes or the electrical wires. The square or rectangular hole is necessary to provide adequate room to maneuver while making the repair. The excavated material should be placed on the plywood.

Repairing the Leak

If the swing joint is at fault, the problem is most often a broken nipple. Replace it, using Teflon tape to seal the threaded connections, but using only one thickness of the tape. Several layers of Teflon tape on a plastic pipe thread can lead to breaks. Galvanized fittings are the major cause of leaky swing joints. They should routinely be replaced by polyvinyl chloride (PVC) fittings.

At times, the cause of a leak may be a cracked sprinkler body. This is often the case in northern climates after a harsh winter. If a sprinkler is to be replaced, releveling the new sprinkler is absolutely necessary. Tilted sprinkler heads cause uneven water precipitation patterns.

The most difficult repairs are those necessitated by broken pipe leaks, because they usually involve a section of pipe that needs to be removed. A longer excavating hole is required to make the repair, and therefore pipe leak repairs are usually more time-consuming to complete. Use a sharp saw to make a clean, straight cut. Bevel the edges of the cut with a rasp or a file. Insert a new section of pipe using gasketed repair couplings.

Backfilling

Once the repair has been completed and the water pressure tested, the excavation is backfilled slowly, with the soil, all the while being packed down with the technician's feet. This helps to prevent settling later on. If the original soil is of poor quality, backfilling with sand is recommended. In the root zone area, the sand should be amended. Replace the sod as level as possible, tamp it down firmly, and finally, fill the cracks with topdressing materials.

Many different tools are used to make repairs to the irrigation system. The following is a list of all the tools and items that should be available to make repairs. Most of these should be carried on a small maintenance vehicle.

- Shovels, both standard and a trenching shovel
- A long-handled sodding knife and an edger
- A fine-toothed general-purpose saw as well as a hacksaw

- A carpenter's hammer and a small 5-pound sledge
- A pipe wrench and a set of vise grips
- A set of screwdrivers, including a large slotted one
- General-purpose pliers and one pair of snap ring pliers
- Valve-insert tools for various makes of sprinkler heads
- Plywood, to keep the job site clean
- Stakes and caution tape to prevent accidents
- GUR (Ground under Repair) signs, to keep the golfers happy

Irrigation maintenance carts are usually equipped with a small vise, a workbench, a low-horsepower water pump, a hand pump, and a bailing bucket. All repair technicians carry a two-way radio or a telephone so that they can respond to emergencies quickly.

The Pump House

If the irrigation system is the lifeline of the golf course, then surely the pump house can be compared to the heart of the system. Without a sound heart with a healthy beat, the system cannot function properly. If the heart flutters at times or suffers from acute angina, it cannot pump properly and the result is fluctuating pressures, which in turn lead to water hammer in the pipes and malfunctioning sprinklers. A typical pump house on an 18-hole golf course may have several pumps with a total capacity of 1,000 gpm or even more. Most pump houses are now fully automated and fully pressurized at all times.

The importance of the pump house cannot be overemphasized. The initial cost of an adequate pump house is a major expense. The necessity of maintaining the pump house in good operating order is, therefore, obvious. Yet many a pump house suffers from poor housekeeping. That is deplorable, because a messy pump house inevitably leads to problems with the watering system on the golf course.

WINTERIZING THE SYSTEM

In climates where a deep freeze sets in at the beginning of winter and solidly freezes the soil to a depth of several feet, it is necessary to winterize the piping system, supply lines, and perhaps even the pump house. Most systems can be drained to some degree, but not all water can be removed in this manner. It is best to connect an air compressor to the main pipe and pressurize the system with air. Once a static pressure of about 50–75 psi has been attained, the sprinklers can be cycled, much as if one were syringing, and the rest of the water will be blown out through the sprinklers. Air pressure in the waterlines

Using an air compressor to blow out the watering system is a yearly ritual on northern courses. (Photo by Kevin Ross, Country Club of the Rockies, Edwards, Colorado.)

can fluctuate dramatically and become very explosive and dangerous. It is not uncommon for the pressure to cause water hammer strong enough to split the pipes.

To blow out a water system is a tedious job requiring much patience. One must make sure that all water is removed from the pipes and that only a thin mist comes from the sprinklers. It may be necessary to move the air compressor around to the extremities of the system, thus making sure that all water lines are thoroughly blown out.

THE WATER SOURCE

Irrigation water may be drawn from many different sources, such as rivers, lakes, wells, and even municipal water mains. Where the water comes from is not really important as long as there is enough. Some courses need as much as a million gallons during the course of a 24-hour period in the heat of summer. Most use much less. Computer-controlled automatic irrigation systems have made watering much more efficient, and as a result we can achieve the same result with less water.

A water reservoir that is fed by a river or from deep wells should be at 10–20 feet deep, so that the water will remain cool and is less likely to evaporate. The sides of the reservoir should be steep, to prevent the establishment of weeds along the shore. Aerating the water by means of fountains will help retard the development of algae. If weeds do build up, they may need to be removed with floating mechanical weed harvesters. Aquatic weed control by means of approved pesticides is governed by state statutes, and in many areas it is a tedious process to obtain the necessary permits.

The quality of the water is very important. Sprinklers, controllers, valves, and other components often have very small tolerances and will malfunction when the water contains silt or other impediments. If dirty water is a problem, filtration devices will need to be installed to screen out the pollutants. At the same time, beneficial additives can be added to the water that will make the precious liquid even more important to the plants. Fertigation, applying fertilizer through the water system, is quite prevalent and so is adding wetting agents. Less common is introducing bacterial cultures through the water system to the grass plants as a means of disease prevention. In all cases, high water quality is essential to make these new systems work to their optimum intent.

SUMMARY

Applying water has become incredibly sophisticated in recent years, and the methodology will continue to advance because water is such a precious resource. Managing the water system is one of the most important functions in a superintendent's job description. Yet it is often the least understood by golfers, because so much of it takes place underground and during the dark of night. For the same reason, it is frequently difficult for superintendents to obtain the necessary capitalization to maintain and improve the watering system. A word of advice: When seeking employment, superintendents should be wary of accepting a position where the water system is in a poor state. It would be difficult to improve the turf on such a golf course. It is important to remember that golf was never meant to be played in a swamp. To avoid overwatering, superintendents should walk the course frequently to experience the physical condition of the turf and the soil water content under their feet. When greens become sparse and pockmarked with ball marks, check the water schedule before blaming the golfers' poor etiquette.

7

Fertilizer

As much as the grass plant needs water, it also requires nutrition to sustain life. Superintendents have many different fertilizers to choose from, and to formulate a nutritional program is a complex task. Virtually all fertilizers have beneficial properties, but there is great variability in their suitability for grass on greens, tees, and fairways. For anyone rising up through the ranks with the goal of becoming a superintendent, a course in basic fertilizer chemistry is an absolute must. After that it is a matter of learning in the field, preferably on a large nursery. An excellent start is to read the fine print on a bag of fertilizer and, as a rule of thumb, apply half the recommended rate.

DIFFERENT TYPES OF FERTILIZERS

One of the best garden fertilizers is bonemeal, a ground-up material of skeletal remains high in phosphorous. For best results, bonemeal is forked into the soil, and for that reason is not used on existing golf greens. At time of construction, prior to turf establishment, bonemeal can be incorporated in the soil mix. Bonemeal has been around since time immemorial, and in recent years has been replaced by a wide range of sophisticated products that require a college degree or a technician's diploma to understand and apply. The terminology of modern fertilizers is so complex that one must have a thorough knowledge of chemistry and be conversant with soil physics. But when all is said and done, there are basically only two types of fertilizers: those that burn and those that don't. That may seem like an oversimplification, but in terms of basic greenkeeping it is best not to cloud the issue with jargon.

Fertilizers That Burn

The most dramatic burn can be achieved by an overdose of ammonium nitrate. Just a few pounds of this deadly material per thousand square feet will kill the grass. This is not surprising, inasmuch as ammonium nitrate can be used to concoct explosives for warfare or industrial purposes. Ammonium nitrate is a water-soluble fertilizer. Place some of it in a jar of cold water, shake it up, and watch it disappear. To make matters worse, ammonium nitrate contains almost 33% actual nitrogen. When the granules are applied to the grass surface, they attract moisture from the atmosphere and literally dissolve in their own sweat. That's why this powerful solution can so easily burn the grass. Similar compounds such as ammonium sulfate and urea act identically and should also be used with caution.

Experienced superintendents know how to handle water-soluble fertilizers, but novices in the field should become acquainted with these products carefully. Many mixed fertilizer formulations contain at least some water-soluble components. As a general rule, the less expensive the fertilizer, the more likely it is to be water-soluble and the greater the chance that it will burn.

Mixed fertilizers contain all three major nutritional elements—nitrogen (N), phosphorous (P), and potassium (K)—in various proportions. Nitrogen encourages growth and color, phosphorous is needed for the roots, and potassium gives strength to the plants. All three can burn the grass, but nitrogen is the chief culprit and should always be handled with respect. As a general rule, mixed granular fertilizers should be watered in thoroughly after every application. Even then, it is possible to see some marking around the cup and between the tee markers at the end of the day when a mixed fertilizer has been applied in the morning. Applying mixed fertilizers during cool weather lessens the possibility of burning. By covering the hopper of a spreader, one can apply fertilizer when it rains and enjoy the benefit of washing the nutrients into the soil immediately. A sensible program, then, should consist of a mixed granular fertilizer that may burn applied during the cool or shoulder seasons, and nonburning fertilizer applied during the heat of the summer.

Fertilizers That Don't Burn

The original nonburning fertilizers were mostly organic in nature and origin, and the most famous organic of all is Milorganite, a by-product of Milwaukee sewage sludge. Organics are low in nitrogen. Milorganite contains just 6 pounds of actual nitrogen per hundredweight, and none of it is water soluble. For that reason Milorganite, and many similar products, can be applied with impunity. Spilling a bag of organic fertilizer is no great disaster. Simply sweep up the granules. There will be no fertilizer burn, but the grass will be exceedingly green and lush in just a few weeks. Occasionally organic fertilizers are fortified with additional nitrogen, which then increases their burn potential. The success of Milorganite has led many other companies to copy the product. Sustane, a by-product of the poultry industry, has recently become widely accepted. Some organic fertilizers also tend to depress fungus disease infestation. Besides the major elements, the organics often contain sulfur, iron, and many trace elements that seem to have a positive effect on the plant's metabolism and its ability to resist diseases. In areas where fungicidal applications are severely restricted, organic fertilizers deserve to be part of the nutritional program.

Many golfers object to the smell that occurs just after an organic fertilizer application. Considering their origin, it is not surprising that both Milorganite and Sustane are guilty in this respect. Superintendents may well take the sensibilities of their customers into account and schedule their fertilizer applications with the golfers in mind. To simply give up on organics because of the smell is to miss out on some great fertilizers whose many benefits far outweigh this one small drawback.

Synthetic Organics

Urea formaldehyde and its many polymer cousins are recent additions to our fertilizer programs. Like the true organics, these products don't burn. The nitrogen and other nutrients that make up these formulations are released at a very slow rate over the course of the growing season, resulting in a consistent low rate of growth of the grass. Many mixed fertilizers now contain at least some of these products.

Fertilizer granulation was a problem when the different elements came in different size granules, resulting in uneven applications. Modern fertilizers are characterized by uniform particle sizes, in which each particle contains the formulation that is written on the bag. Such materials can be applied with greater accuracy and at reduced rates and still ensure that every plant will receive the specified nutrients it requires. Sulfur-coated urea is a pellet of urea nitrogen enshrouded in a skin of sulfur. The idea is that the sulfur skin will crack or dissolve and in the process the nitrogen will become available to the plant's root system.

Manufacturers maintain that all these synthetics can be applied without fear of burning, and that they don't need to be watered in. It is a better policy to be safe rather than sorry and to at least wash these materials off the grass blades. Subsequent irrigation cycles or natural rainfall will ensure that the fertilizer granules filter down into the soil, where they belong.

Liquid Fertilizers

Liquid concentrations of balanced fertilizers or single elements have been formulated that make it possible for superintendents to apply nutrients through the sprayer or even through the irrigation system. The fertilizer elements in the solution are applied to the plant as a mist or a light artificial rain, and some of the solution actually enters the plant's metabolism through the grass blades. The rest leaks down to the soil and the plant roots. The grass responds very quickly and results are visible in a day or two. For liquid applications to be successful, a computerized sprayer is essential.

No two golf courses feed their turf exactly alike and there is great variability in the manner of feeding grass with liquids. Some embrace the liquid technology completely, and others combine liquid and granular applications. Many use the liquids only on the greens and apply granular products to all other playing areas.

Iron

Many superintendents apply small amounts of iron to the turf. Some apply it only on the greens and fairways; others apply iron from fence to fence as part of the preparation for televised golf. Iron applied as a spray is absorbed through the leaf blades, enters the plant's juices, and turns it green within hours. The dark green color will last from a few days to a week. Iron is often used instead of a nitrogen fertilizer; it provides color without the surge of growth produced by a regular fertilizer. Iron is also beneficial because it assists photosynthesis inside the plant. Combine iron with a wetting agent, and you have a magic mix that seems to do wonders for the plants. Concoctions that contain iron, nitrogen, and other materials should always be experimented with in the nursery first. Only after the effects of the spray have been observed and found satisfactory should "cocktail" mixes be applied to regular greens.

Applying too much iron is a scary experience. Too much could be in excess of 3–4 ounces per 1,000 square feet. A miscalculation on the sprayer resulting in 8 ounces per 1,000 square feet will turn the turf black. Watering at that time will not help; the iron is already inside the plant and the damage has been done. Fortunately, the black color of the turf is not deadly, it just looks that way. The turf will lose its dark color in stages and will be back to normal in a few days.

It is important to remember that not all greens are equal. Some are in sunny locations and others grow in partial shade. Some face north and others south. Small greens become compacted quickly and suffer from *Poa annua* infestation. Large greens have no such problems and bentgrass is the dominant turf. As a result, the turf mat tends to vary from green to green. Greens with a sparse plant population react differently to liquid sprays than greens that are healthy and thick. A liquid spray formulation should be based on the threshold value of the weakest green. It is good policy to begin a liquid spray on the strongest green in case something goes wrong. A strong green will survive a miscalculation or a misapplication much better than a weak green.

APPLYING FERTILIZERS

For applying fertilizers to small areas such as tees and greens, a walk-behind spreader is usually quite adequate. Before starting, check out the spreader and make sure that it operates the way it is supposed to. Many of the small cyclone spreaders are not as reliable as one might expect. Test the spreading pattern on a cement or asphalt floor. Make sure the fertilizer spreads evenly, and measure the width of the application. Now is a good time to calibrate the rate of application. Measure the area that has been applied and sweep up and weigh the material that has been used. From these two figures the rate of application can be determined.

For example, if 20 lbs. of material has been applied to 1,500 sq. ft., the rate of application per 1,000 sq. ft. is 20 divided by 1.5, or 13 lbs. per 1,000 sq. ft. If the average green on the golf course measures 4,000 sq. ft., the calibrated setting would require a 50 lb. bag per green. Should the green be fertilized in two different directions, a practice that is always recommended procedure, it would take 100 lb. of fertilizer. If the fertilizer in question should happen to be Milorganite (formulation 6–2–0), it would mean that 6 lb. of actual nitrogen was applied per 4,000 sq. ft., or 1.5 lb. per 1,000 sq. ft. That's too heavy for a summer feeding but not unusual for a dormant application.

For larger areas such as fairways and roughs, one may use a tractor with a power take-off (PTO)-driven spreader with a large-capacity hopper. These large machines are best calibrated in the rough, to avoid causing mishaps on the precious fairway turf. Again, measure out an area, fill the hopper, and pick an appropriate tractor speed. After the measured area has been covered, deduct the remainder of the fertilizer from the amount at the start. Calculations similar to the preceding one should provide a rate of pounds of material per acre of turf.

Rate of application in lbs. per acre = lbs. of material
divided by area covered in acres

As was mentioned before, it is best to apply fertilizer in two different directions to ensure complete and accurate coverage. Experienced operators can make use of the mower patterns on tees and greens to ensure sufficient overlap, thereby avoiding the need to cross-fertilize and saving time. On greens, the aprons, collars, and approaches are generally fertilized at the same time as the greens. On tees, one may fertilize just the tee top but not the sides, because fertilizing the sides merely promotes excessive growth and the need for extra cutting. With tractor-driven spreaders it is best to spread from tee to green down the center of the fairway and then make an extra pass along each side. Extra passes may be needed, depending on the width of the fairway and the contour. Most spreaders are now of the cyclone type, but occasionally one may observe a drop-type spreader. The hopper lets the material fall onto a baffle board, from where it slides onto the grass. It can readily be understood that drop-type spreaders, by their very nature and makeup, can easily lead to poor application patterns. We don't recommend their use for that reason. Spreader technology has not kept pace with the innovations that we have witnessed elsewhere in turfgrass management. The spreaders are still very much the same as they were many years ago. Look for advanced technology in this area at turf conferences, in magazines and on the Internet.

FERTILIZER BURNS

When a fertilizer spill does occur, instant action is required. Use a lightweight square-mouthed shovel to pick up as much of the spilled material as possible without bruising the grass. Be ready with a hose, and use water pressure to wash off the rest of the material. No matter how tempting, don't use a broom to sweep up the material. The bristles of the broom break open the leaf blades and make it possible for the fertilizer to enter the plant juices, killing the grass. Even after careful removal of the spilled fertilizer and washing the remainder off with water pressure, it is very likely that the grass will still burn. There is little choice left but to repair the burn with a sod cutter and new turf. Some have cut the sod at the time of the spill, shaking off the fertilizer, replacing it, and following with a heavy drenching. Using a vacuum cleaner to remove the spilled fertilizer is also a good idea. Last but not least, a power broom or blower can be used to disperse the spilled material.

SOIL SAMPLING

Periodic soil sampling is a well-advised practice to monitor the soil inventory. It is almost impossible to make decisions on plant nutrition without at least knowing what is already present in the root zone. A private soils laboratory or a government agency will specify how samples should be taken, and their resulting report should be the basis for a fertilizer program. Interpreting a soils report requires knowledge of soil and fertilizer chemistry. It may seem like a daunting task but is really not so complicated. The soils laboratories tend to stress the importance of pH and, indeed, a range between 6.5 and 7.0 is probably best for optimum grass growth. These values are rarely actually the case, and excellent golf turf can be grown much above and below these parameters. Although it is relatively easy to raise the pH by adding lime, to lower the pH by applying sulfur is much more difficult. Grass adapts quickly to a variety of circumstances, and rarely is the pH the most critical one.

There are many soil testing kits on the market that allow a superintendent to determine the nutritional requirements of the grass. Testing the nutritional content of the leaf tissue is yet another means of finding out what the grass plant needs for sustenance. A small laboratory house in the maintenance building is an enviable feature that will enhance the superintendent's professional image, as well as make decisions on plant nutrition much easier. It is important, however, that time spent in the lab is not at the expense of more pertinent chores such as managing the crew and making sure that the work gets done.

Knowledgeable superintendents can tell at a glance when turf needs feeding. They recognize when color is fading and when tillering is slowing. They know when turf will respond and what materials are needed. Such knowledge comes from experience and is the result of many seasons of long days spent on the course. Combine this experience with modern technology and academic training, and the result is invariably consistently superior conditions.

FERTILIZER PROGRAMS

A plan to feed the grass must be in place at the start of the growing season. Such a plan should be carefully prepared and be based on soil testing and the nutritional requirements of the grass plant for a specific climatic zone. Older, well-established turf requires less fertilizer than grass on a newly constructed golf course. The game of golf is much more pleasurable on lean turf than it is on lush, succulent grass. Lean turf is equated with healthy turf. More often than not, less is better, and moderation should be practiced not only when it comes to feeding the plant but in all facets of golf course management.

A fertilizer program should specify the number of applications, and the timing, and the amounts and kinds of fertilizer to be used. Remember that after a period of dormancy, the grass plants experience an inner urge to grow vigorously and need very little encouragement at that time. At other times, the grass needs encouragement and a boost in its diet. Knowing when and what to apply is based on judgment, experience, and careful study.

Based on the plan, the materials can be purchased all at once or when needed, although the latter is preferable. There is a danger in becoming stocked with too much fertilizer, bought at discount prices but not needed for several seasons. Fertilizer should be stored in a dry place on pallets. Even shrink-wrapped fertilizer, however, has been known to become moist and thus spoiled for use. Liquid fertilizer is often stored in the chemical building.

CONCLUSIONS

Turfgrass nutrition is an extremely complex subject that requires a thorough understanding of soil chemistry and the materials available to feed the grass plant. Most superintendents are now college graduates of either two- or four-year programs. In both cases they are well prepared to understand fertilizers and their optimum rates and times of application. Why, then, are so many ready and willing to abdicate their responsibility to the first fertilizer salesperson who knocks on the office door? Superintendents ought to take their responsibilities seriously and formulate their own programs. It is wise to seek help when uncertain, but the final decision rests with the superintendent. This well-trained expert is best qualified and owes the employer a degree of frugality that will result in the best program at the most economical price.

8

Topdressing

No other practice but topdressing has such an immediate and positive impact on the health of grass. Whether topdressing with straight sand or with a mixture of sand, soil, and peat, the grass responds almost at once. As the topdressing particles filter down between the grass blades, the plants get a welcome reprieve from the pounding feet of golfers and the shearing action of the mowers. Topdressing that is watered in increases the vigor of the turf and makes the grass look healthier. When such a sward is cut with a sharp mower, it looks smooth and putts to perfection. In fact, it is impossible to create a perfect putting surface without the benefit of timely topdressings. The purpose of topdressing is not only to restore health to weak turf, but also to smooth the surface by filling in pitch marks and other scars and blemishes.

WHAT KIND OF MATERIAL?

Old-time greenkeepers used compost and some still do. Compost has an extra benefit: It is rich in humus and thus becomes a natural fertilizer. For putting greens, the topdressing material needs to be fine so that it will sink in between the grass blades and not be an obstacle to putting. That is why compost is often screened prior to application. The coarser particles are removed, and the rest is suitable to filter into grass mat. Topdressing with straight manure is not a good idea because the material is so difficult to work into the turf. There is another drawback: The rich organic content of manure needs nitrogen to help break it down. This nitrogen is extracted from the soil, but at the expense of the grass plants. As a result, the grass will often look yellow and sick after a dressing with manure. Superintendents who applied manure as a dressing in late fall, before freeze-up, have mostly given up on the practice because it had little value as a preventative measure for winter injury. A thick application of topdressing near the end of the golfing season and as part of a winter injury preventative program has proven to be very effective.

A heavy topdressing is a relative term: How heavy is too much? Smothering the grass with too much topdressing can be lethal. After topdressing, the grass blades should still be clearly visible so that the growth processes can continue and the plants will not suffocate. Anything more than $\frac{1}{8}$ an inch (3.2 millimeters) is too much and will smother the grass. It is better to make frequent light applications than to apply one heavy dose. The height of cut of the grass is another factor that must be taken into account. Greens that are cut very short require frequent light topdressing. On the ultra dwarf varieties, bags of dried sand are often applied with a walk-behind cyclone spreader on a weekly or bimonthly basis.

The choice of material on newly established golf courses is easy: Always use the same material that was used in the original construction of the greens or tees. Superintendents rightly fear the buildup of layers of differing topdressing materials in the soil profile. Successive regimes of different superintendents who all had their favorite mixtures can be documented by analyzing the core sample of a green. Layers of different materials are detrimental to both root growth and water movement in the soil.

SAND VERSUS SOIL MIXES

Straight sand as a topdressing material has found favor with many turfgrass managers. There are some obvious advantages:

1. Washed sand is clean and easy to apply.
2. Golfers can putt even over a light application.
3. Sand can quickly be worked into the existing turf.
4. Sand smoothes the putting surface very well.
5. Watering sand in is a cinch! It washes down after only one or two turns of the sprinkler.
6. As a result, there is very little interruption to play when using straight sand as topdressing.

Repeated dressings of straight sand will build up as a layer on top of the greens profile. Because topdressing with sand is so easy and quick, superintendents tend to do it more often, and as a result the layer can become as thick as an inch or two after only a few years. The layer of pure sand then plays havoc in the root zone. The grass roots have difficulty growing through it, and the sand impedes the vertical movement of water through the soil.

Greens topdressed with sand on a regular basis frequently develop localized dry spots (LDS): small areas ranging from a few inches to a foot or more, where the water won't penetrate and the grass can't survive. Repeated aerations help to puncture the layer of sand and the soil underneath. Sand is a very abrasive material that easily injures the grass blades, especially when a steel mat or a brush is dragged across a sand-covered green. The combination of the sand and the matting action may cause injury to the grass, especially when the turf is under moisture stress. The symptoms are akin to wilt, and a timely syringe cycle will save the grass.

Mixing topdressing material was traditionally part of the art of greenkeeping, acquired through experience under the supervision of the head greenkeeper. Various proportions of sand, soil, and peat were mixed and shoveled through a shredder or over a screen. The old-time greenkeeper would occasionally take a handful of the material, finger it lovingly in the palm of his hand, and then squeeze it. If the ball of earth formed in his hand crumbled easily, he was satisfied and the magic mix was approved for application. During the mixing process bonemeal, sulfate of ammonia, and mixed fertilizers were often added to the mixture. Old-timers guarded the secrets of their mixes carefully, unwilling to share this hard-earned knowledge with their colleagues.

With time, the mixing process became more sophisticated. Loaders and high-capacity shredders were used instead of hand-shoveling the material up a slanted screen. Now it is possible to purchase formulated blends from companies that specialize in topsoil and sands. A physical as well as a chemical analysis can be provided on which to base the selection of the topdressing material.

METHODS OF APPLICATION

For a long time topdressing was spread by shovel onto putting greens. It had to be done carefully to avoid lumping. Workers used square-mouthed aluminum or other lightweight shovels that made it possible to take a sizeable amount from the back of a truck or from a wheelbarrow. With a long, sweeping motion, an experienced worker could spread the dressing to perfection. It would feather out as it left the shovel and never leave lumps. This method was difficult to learn and very time-consuming. Modern topdressing machinery quickly replaced the old-time greenkeeper and his shovel. The topdressing was applied at an even thickness and uniformly over the entire green. The new machines resembled a small version of the farm manure spreaders and were equipped with a rotating brush, the bristles of which propelled the topdressing particles into the turf.

An offshoot of the fertilizer spreader involves a cone-shaped hopper with an oscillating applicator that propels the topdressing material onto the putting surface. This model makes it possible to apply sand as a very thin layer to an entire green in a matter of minutes. Topdressing all the greens on an 18-hole course can be completed in just a few hours. Cutting the greens prior to topdressing is a good idea, because it means applying the sand or the topdressing material to a dry green, which in turn speeds up the drying process and reduces the inconvenience to golfers. Instead of cutting, consider whipping the greens to remove the dew.

Grain on greens can be controlled with repeated topdressings and brushing, but if the control of grain is the primary purpose of topdressing, it is better to verticut first in several directions prior to topdressing. Topdressing helps to control thatch as well, but it is a fallacy to believe that one can bury thatch with heavy topdressings.

Once applied, the sand is left to dry and then brushed into the turf with either a steel mat or a series of brushes. In both cases, a utility cart is used to drag the mat or the brushes. The brushes will bounce when traveling at great speed. As a result, waves or ripples may develop on the putting surface. As with most other maintenance equipment, it is best to throttle down and travel at low speed.

The topdressing material should be watered in either immediately after it has been applied or during the nightly irrigation cycle. The final step in the process is to cut the green, preferably using an old mower. Using a mower with smooth or solid rollers is preferred because grooved rollers and groomers have a tendency to kick up the topdressing particles and make a messy surface, instead of pressing the particles down into the turf. Because of the abrasive action of the sand on the cutting cylinders, the mowers will need to be sharpened frequently. Setting aside an old mower especially for the topdressing operation will spare the regular units.

Scheduling and timing topdressing can be difficult for the following reasons:

- The golfers will complain.
- It is either too wet or too dry.
- It is too hot or too cold.
- It is too close to the weekend.
- There are not enough staff, and there is too much other work.

Single-minded superintendents will weigh all factors and forge ahead anyway. The bunkers will not remember having missed a raking and the rough will not miss a day's cutting. An application of topdressing will benefit all the greens and ultimately improve the putting for all golfers. Always remember a perfect green is the top priority in the scheme of the overall maintenance program.

There is no need to topdress entire greens all the time. Parts of all greens are more heavily used and require extra attention. Fastidious greenkeepers will recognize this, isolate such areas, and treat them separately. In such instances it is often best to omit the high-tech equipment and revert back to the methods of yesteryear and swing a square-mouthed shovel loaded with topdressing. Then take a Levelawn or the back of an aluminum rake and rub the material in.

Brushing topdressing material into the grass mat makes for smoother greens and helps control thatch.

TOPDRESSING TEES

The need for topdressing tees can be even more pressing than for greens. Tees take a terrible beating from golfers who often use several practice swings with their metal-woods and irons before actually hitting the ball. Tees on par 3 holes quickly become scarred with divot holes, and unless such tees are repaired regularly, they suffer permanent damage. Because tees tend to be cut somewhat higher than greens, thatch and grain also develop more readily. Regular topdressing of tees is a must for these two reasons: to repair the divot scars and prevent the buildup of thatch.

It is a good practice to combine overseeding and topdressing on tees on northern grasses. Do not miss such glorious opportunities to apply seed just prior to its being covered with a thin layer of soil. Seed applied with topdressing has a much better chance of germinating and growing into healthy plants than when applied alone. The rate of seeding should be at least 1 pound of bent grass per 1,000 square feet, or 5 pounds of rye or bluegrass seed.

Care must be taken when topdressing tees to preserve the flat surface that

Using a Flymo to force sand into the aerator holes. (Photo by Kevin Ross, Country Club of the Rockies, Edwards, Colorado.)

golfers value highly on tees. There is a tendency, particularly on long, narrow tees, to topdress only the center, where most of the damage is. This is a common and costly mistake, because it involves regrading and returfing the tee tops.

Whereas topdressing greens must be done in advance of the golfers and the material worked in prior to putting, the timing of topdressing tees is not nearly as critical. It can be done while regular play carries on, between groups of players, as long as there is a space between the markers that has been cleaned. Topdressing tees can be scheduled in the afternoon for that reason. There is another advantage: The topdressing material dries up much more quickly and can be worked in almost immediately after application.

TOPDRESSING FAIRWAYS

Applying topdressing to all the fairways of an 18-hole golf course is a giant undertaking. Modern machinery has made the job much easier, but the quantities of material involved are huge. Several truckloads may be required to complete just one fairway. For that reason, topdressing fairways is not a common practice on many courses. There is a case for dressing parts of fairways, such as the landing areas that may be badly divot-scarred. Such areas should be identified and topdressed several times during the golfing season. Because fairways are usually established on native soils, adding sand does not lead to the establishment of localized dry spots (LDS) that may be prevalent on tees

Applying sand topdressing is quick and easy with a cyclone spreader.
(Photo by Scott Brame, Crooked Stick Golf Club, Carmel, Indiana.)

and greens. As on greens and tees, topdressing results in smoother, healthier fairways, less prone to develop thatch.

Recent innovations in topdressing machinery have made it possible to apply minuscule amounts of material to fairways. New technology makes it possible to literally dust the fairways with a light coat of topdressing. If fairways are rough because of improper grading, topdressing using modern machinery may well be the answer to level out the hills and valleys, but it will take repeated applications.

TOPDRESSING SOD

Rarely is a sodding job so perfect that it does not require some topdressing to fill in the cracks and possibly even some footprints. Some prefer to wait until the sod has taken root; others apply topdressing immediately after the laying and rolling of sod. Topdressing sod is always limited to small areas on the short-cut turf of tees, greens, and fairways. A steel drag mat cannot be used to work in the topdressing. It would tear up the edges of the sod. Instead, it must be done with a Levelawn or the back of an aluminum rake. Watering the sod will wash the topdressing material still farther into the cracks where it is most needed.

Aerator holes need to be filled to the top with sand. (Photo by Mark Chant, Aspetuck Valley Country Club, Weston, Connecticut.)

DIVOTING

In addition to regular topdressing applications to tees, there is often a need to fill divot scars on tees with sand, soil, and other additives. This marvelous mixture of several different ingredients is the essence of growth and regeneration. A perfect divot mix contains some of the following ingredients:

$$Sand + soil + humus + seed + fertilizer = divot\ mix$$

The sand can be topdressing sand, bunker sand, or even beach sand. A regular loamy topsoil will do just fine, but for good measure many superintendents add an organic component. For seed, use whatever species or variety that is presently growing on the tees. Do not apply a divot mix containing rye grass on a bent grass tee, and vice versa. A tuft of rye grass will look out of place on a bent grass tee. A fertilizer high in phosphorus is ideal for the divot mix, but sweepings from the floor in the fertilizer shed will do equally well. Although many superintendents manufacture their own special brand of divot mix in this manner, a ready-for-use material can also be purchased from suppliers. In

The divot crew at work. Filling divots with sand to the same level as the tee is critical. Too much sand causes unevenness. (Photo by Michael Dogood, Nassau, Bahamas.)

most cases this material is merely colored sand to which one can add seed as an option.

On the par 3 tees, golfers like to see divot mix stored in containers and available for the players who take pride in their course and wish to take part in its preservation. Divot mix may also be provided in containers on golf carts. There is rarely an excuse not to fill a divot. Divots on fairways, especially in the landing areas, can similarly be repaired, mostly by the greens staff but often with some help from the golfers. Thus, divotting has become a regular maintenance practice on all golf courses.

SUMMARY

Topdressing grassed playing areas is an important part of turfgrass management. Topdressing revitalizes and smoothes grassed surfaces, particularly putting greens. A perfect putting green cannot be maintained without timely topdressings. Too much topdressing material applied at one time, however, can also be detrimental to the health of grass. Ugly divot scars on tees and fairways mar the beauty of a golf course. When golfers fail to repair divots, superintendents must step in to fill the gap.

9

Coring, Spiking, and Verticutting

The cause of compaction and the need for aeration is demonstrated every time a footpath becomes established through repeated use. It happens at a college campus when students find the shortest way from one building to the next. It also happens on the front lawn of most people's homes when the mailman takes the same route, day after day, to the next house. In both instances the soil is compacted, the roots can no longer breathe, and the grass blades wither and die. Repeated foot or vehicular traffic compresses the soil, closes up the pore spaces, and forms a crust that shuts off the movement of water and air. No plant life will survive under those conditions, but long before it happens, superintendents recognize the symptoms and take remedial action: They bring out the aerifier, that hateful machine universally despised by golfers all over the world. Why should a practice that is so beneficial for the grass be so thoroughly disliked by golfers? That is a question that needs to be understood before aeration of any kind is attempted.

Spiking is a modified and less disruptive version of coring. Instead of removing a core of soil and turf, spiking involves making a shallow puncture in the surface of the grass mat and into the soil below. Spiking is much less drastic and hardly interferes with quality putting. Verticutting involves slicing the surface, at times deep into the mat and the soil below. All three, coring, spiking and verticutting, are cultivating practices that improve both the playing surface and the soil when used with skill and knowledge based on experience.

CORING GREENS

The words *aerating* and *coring* are often interchanged randomly, inasmuch as both refer to the same process. *Coring* is a generic term, whereas *aerating* is derived from the first coring machine, which was known as the aerifier and was invented by Tom Mascaro shortly after World War II. Aerating also refers to the process of circulating water in ponds by means of a fountain. As with soil, air and oxygen are introduced into the water.

When greens become compacted, the beneficial grasses such as bent and Bermuda are the first to decline and make way for *Poa annua.* Take note that the popular cupping areas on many greens quickly become infested with *Poa annua.* Compaction can be felt through the soles of one's feet, especially when one is wearing sneakers.

Not all greens are created equal, and some need aerating more often than others. Small greens become compacted quicker than large greens for obvious reasons. Whereas average greens (over 5,000 square feet or 450 square meters) may need to be cored only once annually, small greens may need to be treated two or three times. Large, sprawling greens can be omitted from the aeration program altogether at times. As with topdressing, there is no need to core the entire green all the time. Seek out the popular cupping areas and walk-off areas and reserve special treatment for those portions of the green.

Every possible measure must be taken to prevent the encroachment of *Poa annua,* and none is more important and effective than timely coring. This bears repeating: The only turf that will grow on a compacted soil is *Poa annua.* In fact, when *Poa annua* rears its ugly head, the most likely cause is a compacted soil.

Timing

A thorough greens aeration should be scheduled at least once during the growing season, and a time should be chosen that inconveniences the least number of golfers and is still optimal from an agronomic viewpoint. Because no two golf courses are alike, the best time to aerate should be determined by the superintendent. Some aerate early in the spring to help speed recovery from winter injury. Others wait till early fall to alleviate compaction after a busy golfing season. At some golf courses play is suspended for a few days or even a week during the summer so that all the playing areas can be completed at once.

Because golfers universally despise coring or any other process that disturbs the putting surface, they need to be warned well in advance when coring will take place. Use all of the following methods to warn golfers of pending surface disturbance:

- Post notices on bulletin boards, both in the clubhouse and on the golf course.
- Make announcements in the club newsletter and the calendar of events.
- Use e-mail to alert golfers.
- Include a brief explanation about the benefits of coring, spiking, and verticutting.

Greens aeration is an important management tool that stimulates growth and speeds recovery. (Photo by Anthony Girardi, Rockrimmon Country Club, Stamford, Connecticut.)

- In addition to the golfers, also inform the greens staff, so that they can respond to golfers' questions intelligently.
- Be visible when coring is in progress, and lend a willing ear to golfers' concerns and criticisms.

Aerating a green, a tee, or a fairway is like major surgery on the grass plants that make up the turf. It is a shock to a plant's metabolic system because the grass is often torn loose from its roots. At times there will be a setback instead of an expected improvement to the turf. This happens especially when the turf is weak to start with. As a rule, therefore, it is best to aerate a green when the turf is strong and healthy. The aeration then is a measure to ensure its survival when stressful times arrive. Aerating a sick green with weak, anemic turf is attempted only as a last resort, when compaction has definitely been established as the cause of the trouble. Aeration should never be thought of as a cure-all for all manner of mishaps and maladies that befall grass during the course of a growing season. Be aware of the false phrase, "When all else fails, aerate."

To aerate late in the fall, just before freeze-up, is a mistake. Some superintendents have tried this in the belief that opening up the soil and leaving the cores on the surface is an excellent means of winter injury prevention.

Such is not the case! The open holes will suffer from desiccation along the periphery, and the cores make an unholy mess on the putting surface that is difficult to clean up in the spring and has no benefits whatsoever.

Nature's way of aerating the soil occurs during the winter season on northern golf courses. The freezing and thawing of the soil profile loosens tight soils and makes room for air and oxygen to pass through the pore spaces once again. For that reason, aerating in the spring is rarely necessary, but sometimes aeration in the springtime can be beneficial, especially when winter injury has thinned the sward. In that case the cultivating action of the aerator tines stimulate growth by opening the crust. Applying seed and some fertilizer at this time further promotes growth but remember that seed does not germinate when soil temperatures are less than 50°F (10°C). Superintendents should determine which greens need to be aerated, and how often, at the beginning of the season and schedule this operation as part of the overall maintenance program. Always make a plan first and then work the plan.

Benefits of Coring

1. Relieves compaction.
2. Opens the soil crust.
3. Facilitates entry of water and air into the root zone.
4. Helps to control thatch.
5. When combined with topdressing, coring helps modify the soil mixture.

On the Negative Side

1. Coring makes a mess of putting. Surface disturbance is often very severe.
2. Recovery of the putting surface is frequently very slow.
3. Coring results in increased vigor of the grass, which slows green speed.
4. Coring during the heat of summer can be hazardous and result in turf loss.

Hollow-Tine Coring and Tine Sizing

The purpose of most methods of aeration is to extract a core of soil from the green. The core may vary in size from more than 1 inch to less than $\frac{1}{4}$ inch in diameter. The length of the core or the depth of the resulting hole also varies, from $\frac{1}{2}$ inch to more than 1 foot. The number of holes per square foot varies greatly: The smaller the tine, the closer the spacing. Larger tines may be spaced as much as 6 inches (15 centimeters) apart. The choice of tine sizing depends

Deep-tine aeration promotes internal drainage and breaks up layering in the soil profile.

on the purpose of the operation. For overseeding on greens and to cause minimum disruption, use mini- or pencil tines. For a serious hardpan condition or drainage problems, use the largest size tines of all. In between lie the most common aerating applications: relieving compaction in the top $\frac{1}{2}$ inch of the soil profile and controlling thatch. For those purposes, tine selection is usually $\frac{1}{2}$ inch in diameter and spacings are at 2-inch centers.

If the soil in the green that is being aerated is desirable, the cores can be pulverized by verticutting and worked into the green as a topdressing. If the soil is less than desirable, the cores should be removed and hauled away. In both cases the aerator holes need to be refilled, preferably right to the top of the holes, although that may be difficult or nearly impossible. When the topdressing sand is dry, a Flymo is often used to help to disperse the sand and fill the holes.

Additional topdressing, combined with brushing and matting, will fill the holes and restore the putting surface to its former condition. At times a light rolling after coring helps make the surface smooth. Golfers have cause for annoyance when the aerating practices are not completed properly and putting becomes erratic.

Case History

A worn area on a green infested with *Poa annua,* measuring approximately 500 square feet, has become a source of aggravation for the superintendent and spoils the otherwise perfect appearance of the green. The area should be aerated with minitines at 1-inch square spacings to a depth not exceeding 1 inch. The tiny cores of soil and vegetative material are brought to surface and left to dry for just a short while. Meanwhile, bring out a drop seeder and apply about 1 pound of a favorite bent grass seed. Because the seeds fall vertically, many of them will fall into the tiny holes. Some will fall all the way to the bottom; others will get caught up in the wall of the hole. Now take our favorite greenkeeping tool, the Levelawn, and rub the cores, pulverizing every last one. The core mass will quickly disappear and be converted into topdressing. Some of the ground-up earth will find its way into the aerator holes, where it becomes part of the growing medium. Complete the operation by cleaning the treated area by cutting with a greens mower. Keep the cup away from the aerated area for at least a week, until it has recovered.

Meanwhile down below, in its tiny compartment, the seed has been exposed to moisture, heat, and light and in just a few days the magical germination process has taken place. The seed bursts from its shell and sends a root down and grass blades upward. Since all of this takes place in its very own growth chamber, none of the physiological processes are impeded by foot or mower traffic. The grass quickly becomes established as a small tuft and becomes part of the greensward. How do we know this? Because we have seen it happen, by getting down on our hands and knees, and with the help of a magnifying lens, watching the grass take root. We strongly recommend this method as one of the best means of introducing a new bent grass cultivar into an existing turf.

Shatter Core Aeration

Instead of using hollow tines, some superintendents have substituted solid steel tines. When such tines are forced into a green, they literally shatter the soil profile as they enter the green's surface. Holes are created as the aerator advances, and these need to be filled with topdressing. Many believe that repeated use of solid tines creates a hardpan layer just below the surface of the green, a layer that impedes the movement of both air and water. For that reason, the popularity of this novel practice has never really taken off.

The Hydroject

At the beginning of the last decade, the Toro Company introduced the "hydroject," a self-propelled machine that spouts streams of pressurized water

The hydroject makes aerating a painless procedure. It is a useful tool but has not replaced hollow-tine coring. (Photo courtesy of the Toro Corporation.)

into the soil without disturbing the surface. Obviously, the pressurized streams create channels within the soil profile through which air and water can move. The result is remarkable on compacted greens: There is immediate relief for the struggling grass plants, which are magically provided the necessities of life. It was thought at first that the hydroject would replace core aeration, since it apparently had all the benefits of regular core aeration without the disruptive surface agitation. Although many superintendents use the hydroject regularly and have made it part of their aeration programs, it has not replaced standard core aeration.

The Vertidrain

The Dutch invented the vertidrain and used it for sports fields at first, to improve vertical water movement through the soil. The humongous tines penetrate between 10 and 12 inches into the soil, rock back and forth at their greatest depth, and literally shake up the surrounding soil. The Dutch soon discovered that their new machine was ideally suited to break up the layers of compacted soil on the push-up greens in the Netherlands. The merits of the PTO-mounted behemoth were quickly recognized elsewhere in the developed world, and the machine is now being manufactured and copied in North

America. It can be modified with several different tine sizes and spacings. Many superintendents now use the vertidrain on fairways and in the roughs as well as on the greens.

Recently, Floyd MacKay developed a novel contraption consisting of a series of drills mounted on a metal frame, that can be raised and lowered. The drills, working in unison, bore holes into the green or tee and extract material as they penetrate. Once the desired depth has been reached, which may be several inches to a foot, the hole is refilled with sand or another suitable material. This unique method of aeration is finding favor with superintendents who want to drastically modify and improve the growing medium on greens. It may appear to be a cumbersome method, but it is quite effective.

AERATING TEES

We already know how quickly tees can become scarred during the playing season. No matter how often the markers are changed, the turf on tees takes a terrific beating, especially if the tees are of insufficient size. A regular aeration program for tees is a must. Once a season is rarely enough. Aeration of tees should be a preventative measure. By the time a smallish tee becomes completely worn out, aeration will not restore its cover; sodding will be the only alternative. Before that happens, aerate and reseed.

The wear patterns on tees become established very quickly, and it is these worn areas that need special attention. Once superintendents understand that only small portions of the tees need to be aerated, the task becomes much more manageable and can often be done in a very short time.

It is important on tees not to go overboard on the tine size. It is best to use $\frac{1}{2}$-inch tines or even smaller. If a tee is regularly aerated with large tines, golfers will have difficulty finding solid soil to plant their tees. The larger tines should be used only if the soil needs to be modified, in which case the cores should be removed and the aerator holes filled with desirable topdressing.

CORE DISPOSAL

If cores are raked off tees and greens or harvested with a collecting device, they can be put to good use on most golf courses. Adding the cores to the compost pile is a marvelous idea. A core, in most cases, is a combination of some form of topsoil and organic matter. It is an ideal ingredient to mix with fallen leaves and other debris.

When the grass portion of the core is desirable, such as bent grass, the cores can be used to fill in low-lying areas on the fairways. When such areas are raised, they should be firmed and roped off. It will take a week or two for the

Collecting the cores after aeration can be done quickly with the aid of a mechanical core sweeper. (Photo by Scott Brame, Crooked Stick Golf Club, Carmel, Indiana.)

mixture to grow and form a turf. In the fall, this method of repairing scars and scrapes and low-lying areas is particularly effective because the growing conditions are so much better than in the summer. A word of caution: If the turf portion of the core is *Poa annua,* it is best just to put it in the compost pile, for obvious reasons.

When the soil on an area that is being aerated is acceptable, there is no need to remove the cores. It is much better to pulverize the cores on the spot and use the resulting material as topdressing, thus killing two birds with the same stone. On small areas, the cores can be beaten up and worked into the existing turf with the reliable Levelawn. On larger areas it will be necessary to use other means, such as a verticut mower. Running over an aerated area with a verticut in two different directions is usually all it takes to make the cores go away. Follow this by dragging the steel mat behind a golf cart or a Cushman, and all that remains will be rolls of fluff. The fluff is the vegetative material that was once the roots, the rhizomes, and the grass blades which made up the grass plant. To get rid of the fluff, simply blow it into a heap and haul it away, down the beaten track to the compost pile.

Although a cleanup cut after aerating a tee is not a matter of great urgency, it finishes the job and makes the work look complete. When the tee and the aerated area are subsequently watered, the job is complete and the healthy growing processes can begin and will restore the damaged area to its prior perfect state.

AERATING FAIRWAYS

Fairways encompass a much larger area than both tees and greens, and thus present a bigger problem to the grounds manager. In order not to be discouraged by the magnitude of the undertaking, it is best to tackle the project bit by bit, one fairway at a time. Post the progress on a bulletin board and check off each fairway as it is completed. The process becomes a game, with everyone involved anxious to see the project completed.

Some fortunate superintendents are able to close off nine holes while they aerate the fairways. Others close the entire golf course during aerating week and put all resources to work in order to complete not only the greens, but the tees and fairways as well. The process can be sped up in various ways. Contemporary equipment tends to be speedier than the machinery of just a few years ago. Adding extra units, either by borrowing or renting, will make the operation go faster. Working longer hours without the interference of golfers will also get the work done much more quickly. A thorough aeration with closely spaced tines penetrating to a depth of 3 inches will take longer than using a machine whose tines are spaced at 6-inch centers and penetrate the soil barely an inch. Choices have to be made based on experience, the availability of equipment, and the degree of perfection that is required.

Once a fairway has been completely aerated, it needs to be cleaned off. The cores can be removed, but usually they are pulverized with a verticutter or a steel drag mat and worked in as a topdressing. The residue can be swept off by a powerful tractor-mounted blower. Cutting the fairway, perhaps with the buckets removed, puts the finishing touches on a job well done.

Successfully completing the aerating operation depends a lot on the weather. It must be dry enough so that the cores don't clog the verticutter heads or bog down the steel mat. A sunny day with a bit of wind, and not too warm, provides the best conditions. A word of advice: Don't wait for perfect conditions to start the job. They rarely happen. Rather, anticipate optimum conditions and get on with the job. Make it happen and get the work done.

Once fairways have been aerated, superintendents will note a quick improvement in the water absorption rate during an irrigation cycle. The multitude of aerator holes aids in quickly absorbing the water and transporting it to the roots. The plants show their appreciation by growing more vigorously.

There are areas in the rough that will also benefit from aeration. Vigilant superintendents recognize such areas quickly during their daily tour of the golf course. They may be concentrated traffic areas near bunkers, caused by power carts. Near greens there are frequently congested spaces between traps and fringes that suffer from too much traffic. In such cases the traffic should be diverted and the compacted area aerated, fertilized, and treated with a wetting agent to restore life and improve playability.

Although aeration is a marvelous rejuvenating process that can be used to

Aerating in tandem at the Crooked Stick Golf Club, Carmel, Indiana.
(Photo by Scott Brame, superintendent.)

great advantage, it is not a cure-all. Sparse turf on fairways, turf under stress, and turf with minuscule root systems will probably be worse off after aeration. The weak turf just will not tolerate the severity of the aerating process and often dies instead of recovering. It is best to leave such areas alone and aerate them when conditions improve.

Another pitfall of aerating occurs when the holes are left open and the grass desiccates along the edges. This may happen during the winter, when aeration was done as the last process before freeze-up (a questionable practice at best), or during the summer when drying winds make the grass wilt.

Aerating cultivates the soil while barely disturbing the surface. As such, it encourages renewed vigor of the root system and accompanying top growth. Aerating does not improve the inherent fertility of the soil. One cannot just keep aerating ad infinitum, expecting continuous plant growth. Somewhere along the line the plant must be fed. Timely fertilizer applications combined with aeration will result in a healthy turf cover.

Spiking

Like a verticutter, a spiker consists of a rotating disc with sharp tines. A spiker is most often used on greens, and as it makes its way across a green, it leaves

Verticutting is an important cultural tool that helps control thatch.
(Photo by Thomas Bastis, California Golf Club, San Francisco.)

numerous small holes in its wake. These holes are rarely much deeper than $\frac{1}{2}$ inch (1 centimeter). Spiking breaks the crust that often develops in the course of a growing season. When algae become part of that crust, spiking in one or two directions is an ideal solution. Like coring, spiking can be combined with overseeding. The tiny seeds will gain a foothold in the small holes left by the spiker, germinate, and eventually become part of the grass mat.

Verticutting

Unlike coring, verticutting disturbs the putting surface very little. The process consists of a series of metal blades that are driven in the vertical plane through the mat of the green and, at times, into the soil. In the process, rhizomes are cut and plant material is brought to the surface. When the cutting blades are thicker than a blunt knife, the process becomes more intense and a larger quantity of vegetative material, as well as some soil, is propelled upward to the putting surface. The primary purpose of verticutting is to reduce thatch and grain. It is a vigourous process that should not be attempted when the grass plant is under stress. The best time to verticut is at the beginning of the growing season when grass plants are growing actively. As the growing season progresses, verticutting lightly grooms the grass and improves putting. Superintendents in southern regions often verticut their Bermuda greens prior to overseeding with northern grasses for winter golf and again at time of transition to native Bermuda turf. The new ultra dwarf varieties of both bent and Bermuda grass are very vigorous growers and require frequent verticutting.

When and how to verticut and what machine is best to use require sound judgment based on experience. At times one needs barely to tickle the grass to obtain the desired result. At other times a deep verticutting into the thatch and the soil may be advisable. There is a thin line between success and failure. A perfect green can be likened to a race horse that is bred for speed but in the process has become very fragile.

SUMMARY

When soil becomes compacted it must be aerated. There are no shortcuts or painless remedies. There is a price for postponing the inevitable. It may be summer stress or winter injury. Greens, tees, and fairways must be aerated on a regular basis according to a well-thought-out program. Healthy turf is the result of hard work based on a plan, and that plan always includes aeration.

10

Spraying

From the microbial nematodes feasting on grass roots, to wild boars digging up turf, lies the gamut of pests that confront turf managers in the quest to produce finely manicured golf courses. Many, like the nematodes, fungi, bacteria, and viruses, cannot be seen by the naked eye. Others, such as the wild boars, skunks, crows, and cranes are big enough to shoot, but surely no one would want to do that. In between are worms, grubs, and creepy crawlies that infest the earth and the grass above it. While none of these pests are harmful in small numbers, they do pose a problem when they are present in multitudes.

Besides the members of the animal kingdom, there are pervasive weeds that compete with grass for space and, if left unchecked, will surely take over and crowd out desirable species. All of these enemies that feed on or compete with grass must be controlled to some degree so that grass will prevail, and whatever the activity of the pest, a sprayer filled with some sort of grass medicine is usually involved to achieve the desired results.

It is difficult to be a superintendent and not know how to operate a sprayer, be it a backpack sprayer or a tractor-drawn, computer-controlled tank sprayer with a shrouded boom. Not only does one need to know one's medicines in order to be a turf doctor, one needs to know how to apply the medicines effectively and safely. The mist that is dispensed under pressure from a single nozzle contains the particles per million needed to make a change. Dispensed from a boom with nozzles, it falls gently on the tender leaf of a grass plant or a weed. How can it possibly make a difference? But amazingly, it does. At times the magic solution to achieve the optimum benefit eludes us, and the result is a devastating death through overdose, a horror that every self-respecting superintendent fears but inevitably faces during the course of a career. Equally, a spray may appear to have made no difference at all, and a superintendent may fear having wasted the cost of the application. One never knows for certain unless an area is left untreated as a check plot to compare the results.

Sprayer technology in all its complexities is a fascinating subject that we bypass here. Instead, we focus on the commonsense approach to the application of pesticides and all other ministrations that promote healthy grass plants.

TESTING THE EQUIPMENT

Every golf course should have in its arsenal several backpack sprayers. They are handy for spot treatments, for applications around the bases of trees and ball-washer posts and along fence lines where weeds need to be treated or grass eradicated altogether. Such sprayers must be in good repair, preferably nearly new, for as the equipment ages, it becomes unreliable. The backpack sprayer should be filled with water and tested on asphalt so that the dispersal pattern can be observed. New workers, under the guidance of licensed operators, should be taught how to operate a backpack sprayer filled with water in this manner. The importance of learning to open and shut the stream cannot be overemphasized. An ugly trail of dead grass reveals evidence, for many weeks after the mistake, of not doing it properly. When the superintendent is satisfied that the new operators are sufficiently trained, they can be let loose on the links. But a diligent supervisor will continue to check on the new recruits from time to time.

Larger spray tanks, either mounted on a utility cart or tractor-drawn, should also be checked out thoroughly. Again, with the sprayer filled with water, start up the motor that drives the pump and check the on/off mechanism to make sure it works smoothly. Clean all filters and check the spray pattern of each individual nozzle, and ascertain the overlap. Then drive the spray rig over a paved area again and make the necessary adjustments until completely satisfied that the equipment is dispensing water as it is supposed to.

CALIBRATION

The object of calibrating a sprayer is to calculate the application rate. Once understood, it is a fairly simple procedure. Select a tractor speed that is comfortable: The machinery should run smoothly at a speed that will get the work done in a reasonable time. It should not be too slow, or it will take forever to treat even one fairway, nor too fast, or the tank will bounce, fittings will loosen, and leaks may occur. The best speed is probably a bit faster than a brisk walk.

If the boom is 20 feet wide, one needs to travel more than 2,000 feet to cover an area of just 1 acre. That is not practical. In fact, it makes more sense to travel a distance of 500 feet four times. Plant two stakes in the rough, exactly 500 feet

Algae and aquatic weeds are a common problem, especially on shallow ponds. Manual removal avoids the use of costly pesticides. Water aeration is another option.

apart. Fill the sprayer with water to the brim and spray the area between the stakes four times. At completion, measure how much water is needed to refill the sprayer to its former level. If it takes 30 gallons, then we know that the sprayer will apply 30 gallons of liquid to each acre. If the sprayer is equipped with a 300-gallon tank, we also know that we can cover 10 acres with one tank filled to the top at the speed that we previously specified.

Modern sprayers are equipped with computer controls that monitor the application rates at varying speeds. A sprayer that ascends an incline will slow down; the computer senses the slowdown, analyzes the information, and translates it into a reduced application rate. Computer-operated sprayers function best when they are programmed with the correct information. The rate of application, the boom width, and the speed of the vehicle must be fed into the controller. A computer-controlled sprayer applies exactly the same amount of liquid to every square foot of turf. Such a spray rig results in much greater accuracy in reaching the targeted pest; in addition, immediate savings are gained through greater efficiency. Computers greatly simplify the calibration process, but basic calculations should not be forgotten by modern-day superintendents.

RULES AND REGULATIONS

Virtually all pesticide applicators are now government licensed or work under the direct supervision of someone who is. The licensing process trains applicators to follow the rules. Most of the rules and regulations involve a common-sense approach to spraying operations. Because the rules have been written by people who rarely do the actual work, the language is often cumbersome and difficult to understand. Here we repeat what we know from personal experience in layman's language:

1. Read the label! Much of it is legalese to protect the manufacturer from liability, but there are tidbits of information that are helpful and useful. The product may have certain exclusions for specific plants or there may be some allergy information of interest to golfers and applicators. Most products are accompanied by a fact sheet that can be a treasure trove of information. It is generally best to read all the instructions the night before, so the work will not be delayed in the morning.
2. Be thoroughly familiar with the product that is being applied. One needs to get to know a new pesticide, a wetting agent, or a bio-stimulant formulation, much in the same manner as one gets to know a new piece of equipment. Try it in the nursery, on an abandoned fairway, or in the rough. Never, ever, apply a new product on a problem green. Invariably, Murphy's Law will kick in and the problem green will get worse instead of improve.
3. Determine the recommended rate of application and consider applying half as much. It has been our experience that often half the recommended rate will work just fine. Frequently pests do not need the full dose in order to be exterminated. Think of the savings that can be realized by this simple expedient. But remember that even applying less than the recommended rate may be an infraction. Check on what is permissible in your area.
4. Applying pesticides that are no longer registered is illegal and may result in serious penalties for the operator and the owner(s) of the golf course.
5. Avoid mixing pesticides to save time and labor. Few people would mix a weed killer with an insecticide, but some may try adding a fungicide to an insecticide. Although some pesticides are compatible in tank mixes, most are not, and it is better to be safe than sorry.
6. By all means add a defoaming agent while the tank is being filled, so that it won't overflow with big gobs of bubbles. Adding a dye such as Blazon is also a good idea. It makes it easy for the spray rig operator to see where the pesticide has been applied and what still needs to be sprayed.

7. When filling the tank, it is best to first fill half the tank with water, then add the medicine while the agitator is running, and finally top off the tank. Empty pesticide containers should be triple-washed and the rinsate returned to the spray tank. The containers should be sliced or crushed before being discarded, although they make excellent buckets for the divot crew.

8. The best time to spray is at the crack of dawn when wind is usually absent. With dew on the grass, it's easy to see what has been covered and what has not. It is often possible to complete nine holes before anyone tees off. Consider partially filling the tank with water the night before to gain precious time in the morning.

9. There are many devices that leave a mark in the grass to help the operator decide what areas have been done. The simplest is perhaps a small piece of chain that is dragged at the end of the boom over the grass to leave a trail. There is a need for an electronic device that will help steer the spray rig in such a manner as to provide just the right amount of overlap. In fact, it ought to be possible for sprayers to be operated by remote control.

10. When the job is done and the tank is empty, it is cleanup time. Partially fill the tank with water and spray the rough. Check all nozzles and screens and put the equipment away in such a fashion that it will be ready to go the next time it is needed.

11. A written report documenting the spray application is absolutely essential. Such a report is one of the most important pieces of record keeping in the superintendent's journal. The report should include date and time, weather conditions, the name of the material, and the name of the applicator; the sprayer settings should also be recorded. The pest that is being treated and the extent of the injury should be described as well. In fact, the more information included, the more value the document has for future reference.

DECISION TIME: WHEN TO SPRAY AND WHEN TO WAIT

It is an important part of a superintendent's duties to check the golf course in its entirety on a regular basis. Such an inspection includes the tees, fairways, and greens, and during the growing season one must constantly be on the lookout for signs and symptoms of disease. There are, at every golf course, certain indicator greens that, because of location, lack of air movement, or shade, are invariably the first places for a disease or a pest to show its presence. It need not be a green, but can be the back of a tee or a low-lying area on a fairway. Established superintendents know from experience where these areas are, and they base their decisions about when to spray on what is happening in these indicator areas.

Spraying fairways can be costly and needs to be accurate. (Photo by Anthony Girardi, Rockrimmon Country Club, Stamford, Connecticut.)

When the first signs of Dollar Spot show in their usual locations, and the weather prognosis calls for favorable conditions, a wise superintendent will apply a fungicide just before a three-day weekend. Similarly, if signs of Pythium are prevalent in a damp swale with a southern exposure, danger bells ring in the superintendent's ears. At such times it is wise to stay on the property and monitor developments, especially when hot and humid days and warm nights are also in the forecast.

Not only the superintendent, but also the assistants and the spray technician, should monitor the course for pest invasion. The decision to spray is never taken lightly. The actual blanket application of a pesticide to all greens, tees, or fairways may be preceded by treating localized areas. At times spot-spraying may nip the problem in the bud. The call to bring out the sprayer is based on observation, scientific evidence, and long-time experience. Never hesitate to ask a neighboring superintendent for advice. Check the chat lines on the Internet about the presence of disease. Often the spread of Dollar Spot, Gray Leaf Spot, grub damage, and other pests can be followed by monitoring posts on the Internet.

There was a time when some sprayed from fence to fence at the first sign of any kind of problem. Those were trigger-happy days, when pesticides were plentiful and inexpensive. Few showed any concern about the impact of pesticides on the environment. At the same time, there have always been frugal superintendents who use pesticides sparingly and only as a last resort. Such superintendents know that healthy turf is far less likely to be infected, and therefore they make it their business to grow strong grass that rarely gets sick. They know that vigorous turf is hardly ever infested with weeds. Superintendents who are observant in this manner and practice their grass-growing skills to the highest levels practiced Integrated Plant Management (IPM), long before it became a buzzword in contemporary times.

IPM has now become a maintenance and pest-control philosophy that many superintendents religiously adhere to:

- Scout the golf course for pest infestation a regular practice.
- Determine the specific cause of a pest and adjust cultural practices to contain it.
- Establish threshold values beyond which a pesticide application is an option.
- Spray only as a last resort when all else has failed.
- Verticutting increases effectiveness of pesticides by preventing binding with thatch, thus reducing usage.
- Sharp reels reduce mechanical damage to turf, and therefore susceptibility to pest damage.
- pH greatly affects the efficiency of pesticides.
- Stay away from water courses when applying pesticides.
- Soil and tissue testing determines the needs of plants for nutrients.
- Practice wildlife conservation by installing bird houses and leaving dead trees.
- Use wildflowers and native vegetation in nonuse areas.
- Institute a program of composting and recycling.
- Include the principles of IPM as part of a regular employee-training program.

FATAL MISTAKES

In the process of pesticide applications there have been some horrendous mistakes that have resulted in not just one dead green but several, and at times even all the greens on a golf course have been killed by an overdose, the wrong pesticide, or a lethal combination of pesticides.

- Mixing soluble fertilizers with pesticides should never be attempted until such a mix has been tested in the nursery.

- Problem greens with thin grass cover should be treated very carefully with any pesticides, or almost any product for that matter.
- There is a knee-jerk reaction on the part of many superintendents to blame inexplicable turf decline on some mysterious disease, and out comes the sprayer.
- More grass is killed as a result of mechanical accidents than from any other cause.
- Such mechanical accidents include topdressing or cutting stressed-out turf or cutting with maladjusted mowers.
- More grass is lost on Sunday afternoon than at any other time of week. The reason is that greens staff members are seldom around in the afternoon, and the grass is left to fend for itself. There is no one available to syringe or spot-treat.
- Greenkeeping is a daily endeavor, and the grass takes no holidays or long weekends. Especially during the heat of summer, with temperature and humidity running high, either the superintendent or the assistant should be available to assist the grass.

EDUCATION

The spectrum of plant diseases caused by fungi or insects is very complex, and combatting them requires a continuing stream of information from colleges and research centers. Add to that, weed infestations and nutritional deficiencies, and it quickly becomes apparent that superintendents, their assistants, and key personnel need to constantly update their knowledge of pesticides and their application.

The introduction of surfactants, biostimulants, and growth retardants requires precision sprayers and expert knowledge about rates and timing. Turf managers need to update their information on these products constantly by exchanging learning with their colleagues, by attending specialty seminars, and by visiting the Net. The slack part of the golfing season is an ideal time to go back to school. There is so much to learn.

SUMMARY

At the same time that turfgrass diseases have become more prevalent, a number of important pesticides have been taken off the market. It is becoming increasingly more difficult to control and prevent turfgrass pests with the few remaining medicines still available. Superintendents, now more than ever, need to grow strong, healthy grass that can withstand the ravishment of disease.

In some parts of the world neither pesticides nor chemical fertilizers are permitted to be applied to golf course turf. At first, it was just in a few Europe countries where such restrictions applied. Now there are municipalities in North America that have banned pesticides on lawns, parks, and golf courses alltogether. It is a frightening thought that such legislation may become commonplace in North America. We need to prepare for such an eventuality. A good start would be to reduce chemical budgets progressively and to rely more on old-fashioned greenkeeping methods that have served us well in the past.

11

Flagsticks and Tee Markers

When golfers arrive to play and proceed to the first tee, it is essential that the markers are pointed to the center of the fairway and the flagstick on the green is in a reasonable position. Nothing annoys an ardent player more than a course that has been set up thoughtlessly. Golfers are fussy that way, and for the superintendent to be careless about their wants and needs is jeopardizing his or her professional status. To delegate the course setup to an inexperienced worker is poor management and irresponsible. It also shows lack of concern for the needs of the golfers and for the integrity of the game. How the game is enjoyed on a daily basis is not only a state of mind of individual golfers, but also reflects how the superintendent and crew have set up the course.

THE TEE COMPLEX

There are several tees to choose from on most courses. The forward tees are for women and senior players. The center tees are for regular play, and the tees farthest back are for championship play. The rear tees are of particular importance since they are used by low-handicap golfers. Such players take the game very seriously and have no compunction about voicing their displeasure when the course setup is imperfect. Since the rear tees receive very little play, they need not be large in area but must be maintained with the greatest of care. Not only should the surfaces of back tees be closely cropped, but the surrounds need to be trimmed to an acceptable height. The length of the grass must not interfere with the swing of the club, nor should long grass at the front obstruct or deflect a golf ball. The standard of maintenance of the championship tees should be the guide for all other tees.

The center tee is the largest, since it receives most of the play. There needs

A novel way of pleasing the women on Ladies Day—potted plants instead of regular tee markers. (Photo by John Zinderdyne, Hockley Valley, Ontario.)

to be plenty of room to move the blocks, both back and forth and often sideways. Total teeing area on par 4 and par 5 holes should be at least equal to that of the greens, or about 5,000 square feet. On par 3 holes it is not uncommon for the teeing area to be twice as large as the green.

The forward tees require the same attention as given to all the other tees. Those charged with the responsibility of setting the tee markers use various methods to align the markers with the center of the landing area. One way is to stand between the markers, with arms stretched wide, one hand pointed to each marker. Now, bring the arms forward in a regular uninterrupted motion and, as the hands meet, the fingers should be pointed to the center of the fairway. Another method, not as widely used, involves the use of a T-square made from PVC pipe. Place the crossbar between the markers. The stem should be pointing toward the center of the hole. Problems often arise on dogleg holes. The center of the fairway for long hitters is different from that for shorter drivers. In the case of doglegs, first determine where the pivot point is—that is, the point where the hole changes direction—and line up the markers with the pivot point. Some players will need a driver to reach the pivot point, for others it may be a long iron, but the center of the fairway at the pivot point will be the same in both instances.

The location of the markers on the tee is very important. There is a school of thought that believes the length of a hole should not vary from day to day. When the markers are at the front, the flagstick on the green should be on the back, and so on. This method ensures that the overall length of the course is always the same. There are other means that create greater variation in the length of individual holes, yet the overall length of the course remains the same. A diligent hole changer will keep track of the total yardage while proceeding from one hole to the next. Some holes may be set up a little shorter than indicated on the card and others will be somewhat longer, but at the end of 18 holes the total yardage will always be as stated on the card.

From a greenkeeping point of view, the wear on tees must be spread in the most efficient manner possible so that no areas develop that are void of grass. At times, this means spacing the tee markers across the entire width of the tee. At other times it may be necessary to force golfers to use a corner or a side of the tee in order to give other sections a chance to recover. Unless play is very light, tee markers should be changed daily. At some courses where play exceeds 300 rounds per day, it may be necessary to change the tee markers twice on the same day, except that markers cannot be changed during a golf tournament since the course must play the same for all contestants.

For special events that include female golfers, consider using potted plants or baskets of flowers for tee markers. This extra touch is always appreciated.

OTHER FURNITURE

In addition to the tee markers, there are on most tees several other pieces of furniture that are standard items on many golf courses:

1. Benches are for comfort and for golfers to rest on while they are waiting to make their shots. Benches should be positioned thoughtfully: in shade, to keep golfers cool while they are resting, and out of the way of errant shots from backward tees. Benches should be lightweight so they can be moved easily, but not too light, or someone will take them away or they'll blow over in a hard wind. Benches should be durable because they are out in the open and exposed to the elements. They must be cleaned, scrubbed, and repainted from time to time. The worst sight on a tee is grass growing through the seat of a bench. Keep the grass trimmed around benches, and move the benches often so there is no worn grass where golfers place their feet nor long grass under the seat. On golf courses where power carts are mandatory, benches are often not available.

2. Ball washers are an important part of any tee complex, and at the same time can be a major source of irritation to regular golfers. Most often they lack soap and water. At times the mechanism is broken and the brushes worn. Ball washers need to be checked on a regular basis, at least once a week. They should be cleaned thoroughly by removing them from the post or stand and swishing them in soap and water. Some superintendents use a portable power washer to remove all the grime. Others add bleach to the cleaning solution as a disinfectant. The bleach certainly helps to reduce the smell that emanates from dirty ball washers, but too much bleach in the water may splash onto a golfer's shirt and pants and cause discoloration. The tops of ball washers should be scrubbed with a scouring pad so that the paint looks fresh. Most golfers expect soap to be added to the water in ball washers. Soap certainly helps to make the golf balls sparkle, but too much soap adds to a buildup of grime and the accompanying foul odor. Try adding a small quantity of wetting agent or omitting soap altogether.

3. Permanent markers are made from granite, cement, wood, or some other durable material and are embedded into the tee just a smidgen below the surface so that the mowers won't catch them. A permanent marker is placed precisely at the point from which the hole is measured, usually off to the side of the tee deck but clearly visible. In addition to the yardage, the hole number is also displayed on the permanent marker. The marker should be located in the center of the tee deck. Play should be equally distributed on the tee. If it becomes evident that there is more wear in front of the permanent markers, it means that the course habitually plays shorter than indicated on the scorecard. This translates to golfers' handicaps or indexes being incorrect

4. Trash containers on or near the tee are a must. Unless a receptacle is available, trash will end up on the grass and despoil the golf course. Such containers should be small and unobtrusive so as not to dominate the landscape around a tee. Occasionally a trash container is needed on a fairway, strategically located where golfers finish the soft drinks and coffees that they purchased at the canteen. Wherever trash cans are placed, they should be emptied on a daily basis, usually by the person who goes around changing holes and markers.

5. Signs are found on most tees indicating the number of the hole, the par, the handicap, and the length as well as a schematic of the golf hole. Such information is valuable to first-time players and guests. Members who play the same course regularly, have less need for such detailed information. In addition to tee signs, many courses exhibit signs reminding golfers to fix divots and ball markers and to erase the footprints in the sand. While all of this information is important, there is a tendency to clutter tees with too much furniture and too many signs, and the entire complex may resemble a garage sale in suburbia. In many instances money spent on multicolored signs, fancy ball

Permanent yardage markers on tees should be made of sturdy material,
and the surrounding grass needs to be trimmed frequently so
that the numbers are clearly visible.

washers, and benches could be put to better use in buying fertilizer and top-soil to create superior turf.

THE GREEN

Moving the hole or the cup on the green on a regular basis contributes greatly to the overall quality of the turf. On a large green it is not nearly so critical because the wear can be spread around much easier, but on small greens, less than 5,000 square feet, moving the hole and maintaining quality turf is very difficult. The problem is frequently exacerbated by undulations in the putting surface that limit the number of hole locations. Choices have to be made: Preserve the prime locations for weekends and prime times. During the rest of the week golfers must accept difficult and, at times, "unfair" hole placements. The superintendent will have to learn to grin and bear the wrath of irate golfers for the sake of preserving a quality green. Being a greenkeeper or a superintendent was never meant to be a popularity contest. As a last resort, consideration should be given to rebuilding and enlarging the green.

All the systems that have been invented and instituted to organize a regular movement of hole placements from the front to the center and to the back, work fine on large, sprawling greens. The hole can be placed almost anywhere with impunity as long as the surface nearby is reasonably level and the location is away from the edges and the hazards. The next day the hole can be moved 30–40 feet to a similar location, and so on. Meanwhile the turf does not suffer, because it receives plenty of rest between periods of play. On smaller greens, the moves are more likely to measure 10–15 feet. The hole often needs to be closer to the edge of the green. Contrary to popular belief, there is no rule in golf that dictates that the pin should be at least 15 feet from the edge of the green. A more common yardstick is to use the flagpole as guide for keeping the cup away from the edge. Some superintendents attempt to set up the course with six hole placements in the front third of the green, six in the center, and six in the back. There are some deviations from this simple, straightforward method. But they are all more complex and frequently lead to errors and disgruntled golfers. Others divide the greens into six equal parts that are numbered 1 to 6. The pin position is then posted near the first tee or on the golf cart. For important competitions, pin sheets are made available to the players, with detailed information in feet about the exact location of the cup. By far the large majority of golfers are content to see their shots land on any portion of the green, and for them the front, center, and back method (1, 2, 3) is more than adequate.

To help golfers determine where the hole is located on the green, several systems have been devised:

- Colored flags. For instance, yellow flags are used when the hole is at the back, white for the center, and red for the front. This method requires that the hole changer carry along extra flags or flagsticks with flags attached.
- Pindicator flags are attached to the flagstick and slide freely, except that their downward movement is impeded by a tight rubber ring. Golfers have been known to play tricks on their fellow competitors by moving the pindicator flags either up or down and thereby confusing their opponents.
- An often used variation of the flags is a round ball that also slides up and down the flagstick, but its movement is restricted by a cotter pin.
- The high-tech method of lasering the distance to the pin exactly with an electronic device. A receiver is attached to the pin, and a beam from a handheld gun attached to a golf cart measures the distance instantaneously and prints out the exact yardage. This method is precise and quick and takes all the guesswork out of club selection.

The pin is used as a yardstick for hole location on a green. A location within the length of the pin is too close to the edge; a location beyond is acceptable.

The most common method seems to be using colored flags, and the colors are gradually becoming standardized. That makes it easier for golfers who play many different courses.

CUTTING A HOLE PERFECTLY

Nowhere are the skills of a competent golf course worker displayed more prominently than when a fresh hole is cut into the green and the old hole filled and repaired. It is a simple process, yet so many things can and do go wrong. The hole may be mistakenly cut on a slant, which makes the hole slightly oblong instead of circular. The cup may be too far below the surface of the green, or worse, too close to the surface. When the lip of the cup is less than an inch below the grass surface, golf balls that were destined to drop to the bottom may be deflected and stay out. If it happens to the tee shot on a par 3 hole, it may mean the thrill of an ace spoiled. Replacing the plug in the old hole is often done either too deeply or not deeply enough. Either instance is objectionable but a common occurrence on many courses. Following are seven steps that should be strictly followed when changing a hole:

1. The hole cutter should be in a good state of repair. The blade must be supersharp, and in order to keep it that way, it should be filed regularly. If the hole cutter has been in use for more than five years, it is time to pass it on to a golf course with lower standards.
2. In addition to the all-important hole cutter, there are several other items that are part of the paraphernalia that is carried along:
   a. A cup puller and a cup setter
   b. A sponge to clean the cup
   c. A water bottle to water the plugs under stress
   d. A knife or a flat screwdriver.
   All of these items are carried in a 5-gallon pail or, better yet, in a "soft bucket," a canvas satchel.
3. Select the place on the green where the new hole is to be cut. Most times, this location has been predetermined or its selection is on a scheduled arrangement. It should always be level within its immediate vicinity (2–3 feet). Now, plunge the hole cutter vertically into the green. Twist it down a few inches farther and carefully extract the plug. Remove it from the hole cutter and place it in the pail. Make the next cut to the desirable depth. For inexperienced or novice hole changers, a white mark is often painted on the cutter blade for this purpose.
4. Remove the cup from the old hole and use a moist sponge to clean the inside of the cup thoroughly. Place the new clean cup into the new hole and press it down firmly to the desired depth, using the cup setter. Brush away any bits of soil from around the new hole. Superfastidious greenkeepers will use a pair of scissors to snip off any misplaced blades of grass hanging over the lip of the hole. If the cutter blade was sharp in the first place, this should not be necessary. It is a good practice to keep an extra set of new cups on hand to change the cups at least once during the season. For having clean cups all the time, you'll be a winner with the golfers.
5. Repairing the old hole is the next step. The hole must be filled to just the right level: Too little earth, and the grass plug will sink; too much, and the plug will be scalped by the greens mower. Use a knife or a screwdriver to break the earth between the lower and the upper plug. This is a form of cultivation that helps the roots to find their way downward. The top plug should be broken at the edges so that it fits snugly, pressed down level with the surrounding grass. Squirt some water from the bottle onto the plug, thus making sure that it will survive the heat of day. Clean up any spilled topsoil, making sure that any evidence of an old hole has been removed.

The hole changer carries along all necessary tools in a handy satchel.
Note the impact hole cutter developed in Sweden.

6. Selecting the correct color flag for the new location completes the process, almost. It is a good idea to check on how the pin fits into the hole of the cup. If the fitting is loose, it probably means that either the pin or the cup should be replaced. A loose-fitting pin is easily whipped out by a brisk wind and at times may lean inside the cup in such a way as to prevent golf balls from entering the hole.
7. Finally, when the hole has been changed perfectly, check one more time, from a distance, to make sure that the flagpole is straight on the green.

Changing the hole and filling low plugs with white sand.
Green sand blends in better with the grass.

In addition to changing the hole, the person charged with that responsibility should be aware of additional functions that can be performed in the round of duties. Small scars on a green can be repaired with a hole cutter by taking healthy plugs from the back edge of the green. Similarly, old plugs that have not taken and have turned brown can be replaced in that manner. The hole changer should repair the most obvious ball marks and be always vigilant for the first signs of disease. Because the responsibilities of the hole changer are complex and time-consuming, many 18-hole courses, employ two persons to change holes: one for the front nine and another for the back nine.

The hole changer, better than anyone else, knows from firsthand experience the need for water on any green. The need for water on the greens or tees should be communicated to the superintendent or the person in charge of irrigation. The hole on the green should be changed after about 250 players have passed through. In most instances, this means a day's play. In fact, changing holes is a daily chore except in the shoulder season, when some days can be skipped. Changing the hole on some greens and not on others is a dangerous practice that leads to inconsistencies. If the edge of the hole has been damaged,

Changing the hole requires great skill and attention to detail.
(Photo by Michael Dogood, Nassau, Bahamas.)

it should be changed, regardless of how many people have passed through. The location of a cup, however, cannot be changed once a competition is in progress.

SUMMARY

Golfers come to play with their friends, and they value the comradeship of their companions even more than the condition of the golf course. Their games are memorable occasions long remembered. The condition of the course is soon forgotten. All the more reason, then, that we should try to make their visits happy ones: May they sink many long putts, and may low scores adorn their cards. Nowhere have superintendents a better opportunity to directly affect the state of mind of their golfers than when changing holes and placing tee markers. Let's make sure to make the most of it.

12

Drainage

If there were a choice, most would prefer to play their golf on high land rather than low land. High land is equated with dry land: rolling hills from where the water runs into the valleys, rivers, and creeks. Low land invariably means wet land, unless it is drained. There rarely is a choice, and golf course superintendents are mostly presented with the task of making wet land dry. Golf should be played on firm fairways and greens, and on low land this can be achieved only by the installation of a network of tiles, culverts, and catch basins that facilitate the rapid removal of excess water. Good drainage extends the golfing season at either end and can reduce or eliminate the need for course closures and no-power-cart days.

SURFACE DRAINAGE

When water runs unimpeded from grass-covered land, the natural surface drainage is adequate because there is a fall between the high areas and the low areas. A 1% slope (1 foot vertical in 100 feet horizontal) is the minimum for the free movement of surface water. Somewhat steeper grades are more desirable.

Surface drainage often is hindered by faulty construction methods of long ago. Plow furrows may not have been graded adequately. Hollows may not have been filled to blend with the surrounding terrain. Low-lying areas invariably result in dead grass. Superintendents are expected to take remedial action. Fairways with severe undulations should be regraded. If the turf is of acceptable quality, it can be lifted, the soil smoothed with a landscaping device, and the sod relaid. On larger areas the process becomes more cumbersome, perhaps involving a golf course architect and an experienced contractor. In either case the end result should be a smooth fairway that permits adequate runoff and is compatible with contemporary conditions.

On greens and tees, settling of the soil may take place many years after construction has been completed. Such low-lying areas must be repaired, and the best time is when golfer traffic is low. The work should be completed in short order, probably in just a few days, without much interference to play.

RAISING A LOW-LYING AREA ON AN EXISTING GREEN

A low-lying area on a green is a common problem that occurs as a result of the settling of the underlying soil or faulty initial grading. After irrigation or natural rainfall a puddle results that prohibits putting and impedes the growth of grass. A temporary solution is to remove the moisture manually with a squeegee roller or, in extreme cases, using a pump. The long-term solution is to raise the area by adding a compatible soil mix and returfing.

Step 1

Identify the area and mark it with a paint gun. Place a surveyor's level off to the side and take readings to determine elevations. Record the elevations and outline the working area, making sure that it is two to three times the size of the actual low-lying area. The level should be placed at the back of the green, where it should remain until completion of the project.

Step 2

The large working area is needed to make sure that the finished grade blends in well with the rest of the green. Next, remove the sod very carefully and store it off to the side. Discard sod of poor quality, such as *Poa annua*–infested turf.

Step 3

Gradually build up the depressed area with soil mix a few inches at a time, and firm it as you go. Rake the surface smoothly and compact it still further with a water-filled roller. Measure the progress by taking readings with the level, and add more top mix if necessary.

Subsurface drainage on a typical green construction project includes installing a herringbone tiling system. (Photo by Anthony Girardi, Rockrimmon Country Club, Stamford, Connecticut.)

Step 4

When the desired level has been attained and surface drainage is ensured, apply a starter fertilizer at the recommended rate. Then continue rolling and raking, preferably with a wide aluminum rake, occasionally turning the rake and using the backside with the straight edge. Using a Levelawn is an excellent alternative.

Step 5

When you are completely satisfied that the desired grade has been achieved, it is time to replace the sod. The greatest care should be taken that the sod is placed just perfectly. It is recommended that the best-quality rolls of sod are used for the prime areas in the center of the green. Sod of lesser quality can be used along the outer fringe of the green. If there is insufficient sod, take some from the nursery or a strip at the back of a green. After sodding, roll in two directions. Check the levels one more time with the surveyor's level to be absolutely sure that water will now run off.

Step 6

The final step involves applying a thick coat of topdressing and working it into the grooves between the sod with a Levelawn or the backside of the aluminum rake. Water to wash the soil into the sod and the grooves between the sod, and keep the sod moist but not soggy until it is well rooted. For good measure, fence the work area with stakes and rope, and place a GUR (Ground under Repair) or explanatory sign in the middle. The newly sodded area will be ready for play in 3–4 weeks.

Repair work of this nature exemplifies the essence of greenkeeping: restoring poor turf to better health and improving the golfing environment. Many important skills are included in the process, and unless experienced in these skills one should probably not attempt such a repair, certainly not on the 18th green in front of the clubhouse.

NORTHERN PERILS

Superintendents in northern climates should be aware that snow and ice can hinder the normal runoff on golf course turf. When banks of snow freeze and form obstructions in the path of the water, the submerged turf will die. This can be prevented by the simple expedient of regularly patrolling the golf course during the winter months and removing any obstructions that exist. Dedicated superintendents have been known to remove snow and ice from all greens and tees to ensure the survival of the grass. Such attention is to be commended.

SUBSURFACE DRAINAGE

Water that accumulates in the soil and builds up above field capacity must find a way to get away, or the soil and the turf above will stay soggy and sloppy, unfit for golf and golfer-related traffic. The answer lies in drainage and the installation of a complicated system of tile lines and catch basins connected to larger pipes or culverts that ultimately drain into rivers and lakes. Such an elaborate system resembles an irrigation system in complexity, except that no electric power or controllers are required. If the system is installed in accordance with accepted methods, the force of gravity will make the water find its way, always downhill, to the lowest part of the golf course.

To install a drainage system, it is essential to become thoroughly familiar with the lay of the land. An important step is to identify the areas that repeatedly stay wet the longest, and to mark these on an aerial photograph. All too often an aerial photo becomes a pretty picture on the wall in an office or the clubhouse. That is a waste. Several copies should be available, and at least one should be used to record the location of the drainage system. In addition to an aerial photo, a topographical map should be on hand. The graduated contour lines show the exact course that the natural flow of the surface water will follow.

Plans can now be made as to how the golf course needs to be drained. If it appears that it will be a large-scale project, it is probably best to bring in an outside contractor who has golf course experience. This latter criterion is important, and it should be noted that being able to drain a farm field does not qualify one to drain a fairway. Projects of smaller proportions can be done in-house, even if it involves renting a trencher and a level.

DRAINING GREENS

Unless a green is built on top of a gravel pit, a bed of tiles should always be included in the construction of putting greens. Depending on the contours of a green, the tile drainage bed in the base is usually in the form of a herringbone system: one main drain with several laterals arranged to resemble the backbone of a fish. The tiles are imbedded in gravel, and the outlet is connected either to existing drains in the fairway or rough or to a sump in the rough off to the side. A sump is an underground pit filled with coarse gravel and covered with topsoil and grass. A sump accepts water from connecting tile lines quickly and disperses it slowly into surrounding soil.

The tile lines under a green should be 5–15 feet apart. In greens built according to USGA specifications, a "smile drain," or inceptor drain, is often added across the front of the green and connected to the main drain. Such a drain promotes water movement in this potentially wet area at the front of the green. This is precisely the area subject to most golfer and equipment traffic, and thus prone to wear and tear. Having the approach well drained will ensure good turf. The main drain through the center of the green is often extended to the rear apron and capped. This makes it possible to flush the tile line quickly and easily. A drainage system installed in this manner will function for years to come.

Unfortunately, not all greens are built with perfect drainage. In fact, on many older greens a tiling system of any kind has been omitted. The result is that superintendents are faced with the problem of either improving the drainage or living with a wet green. Installing tiles in an existing green is tricky, but by no means impossible.

Step 1

Lay out the drainage pattern that best suits the green. Spray paint the lines and remove the sod, using a narrow-bladed sod cutter.

Step 2

Place plywood on either side of the proposed trench and excavate the trench to a depth of approximately 18 inches and 3–4 inches wide.

Step 3

Remove the excavated material, clean the trench, and check for the necessary fall with the help of a level.

Step 4

Place a $\frac{1}{2}$-inch layer of pea gravel in the bottom of the trench as a bed for the tile. Install the tile and cover with gravel to 12 inches below grade. Covering the tile with a geotextile stocking is not recommended.

Step 5

Backfill above the pea gravel with greens-mix soil, and compact with a tamper. Add water to the fill to assist with the settling.

Step 6

Replace the sod and roll it well. Apply topdressing over the sod and rub with a Levelawn. Skilled workers should complete an entire green in just a few days.

Follow-up Treatment

1. Water the sod judiciously and never let it dry out.
2. Topdress frequently to ensure that the surface is perfectly smooth.

Installing drains in existing greens is a difficult proposition that can be successfully accomplished by experienced workers.

There are other methods, which involve slit trenching, that are less painful but still improve drainage. Contractors are also available to do this work expeditiously and have the green back in play in short order. Many superintendents prefer to have it done in this manner instead of in-house.

THE VERTIDRAIN

The vertidrain, a unique aerator invented in the Netherlands, punches holes in the soil to a depth of more than 12 inches and extracts a 1-inch core. At 6-inch centers, a tremendous amount of earth is removed from a playing surface. In the case of a green, these holes can be refilled with an approved sand to the top of the putting surface. In the process, whatever layers may have existed in the green's profile will have been punctured in innumerable places and the drainage, at least in the vertical plain, will have improved. The water still needs to be removed from the bottom of the green, and only a tile bed can do that.

DRAINING TEES

Tees, by their very nature, are usually elevated and drain exceptionally well, thus rarely requiring tile drainage. Low-lying tees, however, are another matter. It is advisable in such instances to install a main drain with several laterals, also known as a gridiron arrangement, and drain the subsurface water away from the playing surface. Large flat tees, as well as driving range tees, should be treated as greens and drained accordingly.

Tees that are built into hillsides often require an interceptor drain: a 12-inch wide trench, at least 24 inches deep with a 6-inch tile in the bottom and completely covered with gravel to the top. Such a drain will intercept the water that seeps from the hillside and prevent it from causing wetness on the tee. Interceptor tiles should also be used behind greens that are built in similar locations, as well as along steep banks that border fairways.

DRAINING BUNKERS

Modern bunkers are frequently flat at the bottom, which makes them particularly easy to drain. A tiling system similar to that used under greens is installed, and as under the greens, the tiles are covered with pea gravel. It is best to keep the gravel 2 inches below grade so that it will not mix with the sand and damage golfers' wedges. The outlet of the tile empties into a catch basin, for easy clean-out, and is then connected to the main drain. It is important to remember that bunkers require just as many tiles as greens to guarantee good drainage.

Repairing poor drainage in an existing bunker is best accomplished by removing all the existing sand, shaping the bottom into a desirable form and firmness, and then trenching the lines and installing the tiles. It is advisable not to use stockings around the tiles. The stockings quickly become clogged with sand and finer particles and prevent all water movement.

The same applies to filter cloth liners that are installed in the base of the bunker and tucked into the side under the sod. The main purpose is to stop stones from popping up from the base and mixing with the sand. By necessity, the liners have to be covered with more than the usual amount of sand, as much as 5–8 inches, whereas the normal coverage of sand in a bunker is rarely more than 4 inches. Even under a thick cover of sand, the liner will eventually make its way to the surface, which precludes the use of mechanical trap rakes. Such bunkers are then destined to be hand-raked for the rest of their days. Golfers who find themselves in a lined bunker will not be happy when a ferocious swing of the wedge is abruptly shortened in the web of a bunker liner. It can be a painful experience for the wrists as well as the scorecard.

DRAINAGE ON FAIRWAYS AND ROUGHS

Persistent wet areas on fairways and in the roughs need to be drained to make turf healthier and golf more enjoyable. A surveyor's line level is needed to prepare the plan and stake the lines. Use either a gridiron or a herringbone pattern. Employing a trencher equipped with a laser depth-measuring device will ensure that the trench has the necessary fall.

A small amount of gravel is placed in the bottom of the trench. Dragging a narrow trenching shovel across the gravel ensures a smooth bed for the tile. Covering the tile with gravel promotes the movement of water. At times the gravel can be taken right to the level of the sod, further ensuring that the surface water can enter the drainage system unobstructed. For a while the gravel will be visible and may possibly interfere with play temporarily. Soon the grass on the sides of the trench will grow in and cover the gravel. Do not yield to the temptation to cover the gravel with topsoil; it quickly seals the surface and prevents water from entering the system.

There are some justifiable objections to having pea gravel flush with the surface of the turf. The stones, in all likelihood, will get caught in the mowers and dull the blades. Golfers often object to loose gravel interfering with the lie of the ball or the swing of the club. Covering the gravel with a few inches of sand is acceptable. Tiles installed in this manner not only help remove freestanding surface water, but also draw water from soil adjacent to the tile line.

When the grass completely covers the tile lines and forms a dense mat, it may become impervious to the movement of water. When, after heavy rains, puddles appear over the tile lines, the thatch layer needs to be punctured. A hole cutter is an ideal tool for such an operation.

All tiling systems should include plenty of catch basins. The grate on a catch basin provides an opportunity for more surface water to enter the system. Catch basins also permit a visual check on the performance of the tiling system. Long runs of tile, in excess of 200 feet, should be interrupted frequently by a catch basin to act as a clean-out. Large pipes and culverts require bigger catch basins or drains. During or shortly after heavy rains, superintendents should check how the system performs by lifting the grate and observing the flow of the water.

FRENCH DRAINS

A French drain is a narrow trench filled from top to bottom with gravel, but with no tile in the bottom. The resulting gravel-filled channel should be connected to the tiling system or the outlet taken into the rough. French drains are an effective aid in the removal of water but are no substitute for tile drainage.

MATERIALS

Tiles

There are still one or two factories that manufacture clay tiles for drainage. Such a tile permits water to seep through its wall into the cavity of the tile. Few people go to the expense of buying and installing clay tiles. Most use plastic tile, either with or without holes in the walls. Plastic tiles come in rolls and are easy to handle and to install. Drainage tile made from a bituminous material can also be obtained in straight lengths. Tiles in excess of 6 inches diameter, besides being available in plastic, can also be found in galvanized iron. All small-sized tile is available with fittings that make connecting the tiles easy.

Gravel

By far the best gravel for drainage purposes is pea gravel. The characteristic smooth, round surface of the individual stones makes pea gravel ideal for the passage of water. The pea stones allow the water to slide off their surface and pass freely into the tiles. Clear limestone can be used as an alternative, but only as a last resort. The angular surface of the limestone tends to become clogged with foreign materials such as grass clippings and soil. Granite stone chips are yet another alternative, but have the same drawbacks as limestone. The performance of pea gravel is well worth the extra cost in the long run.

Catch Basins

Plastic catch basins come in all shapes and sizes. They are easy to install and easy to clean. The grate lifts out to permit watching the flow of the water. Plastic catch basins are inherently light. Cement catch basins are very heavy and can be installed only with the help of a heavy-duty lifting device. Cement catch basins are used in conjunction with larger-sized pipes: 12 inches and up. If need be, catch basins can be hand-made from a large-size galvanized pipe, but this method is usually inferior.

Trenchers

There are two important criteria to consider when buying or renting a trencher: How deep will it dig, and how wide will the trench be? In most cases a depth of 2–3 feet is adequate, and the best width for a 4-inch tile is a 5–6-

inch trench. Making the trench any wider than it needs to be only creates excess fill.

There are trenchers especially designed to make narrow slit grooves that permit the installation of flat tiles encased in pea gravel. Such tiles are generally joined into larger main pipes.

SUMMARY

There are many jobs on the golf course that require committee involvement and approval. Drainage is not one of them. Golfers expect their superintendent to take charge and drain low-lying areas, just as they expect the grass to be cut and fertilized. Drains and catch basins should be installed as a routine matter. To drain a full-sized course may take a lifetime, but it should be started, and once begun, little by little, it will be completed. There can never be too many drains and catch basins on any golf course.

After, or preferably during, torrential rainstorms, the superintendent should inspect and observe the performance of the drainage system. There is great satisfaction in watching a drain function perfectly. The result is dry land that can be cut without leaving ruts, and turf that can be played from, without casual water.

13

Seeding, Sodding, and Sprigging

Golf is meant to be played on grass, and the quality of the grass determines the reputation of the superintendent. Bare earth is almost always unacceptable. Every self-respecting superintendent strives to cover every part of the fairways, the tees, the greens, and even the rough, with high-quality turf. It is never an easy task. To establish a turf by means of seeding, sodding, or sprigging requires both skill and knowledge. Once the turf has taken root, we find that grass rarely grows without encouragement. It is a never-ending job to make it grow healthy and strong.

SEEDING

Seeding is probably the least expensive way of establishing turf and is often the preferred method since it does not introduce a layer of foreign soil into the strata. The problem with seeding is that the time window is narrow, and when the soil temperatures drop below 50°F we need to resort to other methods. Since the introduction of superior bent grass cultivars, stolonizing greens is rarely practiced anymore. Sprigging is still widely practiced for the establishment of Bermuda turf.

Seeds need warmth and moisture to germinate, and once a seed absorbs water, its skin is broken. Tiny roots develop and make contact with the soil for nourishment. For that reason it is critical that seeds be surrounded by damp, warm earth. Unless the earth is warm, nothing much takes place inside the seed, and this is precisely why late summer and early fall are the best times for seeding. The heat of the summer is still stored in the soil, and the heavy dews, so characteristic of the latter part of the growing season, help provide the most favorable growing conditions for the small grass plants. Since weeds are not nearly as active in the late season, the lack of competition from weeds is yet another factor that makes the time slot from late July till late September the best opportunity for seeding in northern locales.

Minimum Soil Temperature Requirements for Seed Germination

Perennial rye grass	50°F
Bent grass	60°F
Bluegrasses	55–60°F

Seed can be applied in early spring in the cold soil, but it will just sit there waiting for the temperature to rise. Covering seeded areas with a thermal blanket, such as a geotextile membrane, will speed up the germination process. In fact, it is a good idea to cover the seedbed overnight when the air temperatures are low, and remove the covers during the day when the sun is shining. Judicious manipulation of the growing medium by alternately covering and uncovering the seedbed will speed up turf establishment by several days. To achieve success, it is necessary to nurse the small grass plants. Constant attention is required. Covers need to be removed when the heat under the blanket builds up, and rolled back on with the cool of night. One must always be vigilant about the nutritional needs of the grass and aware that excessively lush growth may spawn fungus diseases.

Seed Sizes and Germination

The smallest seeds are those of the various bent grasses. Their minuscule size makes them almost invisible individually and even a handful of bent grass seed feels light as a feather, but under favorable growing conditions all of the millions of seeds will each produce a grass plant. Bent grass germinates in 5–10 days. Under ideal conditions a haze of green can be detected early in the morning of the fifth day when the grass blades are covered with dew. Not all seeds germinate at once. Over a period of several days more and more seedlings will raise their heads from under the earth and collectively form a cover of grass.

The seeds of bluegrasses and fescues are very much the same in size. The various cultivars of Kentucky bluegrass take at least 14 days to germinate and twice that long to form an appreciable grass mat. The fescues are a little quicker, but the really fast grass is perennial rye. It has been known to sprout a blade in just 3 days, and inside a week a green sward is clearly visible. Coincidentally, rye grass seed is the biggest in size of all the common lawn grasses. It is just as well that it grows so quickly; birds would surely eat all the seed before it had a chance to take root.

Seeding Rates

The following seeding rates are for the application of seed to bare earth only. Overseeding on top of established turf is a totally different matter that requires judgment and experience and is not bound by hard-and-fast rules.

> Bent grasses: 1–2 lb./1,000 sq. ft. or 40–80 lb./acre
> Bluegrasses: 3–5 lb./1,000 sq. ft. or 100–150 lb./acre
> Fescue grasses: same as bluegrasses
> Rye grasses: 5–8 lb./1,000 sq. ft. or 150–250 lb./acre

Overseeding Established Turf

It is very difficult to obtain acceptable results when overseeding into established turf. To simply broadcast seed over actively growing turf is largely a waste of time. Intimate contact must be achieved and established between the seed and the soil for germination to take place. For that reason slit seeders have been manufactured that create a narrow groove in the soil into which the seed falls and quickly germinates. But can the young plants compete with the dominant turf of actively growing grass? Not likely, and at least not to any large degree. If, however, the existent turf is sparse, the new seed has a much better chance to compete and to become established.

Still another method involves implementing what is known as the "scorched earth" technique. Scorching the earth is accomplished by spraying the turf with glyphosate or Roundup, which kills all the green grass in a matter of days. The grass mat is then slit seeded, and in a few weeks the old turf has been killed and is replaced by a superior species. This is precisely how *Poa annua*–infested fairways are converted to bent grass on golf courses in the northern climatic zone.

Another means of establishing seed in existing turf involves combining aerating and seeding. This can be quite effective on greens when using minitines or pencil tines. When the seed is applied with a hopper-type spreader, at least some of the seed will fall into the holes and germinate. The same method works equally well on fairways and in the rough, but it is advisable to use larger-diameter tines, on the premise that larger seeds require larger holes.

Winter Overseeding of Bermuda Turf

Southern grasses are not very tolerant of cold temperatures, and it is an accepted fact that when nighttime temperatures drop below 50°F for any period of time, the grass will go dormant and turn brown. That is not to the fancy of northern golfers vacationing in Florida and other southern destinations. They demand green grass and will settle for nothing less. Knowledgeable super-intendents know just how to look after their discriminating customers: They overseed their southern turf on greens, tees, fairways, and even roughs, with large quantities of bent, rye, fescue, and *Poa trivialis* grass seed. The process is unique, and it requires great skill and judgment to obtain satisfactory results. Since timing is critical and golfing schedules often interfere, results may vary from one year to another.

Several weeks prior to the scheduled overseeding, superintendents cut back on fertilizer programs and so reduce the vigor of the Bermuda turf at a time when falling temperatures also reduce plant growth. To prepare the seedbed still further, extensive verticutting is carried out, thus opening the turf mat so that seed can filter down to the soil level. At the same time, the height of cut is raised to provide a canopy for the seed. On low-budget courses, greens are overseeded with rye grass, and so are the fairways and the tees. At high-end re-sort courses and private country clubs, the seed of choice is bent grass, often augmented with a small quantity of *Poa trivialis*.

Overseeding Rates for Southern Turf

Bent grass on greens and tees	1–3 lb./1,000 sq. ft.
Poa trivialis on greens	10 lb. /1,000 sq. ft.
Rye grass on greens and tees	20–40 lb./1,000 sq. ft.
Rye grass on fairways	200–400 lb./ acre.

Some golf courses overseed the rough as well as the fairways; others leave the rough to its own devices, which means that at least for much of the win-ter it is mostly brown and often makes for an attractive contrast with the lush green fairways. In southern Florida, in a line from Fort Lauderdale to Naples, the Bermuda turf stays green very consistently and overseeding is not a common practice. From there on north, the decision to overseed is often a gamble. A superintendent may guess right one year and be a hero; the next year the su-perintendent could be a villain and lose his or her job.

Immediately after overseeding greens, topdressing is often applied and the greens are watered intermittently to encourage germination. The two-week pe-riod following overseeding can be frustrating for golfers because the greens tend to be excessively moist and very slow. Once the seed germinates and the plants become established, conditions return to normal as superintendents re-duce watering and lower the height of cut. The process for overseeding fair-ways is very similar but not as intensive. Seed can be broadcast by a cyclone spreader, but the outer edge is seeded with a drop-type spreader to make for a distinctive line of contrast. Following the seed application, the fairways are drag-matted or brushed to work the seed into the turf mat.

If the overseeding process is time-consuming and tricky, the spring transition back to Bermuda turf is equally difficult. As soon as air and soil temperatures rise, the northern grasses must make way for southern grasses. That means the height of cut is lowered and fertilizer is applied to pop the Bermuda grass out of its dormancy. If the rye grass is permitted to flourish well into spring, it is often at the expense of the Bermuda grass with disastrous results.

It is obvious that seed size and seeding rates are related. The smaller the seed, the greater the number of seeds per pound. The number of individual seeds per square foot of soil needs to be adequate to achieve complete and thorough coverage of the area to be seeded. There is a danger, particularly with the fine-seeded bent grasses, in applying too much seed. An extremely thick stand can easily give rise to to disease, such as "damping-off" caused by Pythium and Rhizoctonia fungus species. The mycelia of these fungi will quickly wipe out a large stand of newly germinated grass seed. As soon as they have been identified, they should be treated with an appropriate fungicide.

Preparing a New Seedbed

In order for seed to germinate, the seeds must make contact with the soil so that the sprouting root can embed itself among the soil particles for anchorage and to extract sustenance from the growing medium. It is therefore obvious that the seedbed must consist of a layer of fine soil particles. This can be attained by rototilling the area to be seeded and firming and leveling it with a landscaping device that includes a roller of some sort that breaks up the large clods and leaves in its path a bed of fine topsoil. Landscaping tools such as the Gill and the Viking can be attached to the three-point hitch system found on most tractors and do an admirable job of fine-grading the area to be seeded, sodded, or sprigged. Other methods include dragging a steel I-beam, a piece of chain-link fence, a steel mat, or even just the power rake used for sand bunkers. All of these methods work well, except there is the danger that they work so well that contours carefully designed by architects may be obliterated. On smaller areas such as greens, where prescribed contours are absolutely essential, hand-raking may be the only alternative. Debris, rocks, and stones must all be removed from the area to be seeded. Usually such items are hand-raked into piles and carted away. When the quantities are too large, mechanical stone pickers are needed. Nothing must be left to interfere with the growth of the grass and the ultimate maintenance practices.

Fertilizing the Seedbed

Ideally, a starter fertilizer should be applied prior to rototilling so that the fertilizer granules can be mixed into the growing medium. Since this is not always possible, applying the fertilizer to the finished grade is perfectly all right. There may be a justifiable fear that too much fertilizer will burn the root hairs as the grass germinates. We have never seen this happen. On the contrary, we have observed a lot of retarded new grass that suffered from lack of nutrients rather than too much. In fact, grass in its infancy needs to be fed generously, just like a little baby on its mother's knee. Rates of 500–800 lb. of a 10-10-10-type fertilizer or similar material per acre are not excessive.

Seed Application Methods

For the smaller bent grass seeds it is best to use a drop-type spreader. The larger seeds may be applied by means of a cyclone spreader. On steep and uneven terrain, consider using a seeder that is strapped over the shoulder and disperses seed via a cyclone mechanism propelled by a hand crank.

Spreading the small bent grass seeds can be made easier by using a carrier such as sand, or even organic fertilizers such as Milorganite or Sustane. This method increases the bulk of the material and makes achieving uniform coverage much easier. Whatever method of seeding is used, it is best to apply the seed in two different directions to ensure overlap. Wind is an important factor. A brisk breeze can easily blow the seed away from where it is wanted. It is best to seed on still days with little or no wind. After the seed has been applied, the soil should be lightly raked and rolled to create optimum growing conditions and a smooth surface.

For larger areas use a tractor-drawn "Brillion" seeder, which consists of a hopper and a drumlike packer that causes the seed to be covered with a fine layer of soil. The weight of the cast-iron packer draws the moisture of the soil to the surface, thus assisting the germination process.

Mulching

Covering seed with straw mulching is an excellent method of promoting germination. The straw helps provide a damp environment that reduces the need for constant watering. In addition, a cover of straw is an excellent means of preventing erosion. The old-fashioned method of spreading bales of straw with a pitchfork has given way to using rolls of straw interwoven with plastic strands that keep the straw in place. Such blankets are particularly effective on steep hills. Attached to the soil with biodegradable metal staples, these straw blankets provide a wonderful cover and speed germination immensely. They also extend the time frame for successful seeding. Add at least a month in the fall when using straw blankets. The soil moisture and heat are preserved under these cozy covers and the seed germinates quickly, raising its leaves through the straw mesh. The resulting growth forms a thick stand of turf, ready for use in the spring. The plastic netting can be a problem when cutting the new turf for the first time. It does not seem to disintegrate nearly as rapidly as one might like.

Watering

Newly seeded areas need to be watered on a regular basis, but ever so gently. Too much water at a time causes runoff, and once erosion gains a foothold it is difficult to stop. Automatic underground sprinklers can be set with precision, thus making watering an easy exercise. The objective is to keep the soil damp while the tiny grass plants are sprouting their roots. Once the grass plants are established, they must be kept moist to grow actively and form a mat of dense grass. Be careful not to overwater the young seedlings. It may induce a Pythium infestation.

Establishing bent grass on high-sand-content greens can be tricky. The sand dries out so quickly that it needs to be watered frequently, often as much as once an hour, especially during the heat of the day. Even after the seed has germinated, it needs constant attention or the grass plants will wither and die. At such time, the vigilant eye of the professional superintendent must be ever present to ensure success and prevent disasters.

Fertilizer

New turf has an inborn desire to grow, but this process must be stimulated with extra nutrition. New turf requires at least twice as much fertilizer as established grass. Applying fertilizer to newly growing grass can be damaging because of the absence of a wear-resistant mat. To avoid ruts caused by maintenance vehicles, superintendents will often apply liquid fertilizer via the automated sprinklers.

The First Cut

Once the grass is growing actively and has formed a thick mat, it is ready for its first trimming. Prior to cutting it is often a good idea to roll the new turf lightly. This action presses the plants into the soil and promotes firm root contact that will prevent death caused by the tearing action of the mower. A day or so after the rolling, the grass plants, having at first been pressed down, will once again rise up and be ready for a cutting.

It is vitally important that whatever mower is used be exceedingly sharp.

The tops of the grass blades must be sheared off cleanly and with ease and must not be torn, which happens when the mower is dull. On a new green or tee, the first cut can be made with a rotary mower set at a very low height. A regular greens mower may also be used, but conversely, it should be raised to its upper limit. In either case, the clippings should be removed. Gobs of grass left unattended will kill the grass underneath and cause unsightly dead spots. Amazingly, after the first cut, the rate of growth of the new stand increases rapidly, and with successive trimmings a healthy sward soon becomes established.

If the cover of grass is imperfect because of washouts or poor germination, remedial action is required. Spot-seeding for small areas may be necessary. In such cases the seed may be mixed with soil, much like a divot mix. If the washed-out areas are deep, sodding may be the only means of rectifying the problem and preventing it from becoming more serious. Don't wait and waste time. The need for action should be clear very quickly. Repairs must be made so that the success of the project is not impeded by indecision.

New seedlings are prolific growers and, subsequently, big users of nutrients in the soil. These nutrients must be replenished, and a follow-up fertilizer program is essential. During their infancy the grass plants will quickly turn yellow or purple, depending on whether they need nitrogen or potash. Regular applications of balanced fertilizer are essential to overcome these deficiencies. It must be understood that the nutritional requirements of new turf are at least twice as high as those of established stands. Growing in new turf to maturity has now become a recognized art, and a small group of elite superintendents make their living traveling from new course to new course, growing in the young turf to maturity until it is ready for play.

Hydro Seeding

A novel method of establishing seed, especially on steep slopes, involves a process called "hydro seeding." As the name implies, the method involves water. In fact, a mixture of seed and fertilizer combined with a fibrous material, such as chopped up straw, is added to water. As can well be imagined, the ingredients form a slurry that is sprayed under pressure to bare hillsides or other areas to be seeded. Sometimes a dye is added that makes it easier to see what parts have been treated. The slurry tends to form a crust over the soil, which helps prevent erosion and speeds up germination.

Not only are steep slopes ideal for hydro seeding, greens and tees have also been established in this manner. In fact, entire golf courses can be hydro seeded. It is much less expensive than sodding and almost as quick in achieving a grass cover.

A sod cutter is a handy tool for completing renovations in-house. (Photo by Anthony Girardi, Rockrimmon Country Club, Stamford, Connecticut.)

SODDING

Preparing the soil for sodding is very similar to preparing it for seeding, except that at times one need not be quite as finicky. A roll of sod quickly covers a lot of sins, which may come back to haunt a person too much in a hurry to get the job done. Stones and rocks will find their way to the surface and eventually pop up through the sod, hurting the mowers as well as the golfers' clubs.

The surfaces of tees and greens that are to be sodded must be perfectly smooth and firm, almost a bit hard, so that there is no footprinting when the sod is laid. Fertilizer should have been tilled into the soil mix, but it is not too late to spread fertilizer on the finished grade. Planks or sheets of plywood are often used when sodding a green. The workers can now walk on the wood instead of the grass or the soil and prevent footprinting. The first row of sod is laid straight down the middle in a perfect line and the next row butts up against it tightly, the ends being staggered just like the bricks in a wall.

The outline of the green can be painted with a gun, but to obtain a perfectly smooth naturally flowing line, use a heavy water hose. Place the hose in the approximately correct position, then snap and whip the end. The result will be a contour that is cuttable and pleasing to the eye. Use a sharp edger to cut the sod. If the apron is to be sodded as well, sod can now be rolled around and around to the desired width.

Helpful Hints

- When sodding during the heat of summer, consider syringing the dry earth just prior to sodding. That little bit of moisture at the interface of sod and soil will speed root formation and prevent the sod from drying out.
- Rolling sod after it has been laid is essential. The weight of the roller draws moisture to the surface and makes sure that the sod comes into firm contact with the soil. Air pockets will be eliminated by repeated rolling.
- Sodding slopes, bunker faces, or surrounds of tees requires special care. On steep slopes, lay the sod across the fall line; that is, the most direct path from top to bottom. The sods should be attached to the soil with biodegradable metal staples. On severe slopes consider using wooden pegs, and hammer these into the soil to a depth of 6–10 inches. Once the sod has rooted, the wooden stakes may be removed. The metal staples will disappear with time.
- Around bunkers it is best to lay a strip of sod along the edge of the sand and work out from there. It is much the same with tees: Lay a strip of sod perfectly around the perimeter of the teeing area and butt the rest of the sods up against this strip, using staples wherever the grade exceeds 10%.
- Recently, sod producers have started to lift turf in giant rolls, as much as 2 feet wide and almost 100 feet long. Special attachments for tractors are needed to lay the heavy rolls. The obvious advantages of large rolls are that it is quicker to cover a given area and there will be fewer seams to knit.
- Washed sod is also a recent innovation. As the name implies, the soil has been washed away from the roots, and the mass of roots topped with green grass is simply laid on its destined surface, rolled, and presto! it begins to grow immediately. The obvious advantage is that no foreign soil is imported into the soil mix. The lightness of the washed sod makes it possible to ship it by air from coast to coast.

Watering Sod

During the first week or so, newly laid sod requires more water than new seeding. Not only must the grass mat be kept alive, but it must be encouraged to grow roots. It is best to water until the moisture has just passed through the grass mat. Apply too much and you will have created a messy quagmire; too little water and the sod will wilt and die. Dead sod with the edges curled up looks ugly and is one of the deadly sins against the principles of good green-keeping. Strangely, the dead sod is often just dormant and will turn green after a rain. Rather than experiment, it is best to keep the new sod moist by daily watering. Check often for the development of white root hairs. Once they appear, they will quickly find their way into the soil and provide anchorage for the new turf.

Whether sod arrives on pallets, skids, or in rolls, it should be laid immediately, especially during periods of high temperatures. The rolls of sod, tightly packed together, provide anaerobic conditions that produce heat, which in turn will kill the grass in just a few days. In the spring or fall, sod can be stored somewhat longer, but the absence of light will also turn the grass yellow.

Sod may temporarily be stored on plastic, laid out in full. It must be watered regularly. A mass of roots will develop where the soil meets the plastic. The sod can be left in this manner for as many as ten days and used to complete a construction project. The roots of sod that have been stored on plastic will be particularly anxious to renew their contact with the soil. Such sod, when watered, becomes firmly attached to the soil in just a few days.

There are times when a sodding job just has not turned out well. The surface may be bumpy and the grade uneven, not fit to putt on or to hit drives from. Before ripping it up and starting again, consider using a vibratory roller. Place several sheets of plywood on the ugly sodding job and run the vibratory roller several times back and forth. This drastic measure will result in a smooth surface, but the compacted soil will need aeration at a later time.

Aeration can also be helpful to promote bonding between the sod and soil. Washed sod in particular seems to benefit from several aerations early in its establishment. The danger of layering must be avoided at all cost.

SPRIGGING

The process of distributing small cut-up portions of stolons over a seedbed for the purpose of establishing turf is known as sprigging. At one time new greens in the northern climatic zone were routinely stolonized in preference to seeding. The advent of superior cultivars of bent grass and their availability in the seed form has largely eliminated the practice. Sprigging is still used extensively in the southern climatic zone with Bermuda turf on tees, greens, and fairways. Sprigs, or parts of stolons with one or two nodes, can be produced at a turf nursery and shipped to new golf courses in refrigerated containers. The quantities of sprigs are phenomenal. On greens and tees the application rate may be as high as 15 bushels per 1,000 square feet.

Sprigs are usually applied by several workers at a time, and when the green or tee is entirely covered, the sprigs are packed into the soil with a roller or with the studded tires of a small lawn tractor or trap rake. The sprinklers are turned on next, and in two to three weeks' time the sprigs will develop roots and leaf tops and begin to look like a green or a tee. Topdressing begins when the sprigs have rooted and continues at regular intervals until the green is ready for play.

The total area of fairways is too big for hand-sprigging, and mechanical spriggers are employed that spread and push sprigs into soil. It takes more than 200 bushels per acre to plant a fairway.

The First Cut

Be gentle on the first cut, because the new grass is very delicate, and never contemplate performing this important operation in the morning when the grass is wet. When the height of the turf approaches $\frac{1}{2}$ inch, it is time to get the mower out. Don't wait too long or the grass will be too high and the shock of the cutting will set it back. There is merit in rolling the young turf to press the shoots firmly into the ground.

You may use a hand-propelled rotary mower for the first cut. A suitable alternative is to use a walk-behind greens mower set at 0.375 inch. Newly established bent grass or Bermuda fairways may be cut with regular mowers suited for that purpose, but at no lower than 0.5 inch and preferably a tad higher. In all cases it is important to remove the clippings. Clumps of mown grass left helter-skelter may smother some of the grass mat.

The first cut of new roughs is not nearly as critical since the grass species in the roughs tend to be sturdier. Newly seeded, sodded, or sprigged turf areas should gradually be brought down to their desired height. If this process is unduly accelerated, the new turf may suffer a setback, and if the process is too slow, thatch may build up. The height of cut can be lowered at a rate of 0.0625 inch every week.

DECIDING WHEN NEW TURF IS READY FOR USE

With each successive cutting, the grass will thicken and form a dense mat. On greens and tees, the establishment of the turf is greatly assisted by frequent topdressings. On the larger fairways, topdressing may be more cumbersome, although equipment is now available to topdress widespread areas quickly. With each successive cutting, the height can be lowered a bit, but during the first growing season it is best not to lower the height to the eventual setting. This is certainly the case on greens, and perhaps on tees. Fairway turf should be taken down fairly quickly to prevent the development of thatch.

A new green on an established course, having been rebuilt and seeded, is subject to the pressures of impatient golfers to be put into play prematurely. This is a situation where the mettle of a superintendent will be put to the test. Such new greens will look and feel perfect, but they can be destroyed in a matter of just a few weeks or even days. The turf needs to mature before it can withstand the hardship of golfers' feet and the regimen of regular maintenance. In such situations, new golf courses have an advantage. The number of players on new courses is generally low at first and gradually builds up over a period of months or even years, thus giving the turf a chance to mature. On an existing golf course, with 200–300 golfers per day, when a rebuilt green is put into play there is a sudden shock from no play at all to constant foot traffic all day long.

If at all possible, a new green should not be opened till fall, when there is a natural decline in the number of players. To open a new green during the hottest weekend in July is sheer folly. The sudden shock on stressed-out turf will be a sorry sight in short order. The ability to say "No" to the clamoring hordes in such situations is very difficult, and the assistance and support of the greens chairman will be much appreciated.

A new green among 17 established greens presents special problems. For a long time the new green will putt and play differently. Pitch shots won't hold, and the putting speed, whether real or imaginary, will seem at odds with the rest of the greens. This is not surprising. In all likelihood the soil underneath is different. It will take time for the roots to find their way, and it will take lots of watering, topdressing, and fertilizing for the new green to resemble and play like the existing greens.

A new green has to mature. Not just the turf on top but the soil underneath needs to adjust to regular maintenance. Superintendents should be aware that the new green may need to be treated differently for quite a while. Don't be surprised if the turf around the cup wears out more quickly on the new green than it does on all the others. On busy days be prepared to change the cup more than once. New greens should be inspected frequently, and all little imperfections should be remedied immediately. Such greens should be babied until they grow up.

SUMMARY

The magic of new grass covering bare earth is a phenomenon both satisfying and inspiring. It is satisfying for those who do the work and reap the rewards of seeing a landscape develop. It is inspiring because birth and growth signify renewal and the perpetuity of life.

Seeding, sodding, and sprigging present opportunities to demonstrate skill and knowledge of basic greenkeeping. The actual ability to make things grow is a unique and special gift. Hard work and dedication are translated into an almost instant greensward. To a layperson, it is wondrous, even awesome. To the initiated, it is the sweet fruit of one's labor.

14

Traffic and Paths

When a golf course gains in popularity and experiences increased play, the wear and tear of the golfers tramping over the grounds leads to the development of traffic patterns. At first it happens near the greens and tees, later along the hazards, and eventually even on the fairways. Since worn areas make for poor lies and bad bounces, such conditions are unacceptable to discriminating golfers. Superintendents are expected to repair the worn areas or try to prevent the development of paths by spreading the traffic. There are certain threshold values beyond which the damage caused by golfer traffic can no longer be alleviated by the simple expedient of spreading the wear. Then, plans need to be made to construct footpaths and cart paths. Forcing golfers to walk or drive where they don't want to go is at best difficult, if not impossible. Superintendents need to be inventive if not ingenious to devise ways and means to control the golfer traffic and to develop a system of functional paths.

FOOTPATHS

Foot traffic is most severe near tees. By their very nature, tees are elevated and require firm foot pressure to prevent slipping while ascending. The extra pressure wears out the turf much more quickly. A knee-jerk reaction is to install a set of stairs, but rarely are stairs the best solution. Almost immediately after installation the grass near where the steps begin will start to show signs of wear. At the top of the stairs, on the tee deck, the grass will also quickly die. The problem with stairs is that they concentrate the traffic instead of spreading it. In addition, stairs are costly to maintain. Their location invariably interferes with mowing patterns. Adding a railing to a set of stairs may give golfers a sense of security, but it emphasizes the unnatural appearance of the stairway.

A pretty washroom setting on a golf course in Bogota, Colombia.

When selecting materials or methods for footpath construction near tee decks, the most important consideration is to provide sure, nonslip footing. A path of scattered flagstones may have eye appeal, but if the stones are slippery when wet, this method is a poor choice. Rough-textured interlocking paving stones provide a good grip for golfers' footwear. Rubberized tiles can be used in the same manner and with the same effect.

To avoid the need for paths and steps altogether, architects should be encouraged to build tees that are surrounded by slopes that are easy to ascend and that make it possible for superintendents to spread the wear by management practices. Unfortunately, championship tees or gold or back tees tend to be constructed far back and way up, often making the construction of a goat path, combined with steps, a necessity. Slippery wooden bridges, when covered with chicken wire, provide secure footing. The best place to learn about the maintenance and construction of footpaths is in manuals for the construction of hiking paths or foot trails.

After striking the ball, golfers leave the tee in an undefined pattern. Some slice, some hook, and a few drive the ball down the middle. Yet, amazingly, paths often develop quite naturally off the tee, especially if there is an obstruction such as a watercourse or a gorge in the way. A curving goat path through a stand of long fescue can be quite appealing to the eye. Its presence lends aesthetics to a golf hole and often tranquillity to a golfer's turbulent mind.

A common practice is to cut a 6- to 8-foot-wide swath from the tee to the fairway for walking golfers. This closely cropped surface helps prevent golfers from getting their feet wet. Such a strip is known as a dew walk.

On the fairway, much of the wear happens near the hazards. Wherever there is a concentration of traffic, such as between closely placed bunkers or near streams or ponds, foot traffic will pound the grass to death. This is especially true near bridges. On small stream crossings the use of bridges can be avoided by using culverts. The latter are much wider and spread the wear. With very small bridges, the entire structure can be moved at regular intervals.

Near the green, wear patterns inevitably develop between the edge of the green and adjacent bunkers. If the bunker is located in a direct line of traffic, it will be necessary from time to time to stop all foot traffic by means of temporary obstruction devices such as stakes and ropes. A thin metal bar, partially bent like a hoop, can also be quite effective. On occasion, steep slopes near the green necessitate the installation of stairs. Such stairs, just like those near tees, are a maintenance headache. They should be avoided if at all possible.

It is important to recognize all worn areas early in their development and take preventative action. Early in the morning, sparse turf or turf under stress is characterized by the absence of dew. This is an early warning sign that the grass is crying for help. Immediate action is required! Not only must foot traffic be diverted, but the compaction in the soil must be remedied. Bring out the aerator, remove the cores, overseed, and water. Consider using perennial rye grass. Once established, rye grass wears like iron and takes traffic much better than most any other turf.

While many golfers now ride, a core group of health-conscious players prefer to walk, and they should be encouraged to do so. Since wear and tear caused by walkers is negligible, nothing should impede their movements.

Those who pull a handcart or use one of the battery-operated caddy carts must, unfortunately, face some obstructions. The total weight of their carts and clubs is much greater than that of the bags that golfers carry. It is for this reason that all carts must be kept off tees and away from restricted areas, such as between traps and greens.

POWER CARTS

While power carts are a great source of revenue and profit, they may also cause considerable damage to the turf. The traffic patterns of carts must be controlled and the damage constantly repaired. As soon as more than ten power carts are regularly used on an 18-hole golf course, wear will start to show; at first, only near the tees, but signs of wear will soon appear near the greens and the bunkers. In the beginning, the damage can be reduced by changing the traffic and by keeping the grass strong, but as the number of cart users increases, the need for a system of paths, for at least part of the course, becomes apparent.

When a threshold level of 50 power carts is reached, tee-to-green paths on par 3 holes become a necessity. Between 80 and 100 carts on an 18-hole course requires a continuous path from the first tee to the 18th green.

DIRECTING THE TRAFFIC

While cart-driving golfers would probably prefer to drive almost anywhere, some restrictions must apply to protect the turf. Some courses prohibit the use of carts on fairways, others restrict it more severely. Bent grass fairways quickly become infested with *Poa annua* as a result of compaction caused by unrestricted cart traffic. The much stronger Bermuda turf has no such problems. Rye grass fairways are somewhat in between when it comes to wear tolerance.

Limiting the carts to the primary rough is unsatisfactory because the turf in concentrated areas will quickly deteriorate, and restricting carts to the rough also slows down play. As a compromise, some have instituted the "90-degree rule." Under this rule carts may enter the fairway at a 90-degree angle, and after golfers have hit their shots, they must return directly to the rough, also in a 90-degree direction.

There are other well-known methods that involve the use of unobtrusive barricades to divert cart traffic away from sensitive areas. Ropes are often used, and so are stakes and signs.

TRAFFIC-DIVERTING METHODS

1. Exit stakes, uniformly painted either brown or green, can be placed in the rough a short distance from the green on either or both sides of the fairway. Such stakes serve notice to golfers that they are no longer permitted on the fairways beyond that point. In fact, if paths are nearby, golfers are expected to access a path at that point. Such stakes range in height from 2 to 3 feet and are equipped with a spike at the bottom, so that they can be moved with ease.
2. On some golf courses, a white line is painted across the fairway to act as a reminder that carts cannot proceed, but must head for the roughs. The line must be repainted regularly to remain visible, and if left in the same place, the grass will eventually die.
3. Ropes suspended on stakes are also used as physical barriers to stop carts from getting near the green. They are effective but visually unat-

tractive. In addition, they do at times deflect golf balls. Some super-intendents have removed the stakes and stapled the ropes to the grass. The latter is preferable.

4. Signs reminding golfers not to proceed seem to work for a little while but quickly lose their effectiveness. A series of small stakes, placed in a row just far enough apart for pull carts to pass through, form an effective barrier to divert power carts.

5. Near the green, when there are no paths for carts to drive on, the 30-foot rule should be observed. This rule dictates that no power carts should ever be parked or driven closer than 30 feet or ten paces from the green. The aim is to protect the turf and to provide acceptable lies for golfers.

Whatever devices are used, all need timely attention. They must be moved, replaced, and put back again for the mowers that pass and the golfers that forget to replace them. Controlling the flow of traffic is a difficult assignment that should be attended to on a daily basis. The person assigned this responsibility should have a thorough understanding of the need to balance the demands of the golfers with what is best for the grass.

NO CARTS TODAY!

There comes a time when a superintendent must make an unpopular decision. It happens after a heavy rain, a sudden downpour, or a violent storm. The sodden ground on the course is soft and not suitable for power cart traffic. The weight of the cart combined with that of the golfers and their clubs would surely damage the turf. In extreme cases rutting may occur. Carts traversing slippery slopes may possibly even lose traction and spin out.

It is the superintendent's responsibility to bring the unhappy news—that there will be no carts today—to the golf shop and the clubhouse. The message should be delivered in a professional manner. Notices should be posted, including the anticipated time that the ban will be lifted. Irate members with important guests can bring to bear lots of pressure to persuade the superintendent to reverse the decision. At such times it is best to be visible and ready to explain. Reasonable people will understand sound explanations. Irate golfers will want to vent their anger, and an understanding superintendent is a good listening board. To hide in the office on such occasions is poor policy and a professional cop-out.

Who should have the ultimate authority to decide the fate of carts on wet days?

- It should be the person who is best trained to measure the agronomic impact of the potential damage that cart traffic can do to rain-soaked soil and turf.

- It should be the person who is on the job to assess the potential danger that may occur to golfers when carts slip and slide.
- It should be the person who derives no direct financial benefits from cart revenue.
- It should be the person who is committed to do what is best for the grass and for the golfers.
- In all cases that person is invariably the superintendent, the only person who has no axe to grind, who has no vested interest in the outcome of the decision.

It behooves the golf professional, the manager, the club's president, and most of all, the green chairman, to back up the superintendent in such cases. To make unpopular decisions takes a strong backbone, and the total support of the management team is a must.

On "no cart days" there are a number of things a superintendent can do to improve the professional image. Grass-mowing equipment should be restricted to dry areas only or kept off the course completely. Golf course workers should limit their excursions in maintenance vehicles that resemble golf carts. It is a good idea for the superintendent to walk and set an example during course inspections. Golfers will respect a superintendent who adheres to the rules that are good for everyone.

CART PATHS

With increased play the need for cart paths shows up quickly near tees and greens. Par 3 holes that are often characterized by spectacular changes in elevation, water hazards, and plentiful sand bunkers need paths for riding golfers to get around safely. Once a few paths are in place in strategic locations and the number of cart rounds continues to increase, a continuous path system becomes a necessity. A week-long period of wet conditions and no power carts revenue speeds the process of installing tee-to-green paths on all golf holes.

Cart Path Location

Golfers rarely agree on where cart paths should be located on the course. Walkers, who prefer not to have any paths at all, will reluctantly agree to put the paths as far away from the playing areas as possible. Riders, on the contrary, want cart paths in the roughs but close to the fairway, so the walks to the balls are short. A compromise between the two extremes is difficult to bridge. The solution is to hire a golf course architect. The experience and knowledge of such trained professionals qualifies them best to make the final decision. Every

The original turnabout was too small. The extended version lacks curbing.

golf hole is different, and only an architect who sees many, many golf courses and golf holes day after day is capable of clearly visualizing where the paths should go. After careful study, the architect will lay out a routing plan for the paths that will become the basis for a construction program. Such a plan should not be deviated from.

The Width of Cart Paths

Whereas at first, cart paths were narrow, just wide enough for a single cart to drive on, it is now generally agreed that the minimum width for paths should be 8 to 10 feet. Narrow paths tend to crumble at the edges and the turf wears badly along its sides. Narrow paths cannot accommodate the need of golf course maintenance equipment. Wider paths make it possible for carts to pass and for maintenance equipment to use the paths as well.

Surface drainage on and near cart paths is important. Puddles on a path after a rain are unacceptable. Paths should be slanted slightly so that water will run off. It is best to slant paths in such a manner that golf balls that land on a path will bounce toward the fairway, instead of into the rough. An added feature of constructing cart paths is including distance markers at regular intervals. Such markers help golfers decide what clubs to use for their next shot. When a cart path blocks the natural flow of surface water, a catch basin and tile need to be installed to relieve the backup of water.

Cart Path Construction

Ideally, the routing plan prepared by an architect provides not only details about the location of the paths, but also specifics about cut and fill of adjacent mounding. The architect will try to hide the paths from view so that they do not detract from the natural beauty of the golf hole. This is not always possible, but it can often be accomplished by curving a path and placing mounds in strategic places. Nothing is more boring and visually unattractive than a straight line of asphalt or cement along either or both sides of a fairway. An artistic architect will create a design that is practical and pleasing to the eye. Trees in strategic places can assist in hiding and directing paths in an attractive manner. Besides, the canopy of the trees over a path will filter golf shots and prevent or at least reduce the severity of bad bounces.

Paths should be excavated to a depth of 6–8 inches. The excavated material can be used to help create the mounding or can be hauled away for other projects. No matter what topping is used, it is always best to use a solid foundation of gravel that extends beyond the finished width of the path. Most granular materials are satisfactory as long as they are not too coarse. Ground-up asphalt forms a solid base and can be used as an intermediary path until funds are available to put on a topping. As opposed to screenings or fine limestone, ground asphalt does not kick up dust during dry periods. In fact, the heat of summer will solidify the asphalt, and what may have started as a temporary plan may become a permanent solution.

What Makes the Best Top for a Cart Path?

Cart paths use very much the same materials as the highways that span the width and length of a country, but on a much smaller scale.

- Cement probably produces the best-quality cart path. Cement should be poured to a thickness of 4–6 inches, a steel mesh should be included for strength and expansion joints, and cuts provided at regular intervals. It should be broom-finished while still wet to provide better traction. No matter how carefully a base is prepared for a cement path, transgressions of heavy equipment or alternate freezing and thawing in cold climates lead eventually to surface cracks. These are unsightly and difficult to repair.

- Asphalt, by its very nature, is more flexible than cement, and cracks and holes in asphalt are easy to repair. The base for an asphalt path is the same as for cement. Since no forms are required, it is easier to install, but more than one layer of asphalt may be needed to provide extra strength for golf course maintenance equipment.
- Paving stones are yet another solution. While paths paved with interlocking stones are very eye appealing and provide excellent traction for carts and walkers, the cost of installation is a negative factor. Paths paved with stones are easy to repair.
- Graveled cart paths quickly develop potholes and ruts and become very dusty during dry conditions. Gravel is limited to flat terrain since it washes out on hillsides. The use of gravel is at best a temporary measure; the paths can be paved or cemented when funds become available.
- At times recycled asphalt is used. It serves the purpose of a pragmatic cart path very well. During the heat of summer the ground-up material melds and forms a smooth-riding, solid surface that does not wash away on sloped areas. Unfortunately, ground-up asphalt lacks eye appeal.
- Wood chips are used occasionally on flat surfaces where they won't wash away. Paths made from wood chips become very dusty after prolonged usage.

Curbing

Without curbs, golfers will ride wherever they wish. Curbs are installed to keep carts away from tees and greens and other places where their presence is not wanted. The curbs should be 4–6 inches in height and can be poured from cement or shaped from asphalt. Some superintendents use pressure-treated timbers or railroad ties; the latter tend to wear out quickly and are often unsightly. Prefabricated cement can be installed any time. Whatever type of curbing is used, provision must be made for golfers with pull carts to cross the curb. A narrow 30-inch cut is usually sufficient. On the fairway side of the curb, topsoil should be graded to the top and covered with sod.

Diversionary Tactics

1. When a paved path comes to a sudden end, the inevitable result is for the grass to thin and die because of concentrated cart traffic. This damage can be prevented by flaring the path to either the right or the left, thus randomizing where carts may exit.

2. Some constructions use a bubble pattern on the cement surface to indicate that the path is about to end. Riders then exit at random, either left or right.
3. Using barricades such as wooden bumpers or plastic pylons is yet another means of spreading the exit points from the path.

Path Maintenance

Both footpaths and cart paths need to be maintained on a regular basis. Asphalt needs to be patched before potholes develop. Cracks in cement need to be sealed to prolong the life of the paths. Paths need to be swept, and the edges need to be trimmed on a regular basis to stop the grass from growing onto the paths. Poorly maintained paths are a blemish on the face of a golf course and inevitably lead to slovenliness elsewhere.

SUMMARY

Golfer traffic will find its way across the golf course in the most economical way. Scars, scrapes, and worn areas will develop until the installation of designated paths. Unless a qualified architect is engaged to determine the best location for the paths, a committee design, wrought in compromises, will prevail, to the detriment of the golfers. Whatever topping is used, the path must be maintained just like the rest of the golf course. In some ways the paths on a golf course are like the frame around a picture: A poor-quality frame may easily spoil a fine painting.

15

Rules of Golf That Affect Maintenance

Every superintendent should be familiar with the rules of the game, and since most superintendents play golf, many make it their business to know the rules thoroughly and to play by them. In addition to playing by the rules, superintendents are called upon to assist with setting up the course so it can be played comfortably within the rules. A superintendent should be prepared to define accurately the course and the out-of-bounds, the margins of water hazards and lateral water hazards, ground under repair, obstructions, and other integral parts of the course. It is imperative that the staking and marking are done in such a manner that even the most pernicious interpreters of the rules will be satisfied.

WATER HAZARDS

Golf is played either alongside a water hazard or across it. Different rules apply, and different colored stakes or lines should be used to define the margins of the hazard. Water to the side of a hole is generally a lateral water hazard and should be marked with red stakes or red lines. When play crosses a body of water, the hazard is generally marked with yellow stakes or lines. Stakes defining the margins of the hazard should be placed in the grass as nearly as possible along the natural limits of the hazard. The distance between stakes is important. At all times, an imaginary line between two adjacent stakes must be on dry land. Such a line of sight must be clearly apparent when one lines up behind one stake and looks toward the other. The stakes cannot be too far apart or else the margin of the hazard may be hard to define. It is seldom advisable for stakes to be more than 30 yards apart. Stakes should be closer together when play is around an irregularly shaped pond or riverbank.

When a golfer is playing a hole and the ball is in or lost in a water hazard or lateral water hazard, the player needs to able to determine where the ball last crossed the margin of the hazard, in order to apply the rules. Complicating the procedure, if hazard stakes are placed on sloping ground, it may be difficult to drop the ball and have it stop. It is far better to place hazard stakes on somewhat flat ground, so that a ball can be dropped without complications.

Hazard stakes are often moved by both golfers and maintenance personnel. It can be difficult to replace a stake in its original place when the hole cannot be found in the long grass. Both golfers and greenkeepers have been known to just drop the stake somewhere and let someone else worry about it. This causes confusion and irritation to the golfers who follow.

To avoid this problem, permanent hazard markers can be installed precisely at the natural limits of the hazard. Made from cement or other durable material, they are permanently in place, flush with the ground so that mowers can cut over them. They are marked with a detachable stake to make them highly visible from a distance. These permanent markers along the hazards, just like the permanent distance markers on the tees, are in place forever until someone decides to change their location. At the end of the golfing season the detachable stakes can be taken in, but the permanent disk remains. At the start of the new season, the stakes are replaced in their permanent locations.

For tournaments and special events the hazard margins are usually painted with red or yellow paint. The presence of the painted line takes the guesswork out of the decision as to whether a golf ball is in or outside a hazard. Many superintendents now paint hazards on a regular basis, a popular move that is much appreciated by ardent golfers. When hazard lines are painted regularly, there is no need for stakes.

OUT-OF-BOUNDS

At most courses the perimeter of the property is clearly marked with fences that serve as boundaries, thus making it easy to determine whether a golf ball is in- or out-of-bounds. In the absence of property fences, out-of-bounds (OB) is designated with white stakes. Such stakes should be placed on the property line. When there are no fences that serve as property boundaries, the property line must be determined from a registered survey. Once it has been decided where the exact property line is, it should be marked with white stakes. The possibility that the stakes may be knocked over and their location become obscure should be taken into account. It is advisable to use sturdy white posts or permanent cement markers that can not easily be relocated. When using permanent markers for boundaries or hazards, it should be clearly understood that the edges of the markers facing the golf course designate the boundary or

Out-of-bounds (OB), as indicated by property line fence.

hazard line and that the stake is merely a visual aid that helps the player determine where a ball has crossed the line.

As with water hazards, the actual out-of-bounds line may need to be painted for important events or on a continuous basis, if desirable. Occasionally, out-of-bounds stakes may be installed to define the out-of-bounds between the play of two adjacent holes, as, for example, in a dogleg golf hole. A better solution, if feasible, is to have a golf architect remedy the design and eliminate the need for an internal out-of-bounds.

GROUND UNDER REPAIR

There are often areas on a golf course in less than perfect condition that are slated to be repaired in the near future. Such areas should be marked as Ground under Repair (GUR), as approved by the committee or its authorized representative, by using either a small sign, or preferably a painted white line, that distinctly outlines the limits of the work area. A dug-up irrigation leak may be

Ground under repair (GUR) may be roped off to give golfers a free lift.

GUR, as is a scar or a scrape caused by a maintenance vehicle. Dead turf caused by winter injury or summer heat stress is GUR. Any of these conditions and others may be marked GUR by order of the committee or so declared by its authorized representative, which in most cases is the superintendent.

For tournaments and important events, such areas are outlined with white paint by an official or, more often, by the superintendent. It should be noted that GUR areas should rarely be painted beyond the fairway and the adjacent primary rough. Careful consideration should be applied in determining GUR. Landing areas and areas near putting greens should be the primary concern. There is a tendency on the part of overambitious club officials to paint any imperfection white, even if it is 100 yards beyond the line of play. In such instances, the superintendent should seek the assistance of the golf professional and work cooperatively for the benefit of all golfers.

Grass clippings that are left in piles to be picked up later are considered GUR, and golfers once again get to move their balls, if they are in or close to the pile. Grass clippings, poorly spread in the rough, can provide unplayable lies, but no relief is granted. No wonder greenkeepers often become unwitting victims of a golfer's misfortune.

Key maintenance staff should carry along GUR signs or a can of white paint on their utility vehicles. Less than perfect areas can be marked on the spot and scheduled for repairs. In fact, all GUR areas should become part of the maintenance schedule and checked off when they have been repaired.

CASUAL WATER

Casual water by definition is "any temporary accumulation of water on the course which is visible before or after the player takes his or her stance and is not in the water hazard." Golfers may take free relief from temporary accumulations of water on the course, as long as the accumulation is not part of the hazard. Such water is considered to be of a temporary nature and so is referred to as casual water. A player's golf ball can then be moved to drier land.

If casual water is a continuing problem on the golf course, the causes should be explored. Invariably such conditions are drainage-related and should be addressed. Casual water during the heat of summer can lead to scald, the actual cooking of the grass in freestanding water that is heated by the sun. This is not an unusual condition and is totally preventable by the simple expedient of pumping the excess water away.

OBSTRUCTIONS

When maintenance equipment interferes with the play of the game, the players once again are entitled to relief. Whether they are mowers, tractors, or maintenance carts, such items are collectively referred to as movable obstructions. "Moveable obstructions" does not refer only to maintenance equipment; it can also include a pile of lumber scheduled to be used for the construction of a shelter, or a skid of fertilizer destined to be applied to a fairway.

Superintendents should strive to make sure that such conditions are indeed temporary. If the pile of lumber, the skid of fertilizer, or the set of gang mowers is left in the same place for a prolonged period, someone may very well decide that this has become a permanent obstruction and a whole new set of rules will apply. Permanent obstructions are bridge abutments, rain shelters, irrigation controllers, and the like.

LOCAL RULES

Local rules are supplementary regulations to the rules of golf to deal with abnormal conditions. Local rules may apply to newly planted trees that need to be protected from erratic golf swings. A local rule may state that relief may be taken from staked trees. Similarly, at the start of the season when conditions are less than perfect, club officials may decree that "winter rules apply," allowing golfers to move the ball.

Local rules can also be instituted when major construction projects are under way. A sodding job, a bunker renovation, the installation of a water line—all involve temporary inconvenience to golfers. Areas on the golf course that are under construction in this way should be declared GUR. No fuss, no bother; golfers simply take their balls from these areas and drop them at the nearest point of relief, no closer to the hole, and carry on.

SUMMARY

If ever there is a case for the need of further education on the part of the greens staff, a seminar on the rules of golf as they affect maintenance should be highest on the list of priorities. Superintendents need to know the rules as they apply to their daily operations. They need to be able to advise their golfers on what rules apply and what type of relief is permitted. Superintendents need to work with their golf professionals to make sure that the course is marked correctly and consistently, so that all golfers can play by the rules enjoyably. Most important, superintendents should set the example by playing golf regularly and according to the rules.

16

Trees

Whispering pines, waving palms, giant sequoias, flowering jacarandas, weeping willows, and many other kinds of trees line the fairways of the world's diverse golf courses. Yet some maintain that golf is a game for wide-open spaces, and what's more, they have St. Andrews to prove it. Many other courses, built on landscapes that are not suited for their growth, are characterized by a scarcity of trees. There are many more who are proud of the trees that grace their properties and even include the names of trees in the names of their golf courses. To name but a few, there are Maple Ridge, Old Elms, Burnt Tree, Pine Valley, Magnolia, Royal Poinciana, and, of course, Cypress Point.

Beautiful trees provide the setting for the game to be played to its fullest enjoyment. The shapes of trees, the gnarly roots and strong trunks, the crooked branches, the towering heights, the whispering leaves, the cool shade, all combine to give trees an aura of permanency and at times an atmosphere that can be both forbidding and inviting.

When trees are too tightly spaced and encroach upon the playing ground, they tense the muscles of all but the most expert players and cause erratic golf shots. Trees at a distance provide peace of mind, relax the body, and make one swing freely. Single trees on the fairway between player and green, are often best ignored; they are, as has so often been pointed out, mostly air anyway. On a bad golf day, trees can be therapeutic for a troubled mind. Who but the most self-centered, ardent golfer can possibly ignore the beauty of flowering magnolias in the spring or the brilliant hues of maples in the fall? Such is the world in which superintendents live and ply their skills to make the landscape ever more beautiful.

Golf course superintendents have unique opportunities during the course of their working lives. At the beginning of their careers they often find themselves on properties that need help, golf courses that have been ignored and neglected. Trees are planted and looked after, and the grass thrives. At the end of a lifetime, hard work and dedication have converted a barren plain into a veritable Garden of Eden. Birds sing in the trees, rabbits scamper through the bushes, and hawks circle overhead. There is a tremendous satisfaction in such an accomplishment, and few other professions provide opportunities to leave a legacy of such proportions.

TREE SELECTION

It is best to check with the experts before deciding on what trees to plant. State colleges and research stations all have such information readily available. It is even better to visit neighboring golf courses and find out what trees grow best and where they are available. Check also with tree nurseries and learn about availability and planting times. A slack time for nurseries is often midsummer after the spring rush and before the fall planting season. That is a good time to examine their picked-over stock. Some real gems can be found among the discards: trees with crooked trunks and misshapen heads. Such "Charlie Brown" trees can be bought for very little and will thrive under a watchful eye and the nurturing golf course environment. Remember that perfect trees are often statuesque, much better suited for the straight lines of cemeteries than the free-flowing curves on a golf course.

There are many trees that have undesirable characteristics that make them unsuitable for golf courses in large quantities. Willows and poplars have extensive and fibrous root systems that spread well beyond the drip lines of these trees. Such roots inevitably become entwined in drains and stop the flow of water. In addition, both species are very brittle and even a minor storm will knock off many branches. As a result, the grass under and near willows and poplars needs to be cleaned constantly.

Certain types of maples, such as the Norway varieties, provide dense shade and make it difficult for grass to compete. A group of Norway maples, although attractive and fast growing, is earmarked by bare ground at the bases. Soft maples have objectionable roots that stick up aboveground, and they can be just as dirty as willows and poplars. Ash trees are slow in the spring and make one wonder if they have died. Catalpas are even slower, frequently not showing leaves till June. The female of the species of the exotic ginkgo tree produces fruit with an objectionable odor. Many species of palm trees need annual pruning to remove dead and ugly fronds.

Are there any trees that can be safely planted without arousing the ire of the golfers or the greens committee? We feel that there is a place for all trees. Certainly, some trees are more desirable than others, but all have a place. It's just not a good idea to plant a ginkgo near the golf shop, a willow over the clubhouse septic bed, or a chestnut tree near a neighboring schoolyard.

Evergreens such as pines and spruces make for wonderful partitions and backdrops. After a number of years, a bed of needles will develop at the bases of evergreens that titillates the nostrils and makes it unnecessary to trim the grass there. Beeches and maples are solid citizens in the forest but they produce leaves in abundance. The strong oaks last forever and keep their leaves, although dead and brown, into the winter long after the golfing season has ended.

The best selection of trees for any golf course includes a wide variety of many species. Plant just a single species, and suffer the consequences. The Dutch elm disease killed many feature landmarks and left golf courses looking naked without greenery. Austrian pines were likewise decimated by the Diplodia fungus that left brown skeletons in its wake. When disease strikes, it is always best to have a diversity of species, so that many will survive the devastation of an epidemic.

Ccriteria for Tree Selection

It is best to avoid trees with certain characteristics:

- Roots underground that compete with grass for nutrients and clog drains
- Roots aboveground that interfere with mowing operations and present unplayable lies to golfers
- Foliage that is so dense that grass cannot grow underneath
- Branches that are brittle and a danger to golfers and present a constant maintenance problem
- Longevity—trees that grow fast and die quickly

A TREE PLANTING PROGRAM

Not all golf courses are blessed with an abundance of native forests or widely spaced specimen trees. When, in addition, there are few inherent features such as streams and ponds or hills and dales, trees may need to be planted to separate the fairways, to screen the perimeter, or to give character to the holes. Groupings of trees break the monotony of an otherwise bleak landscape. Trees can be planted to accentuate the strategy of individual golf holes. Trees that are small when first planted are no hindrance, but can quickly grow up to become formidable obstacles. Trees planted in the wrong places can obscure vistas and views. Trees and tees almost never go together. Nor are trees a good idea near greens. Yet a wisely planted tree can take the place of a bunker and does not need raking every day. For all these reasons and more, a tree planting program is a necessity, but it must be carefully prepared. Since in most cases the location of the trees affects the strategy of the golf holes, a qualified architect should be engaged. The plan prepared by the architect should show where to plant trees. The plan should be preserved, encased in glass or foil, and hung in a prominent place where it can stay for a while, because planting trees is a long-term project. Committees and functionaries should make a firm commitment to adhere to the plan.

THE TREE NURSERY

Planting baby trees in a nursery is a very satisfying experience. Trees selected for the nursery may be as small as a few inches or as thick as the small finger on one's hand. Small trees should be planted in fertile soil that can be watered when needed. It is best to plant the saplings in rows, a few feet apart. They may need to be protected with tree guards or stakes. Small trees grow quickly and may need to be transplanted after just a few years or they will grow into each other. Planting small trees provides an opportunity to use a wide selection at very low cost. There is an opportunity to experiment with unusual trees in the nursery; to watch them grow and see how they adapt to local conditions. A nursery should be weeded regularly or treated with glyphosate, a grass killer. Leaving the nursery unattended will result in the trees being overgrown with grass, and the nursery experiment will be a dismal failure. Using string trimmers or rotary mowers in small tree nurseries is not advisable. More trees have died from string trimmers than from any other cause.

Trees should be moved from the nursery to their permanent locations according to the master plan and with the passing of time. Not all trees need to be moved at once. Leave a few; it's like insurance and money in the bank. If at all possible, the tree nursery should be located near the maintenance building. If a nursery is created in some out-of-the-way spot on the golf course, chances are that it will be out of sight and will be forgotten and neglected. The advantage of having a tree nursery on-site is that the planting can be done on short notice. Rainy days are ideal for transplanting trees from the nursery. The work may be messy, but its success rate is very high.

PLANTING TREES

For most trees there is a preferred planting time, but small trees can be transplanted with less pain than their bigger brothers and sisters. When the soil is moist and the buds on the shoots have not broken yet, that is an ideal time to transplant a tree. It will surely survive and grow if the following precautions are taken:

1. Digging the hole that is to receive the tree is critical. The old adage to dig a ten- dollar hole for a five-dollar tree still applies today. Make sure

*Double trouble: in the sand behind a tee. Such gimmickry rarely survives
the tenure of the greens chairman or the superintendent.*

that the hole is twice as big as the root ball of the tree that will grow
there. If the existing soil is undesirable, as is often the case on new golf
courses, add some superior topsoil mixed with fertilizer.

2. Plant the tree to the same depth as it grew before, or slightly higher.
   This is to encourage drainage. Freestanding water should not accumu-
   late around the base of the tree. It will result in the tree's having wet
   feet, a condition that will ultimately lead to its death.
3. Backfill carefully around the roots of the tree. Use good-quality topsoil, and stamp it down with the heel of one's boot. The earth around
   the tree must feel firm so that the tree is securely anchored and there
   are no air pockets in the soil surrounding the roots.
4. Create a well around the base of the tree. It is for water that will remain
   in place and gradually soak down to the roots every time the tree is
   given a drink. Newly planted trees are very thirsty at first and must be
   watered regularly. The well, however, will have to be leveled at a later
   date, or surely some poor golfer will find an unfair lie.
5. Finally, the tree must be staked to protect it from the elements and
   from people. Even small trees must be staked so they won't get run

Mechanical tree diggers create instant landscapes, but the trees still need to be watered. (Photo by Anthony Girardi, Rockrimmon Country Club, Stamford, Connecticut.)

over. Larger trees may need more than one stake and even guy wires to secure them in position.

All of these steps can be performed quickly by the simple expedient of using a tree spade. Such contraptions come in all shapes and sizes and can be used for small trees and, especially, for very large trees. Tree spades can move trees with a caliper of 10 inches and a ball of earth measuring 6–7 feet, weighing more than a ton. Several such trees planted in a group create an instant landscape, or an instant hazard, depending on one's viewpoint. Trees that are planted with a large tree spade need postplanting care just the same. The spaces between the ball and the hole need to be filled with topsoil and tamped down with a two-by-four or a shovel handle. It is also advisable to create a well around the base of the tree for water retention purposes. Large trees that are planted during the heat of summer need to be watered often.

Smaller trees will continue to be planted manually, because it is quick and easy. At certain times of years, deciduous trees can be planted with bare roots as long as the roots are kept moist. An unusual planting method involves filling a hole with water, adding soil, manure, and fertilizer, and mixing them thoroughly. The resulting slurry is used as a bath for all trees to take before being planted. A bare-rooted maple that is dipped into such a mud bath finds its roots dripping with a concoction that contains all the essentials of life, and when planted, is ready for certain growth.

DISTANCE BETWEEN TREES

It is important to visualize what the newly planted trees will look like once they grow up. They must be planted far enough apart so that they will not crowd each other. There must be sufficient space for mowers to get around and in between to trim the grass. When trees are planted too far away from each other, they seldom do well. Trees like company as they grow up, and they survive better as a group than when planted alone. As trees mature, they can be thinned or transplanted.

Trees on a golf course seldom look good when planted in a straight row. Even along a fence line or perimeter, trees should be planted in an irregular manner, to create interest and to avoid monotony. Groups of trees should be made up of different species and be of varying sizes for the same reason.

TREE MAINTENANCE

Taking care of small trees is an easy task. They must be fertilized from time to time, watered if need be, and pruned to keep growth under control. Superintendents should carry along a small set of pruning shears to nip off branches that look out of place, or low branches that hit the roofs of golf carts. Pruning, however, is not a part-time assignment for the superintendent. Regular pruning of trees is part of the overall maintenance operation and should be done on a timely basis.

As trees grow bigger, pruning becomes cumbersome, requiring the services of experts that climb trees and are trained to sever branches. Deadwood must also be removed and crossing branches eliminated. Wood chippers are used to pulverize the branches, and the larger parts are cut for firewood.

Many golfers do not take kindly to the cutting of trees, even trees that are past their prime or obviously dead or dying. Trees that were planted with good intentions originally may have lost their usefulness and become a hindrance. Such trees may at the same time have become "sacred cows" to many golfers, and their removal sparks a rallying cry to stop a project. Otherwise sensible people become quite emotional and irrational when it comes to trees. To avoid these confrontations it is best to have a golf course architect make the final decision. As a last resort, trees can be cut down when there are no golfers around. Remember to remove the stump as well and cover the area with fresh sod. Golfers rarely miss a tree once it is gone. There is the tale of a superintendent who carried two chainsaws on the utility vehicle, one called "thunder" and the other "lightning." Both were used to remove unwanted trees. When asked

A PTO-driven leaf blower clears the playing surface. Another method involves mulching the leaves with a rotary mower.

by golfers what had happened to certain familiar trees, the response was always the same: "Thunder took it down" or "It was struck by lightning." The answer was the truth, but with a twist.

No responsible person likes to heartlessly take down the giants of a forest or specimen trees on a golf course. In most cases the trees that we planted many years ago eventually grow to maturity but, for whatever reason, are in the way and need to be removed. There are few that meet such a fate in comparison with the many hundreds or even thousands that have been planted during a superintendent's career. For the golfers, the pain associated with the felling of trees can be lessened to a small degree by making the firewood available to those who need it.

LEAVES

As pretty as the colors of the leaves may be in the fall, they cause tremendous problems for golfers who lose balls among them. Leaves must be blown in piles or windrows, then swept into hoppers and hauled away to be composted or

Bushes and trees that obstruct a view of the target need to be trimmed periodically.

otherwise disposed of. The smell of burning leaves is now just a fond memory in the minds of gray-haired greenkeepers. The practice is now forbidden by regulation and has slipped from the golfing scene just like hickory-shafted clubs.

On golf courses that are well known for their numerous trees, leaf removal is a big-time operation involving large machinery and several workers for weeks at a time. The highest order of priority is to keep the greens and surroundings clear of fallen leaves. Since leaves fall continuously but gradually, the greens may need to be cleared several times a day. The next order of importance is the landing areas, and after that the roughs, the bunkers, and the tees. It is an ongoing process, not finished until the last leaf has fallen and is swept away. Sometimes there is help from a friendly wind that blows the leaves into a nearby forest or a stream whose current will carry the leaves away. Mostly it's just hard work.

Special attachments are available for rotary mowers, the large up-front varieties. Screens are placed inside the cutting units, and these powerful grass cutters can be turned into very useful leaf mulchers. The fast-rotating blades grind the leaves into tiny snippets that disappear among the grass blades. Mulching leaves in this manner quickly converts a leaf-strewn fairway or rough into a clean and playable turf. Once the snippets of leaves break down they will add organic matter to the soil.

SUMMARY

When we were young and inexperienced we searched for fast-growing trees and could not find any. As we grew older we began to realize that most trees are fast-growing trees, and that somehow trees grow bigger and stronger as we grow older and weaker. Superintendents will continue to plant trees and, on occasion, be horribly ruthless and cut down a perfectly healthy tree, but when they leave this earth there will always be a living legacy of their toil.

17

Landscaping

On the way to the course a golfer receives a first impression of what is to come at the entrance to the grounds. This first impression often sets the tone for what lies ahead. A messy flower bed, a weedy lawn, or a cracked pavement can be indicative of what the golf course or even the clubhouse will be like. Add a cool reception in the pro shop and some poorly cooked food in the grill, and no matter how well manicured the golf course, the stage has been set for a miserable golfing experience. That is precisely why golf club management is so much a team effort. All the components of the team must work synergistically, like the gears in a well-oiled machine, to produce a smooth-running organization. Nowhere is such cooperation more important than at the entrance to the golf club. It does not need to have an elaborate rock garden with cascading waterfalls and splashing fountains. There is no need for statues, hanging baskets, or cunningly trimmed bushes. The golfer in a rush to the first tee will barely notice such extravagances, but the subconscious will pick up the imperfections—the lawn not trimmed, thistles among the petunias, and trash on the pavement. Such blemishes are registered indelibly on the mind, only to be recalled when the putts don't drop and the service is slow.

TREES AND SHRUBS

Landscaping around the clubhouse is meant to dress up the buildings and to create attractive and colorful scenes. Everyone likes showy flowers and bushes and specimen trees. To arrange them to their best advantage is landscaping, and even the most modest clubhouse needs some landscaping to enhance its visual appeal.

Whereas on the golf course the emphasis is on the quality of the turf and the design of the holes, around the clubhouse there is an opportunity to showcase unusual trees, flowering shrubs, and rose beds. Trees such as flowering crabs, tulip trees, and Japanese cherries, which would detract from the strategy of individual golf holes on the course, are ideal around the clubhouse. Groupings of showy shrubs look magnificent on grassy banks near the locker room. In the shelter of the clubhouse buildings, plant material that may struggle on the golf course manages to survive when protected from wind and cold. Precisely because of the favorable clubhouse location, plant material will grow faster to maturity here than on the golf course. It is for this reason that one must at times be ruthless and trim bushes and trees severely or even remove them completely.

The clubhouse grounds can be converted to a veritable botanical garden with a wide variety of plant material that is of interest not only to the golfers but to all visitors. Superintendents with a horticultural bent will find a perfect opportunity to display their knowledge on the grassy slopes that surround the clubhouse. Often the trees are donated by members or are planted to remember deceased golfers. It is not unusual to tag trees with both their Latin and common names. This encourages visitors to stroll through the gardens and admire the beauty and, at the same time, learn the names of the plant materials.

It is important to screen service areas with plantings that will hide the storage bins and the inevitable trash that accumulates. Groupings of dense evergreens give an immediate effect, but deciduous shrubs can also be used to good advantage.

Visiting golfers need a place to drop off their clubs, and a bag rack should be provided for this purpose. It is no sin to copy the design of the bag rack from a neighboring golf course. That is why superintendents carry cameras: to visit other golf courses, take photographs, and imitate ideas.

FLOWER BEDS

To design the shape of a flower bed takes artistic ability, and unless the superintendent, the gardener/horticulturalist, or someone else has specific knowledge of landscape design, it is best to engage the services of a landscape architect. Such a professional will prepare a plan showing the shapes and locations of all the beds, as well as features such as rock gardens and waterfalls. Often the trees are already in place by the time the landscape architect arrives. Most of these will be preserved and others added in prominent places. The architect's primary function is to create a plan with flowing lines that fits in with the existing buildings. Once the plan is in place, the superintendent and the gardener combine their talents and make the plan a reality.

The use of quality topsoil is just as important for the flower beds as it is under the grass on the golf course—perhaps even more so. Don't hesitate to dig out a new bed to a depth of 2 feet. Use the excavated material to build a mound and then fill the flower bed with topsoil that is rich in humus. Take a handful of the soil and hold it close to the nose; it should permeate the nostrils with the musty smell of animals and manure. Don't mistake black loam for quality topsoil. Black loam smells like the bottom of a bog, where it came from, and is slippery to the touch. Such material is not worthy of the name "soil" and it will never grow anything but weeds.

Add plenty of fertilizer to the new flower bed, particularly bonemeal, which is high in phosphorus and makes for excellent rooting. Don't be afraid to work in some manure, but be cautious with certain kinds of manure. Too much horse manure can actually retard plant growth. For good measure, add some 10-10-10 fertilizer, and fork or rototill these materials into the topsoil. Such a well-prepared flower bed, high in fertility, will grow large plants with huge blossoms for years to come and will be the envy of neighbors and visiting friends.

Flowering Bulbs

In the springtime no garden is complete without at least some flowering bulbs. A show of tulips and daffodils always attracts attention. So does a border of crocuses and hyacinths. Large grassy areas can be naturalized by planting bulbs in a random pattern. This can be done simply by taking a handful of bulbs, throwing them over your shoulder, and planting them precisely where they have fallen. Any other method invariably results in straight lines that are distracting and look artificial. When the bulbs sprout in springtime, be aware that the grass in between cannot be cut without spoiling the naturalized appearance of the area. As soon as the bulbs begin to fade, it is time to cut the grass as well as the remaining flowers. Bulbs in flower beds are best left until the leaves begin to brown. This helps to store food inside the bulb below ground and ensures plentiful blossoms next spring.

Annuals can be planted between the flowering bulbs. It may look messy for a week or so, but if the beds are carefully tended, the overall appearance will soon improve. Some dig up the bulbs and store them until fall. Others leave the bulbs underground, thus ensuring that no one will have to remember to plant them in the fall. Once bulbs are past their prime after two or three years, they can be dug up and planted on the golf course. Southern exposures along a tree line make excellent locations. Their early blossoms will greet the golfers when they return to the course for their first game in the spring.

Annuals and Perennials

There are many annuals to choose from each spring, and it takes some experience to make the right selections. It is important to select matching colors or the flower beds will resemble patchwork quilts. Instead, stick to just a few colors for best results. Individual beds often look better with just one species with a border for emphasis. Obviously, the height of the plant material is important, with the tallest specimens always at the back and the smaller plants up front.

For immediate effect, plant the annuals close together. However, patient gardeners will allow for more distance between plants. Once the plants take root and receive encouragement, they will quickly fill in. Newly planted annuals need lots of water at first. Once they have rooted, they benefit from regular hoeing to break up the crusty earth and let in the air. Timely fertilizer applications are also essential, although beds constructed as described here will need very little in the way of nutrients for quite some time. Hanging baskets and standing pots thrive on a regular feeding of liquid fertilizer to provide continuous blossoming.

Perennials are the hallmark of English gardens. Nowhere do perennials look richer and more profuse than in English country gardens near a Tudor manor or a Victorian mansion. There are a multitude of plants that blossom all season long and provide color and interest on a continuing basis. Study English gardens and apply the knowledge gained around the clubhouse in suitable locations. Remember that English gardens are tended by hardworking and dedicated English gardeners. A perennial garden requires lots of attention, indeed devotion, to make it look supreme.

Interested club members can be recruited to help with the gardens. A Garden Committee may lend valuable support to the horticulturist. Combining the talents of volunteers with those of the professional can lead to a profusion of color around the clubhouse.

PHOTO AREAS AND VIEWING OPPORTUNITIES

Golf courses are favorite settings for weddings, anniversaries, and other important events. Such memorable occasions are often recorded in photos and videos. The most suitable locations need to be identified and enhanced with arbors and garden furniture. Visitors to the golf club also like to observe golfers in action. Perhaps there is an opportunity to provide a vista of the property from a high promontory. Such a viewing area should include a comfortable bench, possibly a table and some chairs, and an abundance of flowers.

At exclusive country clubs the extent of the landscaping can become quite extravagant. One may find some of the most elaborate rock gardens with cascading waterfalls and fountains spraying colored water. Impressive as such landscaping may be, it should never be done at the expense of the golf course. The vast majority of the club's customers come to play golf and not to look at an artificially created landscape. The real landscape of grass, trees, water, and sand is a piece of beauty seldom equaled in any other way around the clubhouse.

A GREENHOUSE AND A GARDENER

Any kind of extensive clubhouse landscaping will need the full-time attention of a gardener. There is the daily routine of watering and weeding, of trimming the bushes and the grass. The work is never-ending, with peak periods of activity in the spring, followed by regular routines all season long. Lawns need frequent cutting and fertilizing. Sprinklers must be set to ensure that both the grass and the landscape plants are watered properly.

A gardener's reputation depends entirely on the quality of the work that is produced. When the women "ooh and ah" as they admire a flower bed, when the men take pictures of the bushes, and when visitors want to know the names of plant materials, then an astute gardener knows that the good work is being appreciated.

Almost any professional gardener will want the convenience of having a greenhouse. It can be used to start new flowers from seed, to pot plants, and to create hanging baskets. The greenhouse is a perfect place to overwinter plants that might otherwise not survive. A greenhouse is a valuable addition to a gardening enterprise, and no respectable clubhouse grounds should be without one.

SUMMARY

For many golfing establishments, the need for elaborate clubhouse landscaping is entirely superfluous. Their reason for being is to provide golf, and golf only. For many country clubs, the quality of the gardens is almost as important as that of the golf course. Such clubs go to great lengths to beautify their grounds, and a competent gardener is invariably the person who makes the clubhouse grounds shine. That all-important first impression starts with the appearance of the clubhouse grounds. It does not need to be elaborate, but it must be thoughtfully composed and neatly tended.

18

Managing People

When the workers arrive at the crack of dawn, or even before, they will all be assigned certain tasks, which will to a great degree determine the condition of the golf course. How they are organized and how they are managed will directly impact the golfers' enjoyment of their game for that specific day. As a rule, many of the decisions of who does what and who goes where have already been made the day before, but often there are last-minute changes caused by the weather, the change of a function, or an event.

STAFF MEETING

In most cases the superintendent and the assistant will have a last-minute meeting to decide the day's work. Often other key players also get involved. Then it is time for the superintendent to address the troops. Speaking to the assembled workers is much like giving a talk at a turfgrass meeting or conference. It requires preparation and confidence. The assistant should be close at hand to help look after the details.

An address to the troops should start with general information about what kind of events are taking place on the golf course that day. Outings that are scheduled for the future can also be mentioned. Perhaps there is a major tournament in the offing and special preparations need to be made. During the opening remarks it is a good idea to single out one or two employees who have performed well the previous day or week and praise them in front of their peers. Such public praise is great for the morale of the crew.

Next, assign all individual routine tasks such as mowing, changing holes, and raking bunkers to specific crew members. Address them by their first names and make them feel that their tasks are important. Change the sequence of assignments frequently. If bunker raking is always the last job mentioned, the trapper will feel that bunker raking is least important, and the quality of the work may suffer. Start with the rough cutters one day and finish with the hole changers. Then turn the sequence around. If a certain worker has started earlier than usual, inform the rest of the staff what is taking place.

If a greens cutter is expected to be finished by midmorning, spell out the work that needs to be done for the rest of the day. It is best that each employee knows what is expected all day long. It is even better that all employees know what everyone is doing. Therefore, be specific in spelling out exactly what is expected. Emphasize the need to repair ball marks to the greens cutters, and remind the hole changers about the need for clean cups.

The address to the troops should not be a long one. Be precise and to the point. A long-winded chitchat quickly loses its effectiveness. Save the favorable comments from golfers to the last. That way the day begins with a positive note.

START UP THE ENGINES

While the crew receives its instructions, the mechanic or an assistant should put out all the mowers that will be needed that day and start up the machines to warm the motors. Right on the dot of the appointed hour, maybe earlier but never later, the operators mount their machines and are off. The superintendent should stick around for a while, in case there is a breakdown. While the mechanic fixes the problem, the assistant or another pinch hitter is already on the way to fill in the gap.

CHECK, CHECK, AND CHECK AGAIN

About a half hour after the greens crew has left and is busy working on the golf course, it is time for the superintendent to make the rounds. Check the greens to make sure the mowers are cutting right and the lines are straight. Check a hole location to see that it is on a level spot. Pull up on a ball washer handle to test for soap and water, and pace off the tee markers and line them up with the center of the fairway. Stop and talk to the lonely trapper or help rake the edge of a bunker. It shows you care and sets an example at the same time. By all means pick up all trash, such as napkins and soda cans, as you travel across the golf course either by foot or in a cart. Praise the jobs that are well done and assist those who need help and additional training. A wave of the hand or a smile at a passing fairway mower or rough cutter will do wonders for the morale and the attitude of the workers. It is reassuring for the workers to know that the boss likes them personally and appreciates their hard work.

Occasionally stop and converse with the golfers. Don't intrude on their game when they are obviously engrossed in concentration, but be approachable if they seem to want to talk. Listen to their concerns with undivided attention, even if you have heard their particular gripes a hundred times before. Apologize for work that may interfere with their game and explain the reasons for inconveniences. At all times present a congenial image, even when the grass is wilting and the machines are breaking down. Try to remember the names of your regular customers. It is much more pleasant to have an intelligent exchange with a person one can address by first name than an angry confrontation with a total stranger.

LOOK THE PART

Whereas old-time greenkeepers wore collared shirts and ties, and even jackets, the casual look seems to be universally acceptable today. But even when our golfers now wear blue jeans around the clubhouse and sometimes on the course, it still behooves the superintendent to look respectable. You will be treated in the manner in which you dress. If the golfers cannot tell the superintendent from the workers, one should not be surprised that respect for the position will diminish. It is not necessary to make a fashion statement; simply wearing clean and functional clothes is sufficient. Many of the outdoors stores now sell clothes that are appropriate for the superintendent. The cotton mixture material is durable and attractive. When golfing, a superintendent should look the part of a golfer, with a clean shirt and pressed trousers. For greens committee meetings, dress up in slacks and a jacket and possibly a tie.

COFFEE BREAKS AND LUNCHTIME

Few people are willing and able to work continuously without an occasional break. We all like to sit down from time to time, to relax and have a coffee or a soft drink on a hot day. Our workers are no exception. Many will take along a thermos filled with coffee or tea and take a break under a shade tree or on a bench on a tee. Others will visit the canteen on the golf course. A problem arises when all congregate at once near a halfway house or a snack bar. The overwhelming presence of a large group of workers tends to inhibit the golfers, who may bypass the canteen as a result.

Coffee breaks should be organized in such a way that they break up the greens staff into small groups that are spread out and do not interfere with the regular customers who frequent the canteen for their convenience. At lunchtime all staff members are expected to return to headquarters to take a rest and a break. While they eat their sandwiches, they socialize and establish bonds of friendship and camaraderie. Just before the conclusion of the lunch period, the superintendent or the assistant once again discusses the work assignments for the rest of the day. Mostly this is just a rehash of what was already decided in the morning, but sometimes there are changes and the staff needs to be advised of what is expected.

At some golf courses no time is allotted for coffee or lunch breaks. Workers are expected to eat and drink on the run. Before embarking on a continuous shift system without breaks, it is well to check the local labor code that governs periods of work.

CHECK, CHECK, AND CHECK AGAIN

It is only by persistent checking on the workers that one can be sure that the work is being done. It is not necessary to interfere with the work of well-trained personnel, but by visiting and checking the progress, one shows an interest that is contagious and leads to a higher-quality performance and pride in the project. In addition, many of the little things that may be overlooked by otherwise diligent workers can be noted and corrected by the timely visit of the superintendent.

THE END OF THE DAY

At least for the hourly workers, the end of the day comes by midafternoon. All the machines and the operators make their way back to the Turf Care Center. It's washup time! Fuel tanks are topped off and equipment is cleaned and put away in an orderly fashion. The floors are swept, the washrooms cleaned, and the staff room tidied.

It is best to appoint one or more persons on a weekly basis for cleanup and lockup duty. Prepare a checklist and have the person in charge make sure that everything is taken care of, put away, and locked up safely. It is time for everyone to go home except those few who are working overtime, perhaps the irrigation crew, the assistant, and almost certainly the superintendent. When all is peaceful and quiet around the shop there is a wonderful opportunity to get caught up on the administrative work. File the fertilizer or the chemical application report. Record all daily activities in a running log. Make telephone calls and check on your e-mail. Get ready for meetings with committee members or other department heads. Relax for a while with a turf magazine, and make one more swing over the golf course. Then it is time to plan the activities for tomorrow.

HIRING AND FIRING

To recruit and train greens staff is arguably the most important task in a superintendent's domain. No other factor than a hardworking greens staff has such a profound impact on the condition of the golf course. At most courses there is a nucleus of workers who are employed year-round, and seasonal employees are hired as the need dictates.

To buy a new mower or a tractor, one simply needs to obtain quotes and make a choice. To hire a new worker requires more time and deliberation. Hiring a new person has the ultimate potential of being either a disaster or a great success. Machines can be returned for warranty if they break down or are unsuitable. Workers are human beings with feelings, who at times need to be scolded or praised, encouraged or dissuaded, as well as trained to be hardworking and devoted greenkeepers. The object is to hire carefully.

The Interview

There are many ways to advertise for help, and the want ads in the daily newspapers probably offer the greatest opportunity. Don't overlook local newspapers, bulletin boards in grocery stores, and word of mouth via current employees. Some of the senior workers with roots in the community can spread the word that the golf course is hiring. Be wary of hiring family members of current staff or the sons and daughters of golf club members. Never hire workers who are difficult to fire. The greens chairman's son falls into this category, and so does the manager's daughter. Stay away from these potentially difficult situations.

It is preferable to hire people who live in the community so that they do not need to travel far to work. Give preference to persons who are active and play sports, but not necessarily golf. Such people are apt to be physically fit and won't need time off work to see doctors. The interview is conducted in a quiet place where there will be no interruptions by the phone or by people intruding. Usually there is another person present to make sure that all the questions are acceptable and that there cannot be any misunderstandings at a later time. It is not uncommon that for everyone who is interviewed, there are at least three others who have been eliminated on the basis of their resumes or as a result of telephone interviews.

Picking the right person for the right job takes an uncanny ability that is learned after much practice and many mistakes. The first impression of any new recruit can be crucial. Be prepared to give applicants a second chance if they make a poor first impression. Never hire impulsively or reject quickly. Do remember the need for all employees to fit into the golfing environment. Most suitable are those who like working hard in the outdoors and with smiles on their faces.

It is also worthwhile remembering that each new employee needs to be trained for several weeks or months. If, at the end of this training period the new recruit does not fit in and proves to be unsuitable, then a lot of time and money has been wasted and the unfortunate employee who did not measure up suffers an emotional jolt. Therefore, hire carefully. Don't make impetuous decisions. Check out the references, particularly the ones from other golf courses. It makes no sense to hire someone else's problem. Better wait till the following morning before making a decision. Once a decision has been made, act promptly and bring the new recruit aboard as quickly as possible. Discuss the rules and regulations and have the new worker sign a copy of a document explaining them, so that there will be no misunderstanding about the conditions of employment.

The Training Process

If a new worker has been hired to cut greens, have one of the experienced hands or the assistant do the training. The nursery is a good place to start. Once some fundamentals have been mastered, a training video provided by a manufacturer should be shown. Now the time has come to take the trainee to an isolated green and have him or her make the first attempt to cut this green. In fact, it may need to be cut two or three times just to gain experience. There may be other greens on which the trainee can practice. The next day is time for solo flying, with the assistant lurking behind in the bushes, keeping an anxious eye out and waiting for disaster to strike.

Similar procedures are followed for fairway and rough mowers. Make sure that there is always a senior employee present to assist and supervise. Everyone needs to learn, and we have to be patient with the newcomers. Unlikely as it may seem at first, they will eventually learn and turn into respectable workers. Some may even become superintendents at some distant future date.

Hiring an Assistant

Once word gets out that a golf course is hiring a new assistant, the resumes, the phone calls, and e-mail messages will arrive in large numbers. Select 10 to 12 whose qualifications meet the job criteria and set up the interviews at least an hour apart. Try to arrange the interviews in a concentrated time period so that a decision can be made in a methodical manner. Use the following criteria as a basis of comparison, and grade each applicant according to merit.

- *Appearance.* A favorable appearance increases the chances of success in life as well as on the job. The all-important first impression opens doors or closes opportunities.
- *Education.* Educational requirements for turf managers have increased substantially as their duties have become more technical and complex. A minimum requirement for assistants is now a two-year diploma from

a recognized turf school. A bachelor of science degree in agronomy will open more doors.

- *Experience.* Several years on a greens crew and familiarity with all operations are essential. Do not discount nine-hole experience, since workers on small golf courses have to be more versatile to do all the various tasks.
- *Health.* Good health translates into better job performance and fewer days off. That's why applicants who participate in sports are often a good choice.
- *Attitude.* Without a positive attitude, all other criteria are meaningless.
- *Maturity.* Since an assistant will be a leader, you will need a person who will command respect. The degree of maturity that is desirable for the position is a subjective decision on the part of the interviewer.
- *Golfing Ability.* While some outstanding superintendents are known to be non- golfers, in the golfing environment knowledge of and the ability to participate in golf are essential. The applicant does not need to be a single-digit handicap player, but being able to break at least 100 is a desirable objective.

Always check the references of the persons who rank highly during the interview. Then arrange for two or three candidates to be interviewed for a second time. During the second interview, working conditions and salary may be discussed in greater detail.

Before making the final decision, ask yourself the following questions:

1. Can I work and get along with this person?
2. Will this person take direction and follow instructions?
3. Does this person have leadership qualities and the ability to get along with the greens staff and the golfers?
4. Will this person represent our club respectably?

On the basis of such a thorough process, mistakes are rarely made and the new assistant will almost invariably work out well and become a valuable asset. The same process, with minor alterations, may also be used for mechanics, secretaries, and other key personnel.

Performance Reviews

Each worker and all key personnel should have a file detailing the history of employment. Part of the record-keeping process involves making timely notes in these files. Sick days, vacation periods, and lateness are all reported in the employee's docket. Any unusual occurrences in which the employee was involved should also be noted for possible future reference. In addition, once a year there should be a thorough performance review. Such a review should be in writing and starts by listing all the positive accomplishments that the employee has made during the past season. In addition, shortcomings should also be noted. Perhaps a worker has been lingering at the coffee table. Possibly a worker has developed an unpleasant attitude problem. The review is an opportunity to discuss drinking problems or antisocial behavior. By documenting such imperfections they become part of the record and serve as motivation for the worker to improve performance. The document is discussed and agreed upon, then signed by both the superintendent and the employee.

Firing

To dismiss a person for unsatisfactory performance is a dreadful deed that must be done, ruthlessly sometimes, but done just the same. While a new employee can easily be let go during the probationary period, it becomes more difficult as time progresses. Longtime workers who were excellent performers at one time but have developed bad habits should be given every opportunity to improve. When no improvement is discernible, swift and drastic action is required. A severance payment based on the period of time the worker has been employed will sweeten the sting. The reason for firing never makes sense to the person who is being let go, but if the transgressions are well documented there is very little argument and the decision is irreversible. Never keep on, for an extended period, an employee who has been fired. It is better to cut out the rot with one swift twist of the knife and let the healing process begin. A crew cannot function to its optimum performance unless all participants, workers and managers alike, work as a team to the best of their ability. The rotten apples must be removed, and swiftly.

DEALING WITH SALES AGENTS

Sales agents can be a great help to golf superintendents, especially novice superintendents who need assistance and often have few friends to call on when they take a new position. Company representatives carry a wealth of information, but one should be reminded that their primary goal is to sell product. Modern technology makes searching for information much easier, and comparing products and prices can now be done with ease. We should not become totally absorbed by price. Service, the willingness to help a customer, is usually more important than the cost of the product and is really the foremost consideration.

SUMMARY

Managing people involves building relationships with fellow human beings. It means getting work done, motivating the workers, and often delegating certain tasks to assistants. One should always remember that workers are often not very well rewarded for the work they do on the golf course, and when they perform extraordinarily well it may be because they are treated with respect and kindness by the superintendent.

19

Budgeting for Tools and Machinery

To maintain a golf course in playable condition requires a minimum number of mowers, tractors, and various other machines and utensils that are collectively known as the tools of the trade. The number of mowers may vary from one golf course to another and depends largely on the maintenance and capital budget available for the golf course. Exclusive country clubs and high-class golfing resorts often do not tolerate workers with noisy machines scurrying about while golfers play. This makes it necessary that the maintenance work be done in advance of the golfers' play and results in a substantial increase in the number of mowers, utility vehicles, and so forth. needed to do the job. Golfers at low-end golfing facilities are far more tolerant of workers on the course while golf is in progress. Thus, it can happen that a 9-hole course makes do with just one riding greens mower while an 18-hole course next door has six or more walk-behind greens mowers available. The same applies to all other mowers and cultivating equipment. Some courses have very little and perform admirably, others have a plentiful arsenal and at times achieve only mediocre results. It all depends on the budget.

THE BUDGET

In its simplest form, a budget is a forecast of expenditures for the coming year. The budget may have started as a wish list by a dreamy superintendent but has been pared down by the realities of expected revenues. In most instances a budget is based on financial records of the previous year, but at times prudent administrators may wish to start from scratch and require detailed justification for every expense that may be incurred. Superintendents need to know how many hours it takes to cut the greens and how many times the greens will be cut during a golfing season. They need to know their labor cost, how much fertilizer and pesticide is needed annually, and many other requirements that are based on accurate records of the previous year. Without good records it is well nigh impossible to arrive at correct predictions.

There are two types of budgets that turf managers need to know about: capital budgets and operating budgets.

Capital Budget Line Items

- New equipment purchases
- Major golf course repairs, such as new green and tee construction
- Installation of a new irrigation system
- A new pump house or a well
- A tree planting program

All capital expenses show up on the Balance Sheet as increases in assets. Such items will be depreciated annually based on the projected life span.

Operating Budget Line Items

- Salaries and wages
- Materials such as sand, gravel, and divot mixes
- Fertilizers and pesticides
- Repairs and parts
- Gas and oil
- Equipment rentals
- Administrative costs
- Educational expenses for the superintendent and the assistant

All operating expenses show up as line items on the Statement of Revenue and Expenses and have a direct impact on the profit or loss of the operation. Golf operations such as resorts and individually owned courses are expected to produce a profit. There is no other reason to be in business but to make a profit. Member-owned golf courses expect to break even, and the occasional loss is divided equally among all members and charged as an assessment.

LEASING VERSUS BUYING

At times a golf operation lacks resources to purchase equipment. Leasing then becomes an attractive alternative. Leasing makes it possible to acquire all new equipment at once, and at the same time dispose of decrepit old machines that require constant repairs. The monthly lease payments are a direct expense against revenue instead of the yearly depreciation that will be much less. New leased equipment comes with extended warranties and dramatically reduces the cost of repairs. Since leasing usually involves a package of several machines, the initial cost tends to be less than when they are bought outright. Leasing does involve finance charges. Those with ample resources who buy their machinery escape these charges.

TOOLS TO CUT THE GRASS

To determine the number of mowers that are needed to cut the greens on an 18-hole course, one should think in terms of running a shotgun tournament early in the morning. There may be only one hour to cut all the greens, and it will surely take three riders and at least six pedestrian mowers. For regular play two riders or four to five walkers would be sufficient. Since cutting greens is such a critical part of golf course grooming, extra units should always be on hand in case of breakdown.

For the tees, two riders will be sufficient, or double that number if walkers are used on the tees. If the golfers start early or if the pro shop runs many shotguns and crossovers, additional units may be necessary.

There are many different ways to cut fairways but no matter which way is preferred, at least two cutters are needed, and many clubs have twice that number. One should be prepared for emergencies and backup units can save the day, especially when important functions are scheduled.

All golf courses need at least one specialty mower and preferably two, for surrounds—around bunkers and tees. These hard-to-get-at areas, frequently with very steep slopes, require ingenuity and lots of experience to produce satisfactory results. Sturdy machines with good climbing ability are needed.

The roughs on most golf courses encompass the largest area and need the most machinery to get the grass cut. Consider several up-front rotary mowers and an equal number of triplex trim mowers. The rough is a never-ending job and requires lots of attention and dependable machines to stay ahead of the fast-growing grass. Include four to six rotary mowers and string trimmers to do the fine-tuning.

TOOLS TO CULTIVATE THE GRASS

Walking aerators are for tees and greens; larger, tractor-drawn machines are meant to do the fairways. Spikers and overseeders are important tools as well, to augment the aerators, and are also useful as a means of introducing seed into established turf. Verticut units are needed on greens and tees to thin the turf and are often also used to pulverize the cores after aerating. They can be employed for the same purpose on fairways. There are other means worth considering, such as core processors and drag mats or brushes. Much of the aerating equipment is used infrequently and many golf courses are contracting out such work, thus eliminating the need for investing in and maintaining expensive equipment.

Topdressers are regularly used on tees and greens, and every golf course should have at least one or two of these machines. Topdressing fairways is gaining widespread acceptance. Many courses now include fairway dressers in their inventory.

MAINTENANCE VEHICLES

The greens staff needs to get around to change holes and markers, to make irrigation repairs and fix bridges and benches, and to perform a myriad of small chores. There are some fine personnel carriers equipped with hydraulic lift boxes and extra seats. A rule of thumb dictates that almost half the greens staff needs to be mobile. Therefore, one should count on between five and ten maintenance vehicles for an 18-hole golf course.

SPRAYERS AND SPREADERS

Most operations now require computer-operated sprayers for tees and greens. Such units are usually self-propelled. If there is a necessity to spray on a regular basis, a backup unit is easy to justify. For fairways, many superintendents use a tractor to pull the heavy spray rig. Reliable fertilizer spreaders, both big and small, are needed to apply fertilizer to fairways, tees, and greens as well as in the roughs.

TRACTORS AND TRAILERS

It is easy to establish the need for four tractors to do miscellaneous work on an 18-hole course. At least one of these units should be equipped with a front-end loader, and a backhoe can be put to good use on most any golf course. It is customary for golf course tractors to be equipped with turf-type tires. Several small utility trailers are needed for construction work and cleanup chores.

TRUCKS

No golf course is complete without at least one pickup truck and most would like to have a small dump truck as well. The first is used for a runabout, both on and off the golf course. The latter becomes handy for construction work and, in northern climates, equipped with appropriate attachment, as a snowplow.

IN THE SAND TRAPS

At least two powered bunker rakes are needed to rake the 50 or so bunkers on an average 18-hole course. Where bunkers are small, they may be raked by hand. In addition, power edgers are needed to trim the bunkers.

MISCELLANEOUS EQUIPMENT

- Most courses would not do without a sod cutter, and an essential component of the sodding operation is a self-propelled roller.
- A trencher to install both irrigation and drainage pipe is high on the list of most superintendents' needs.
- A wood chipper to grind up branches and twigs.
- Leaf blowers and sweepers.
- Mower-grinders and a generator.
- Water pumps and a power washer.

SMALL TOOLS

Let a superintendent loose in a hardware store, and there would not be a shopping cart big enough for all that is needed on the golf course and in the Turf Care Center. High on the list would be several quality chain saws, some line trimmers, a couple of hedge trimmers, and too many shop tools to mention.

SPECIALTY GREENKEEPING TOOLS

Our profession requires certain specific tools that are needed to practice the ancient art of greenkeeping, and one must learn to be proficient in their use. Such skills are learned from wise old men who, in turn, learned from their predecessors. The tools that are specifically greenkeeping tools include:

- A sodding iron to lift sod and to make small repairs on tees, greens, and even fairways.
- A turf doctor, or a square-hole turf repair tool. This tool makes it possible for square pieces of thick sod to butt against each other for an instantly playable surface. Besides square, other shapes are available.

- A Levelawn used to work topdressing and aerator cores into the turf by pushing it back and forth. This tool is ideal for small areas and in-between tee markers at the end of the day.
- A dandelion rake with many small teeth to scratch the grass.
- A large square-mouthed shovel, which can be used with an educated swing, to apply topdressing to small areas.
- Whipping poles, formerly bamboo poles but now often made from fiberglass, to whip the dew off the green. They also come in handy to clean spilled grass clippings from the apron.
- A push-type sod cutter with a narrow blade that is ideal to replace the turf killed by a hydraulic spill.

AN INVENTORY

As has already been mentioned, there is wide divergence among different golf courses and the tools that they use for maintenance. It all depends on golfer expectations and the size of the budget. For an average 18-hole golf course, the following are required:

Tractors

Three towing tractors, a loader with backhoe, and a trencher with a blade

Trucks

One dump truck and a pickup truck

Utility Carts

Some carts with hydraulic dump boxes and some personnel carriers, totaling at least ten units.

Mowers

Eight walk-behind greens mowers and four riding greens mowers that are mainly used for tees.
Four fairway mowers

Four rotary mowers, three triplexes or trim mowers
Four small Toro rotary mowers and two string trimmers

Bunker Rakes

Two mechanical sand bunker rakes

Spray Rigs

One 300-gallon sprayer and one 150-gallon sprayer

Renovation Equipment

Aerators, topdressers, overseeders, a sod cutter, and a power roller

Miscellaneous Outside Equipment

Trailers, spreaders, pumps, trimmers, edgers, chain saws, etc.

Miscellaneous Inside Equipment

Power drills and saws, a welder, a pressure washer, and mower grinders

It is not uncommon for the total replacement cost of all the equipment and machinery for an 18-hole golf course to exceed one million dollars. If that seems excessive, it is well to remember that the vast majority of North American golf courses manage with much less. Big-name resorts and exclusive private country clubs that host televised tournaments are well endowed with the latest and the best. Thousands of mom-and-pop-type operations scattered across the continent manage with much less and still provide plenty of enjoyment to millions of ordinary golfers.

SUMMARY

There are stories of heroic superintendents who make do with hardly any equipment at all. The reality is that greens specifically, and grass generally, cannot be cut satisfactorily nor maintained with broken-down old mowers held together by binder clips. There comes a time when the old junk needs to be pitched out and replaced by modern machines. Golf course owners and club committee people ought to realize that a new piano in the dining room does not cut grass and that the soft rug in the grill is less important than fertilizer for the greens. There will always be clubs and courses that have their priorities mixed up, but only for a little while. Ultimately, the golfers will vote with their feet and go to where course conditioning is uppermost on the list of necessities.

20

The Turf Care Center

The maintenance facility at any golf course is the center of operations, where each day often before dawn many important decisions are being made that determine the condition of the playing surface for that day. The staff arrives and is put to work. Machinery is started up, carts are loaded with fertilizer or top-dressing, and sprayers are filled with water-wetting agents, growth retardants, and other materials. The maintenance building is a beehive of activity all day long, but especially early in the morning, with workers scurrying in all directions and gradually leaving for their assigned tasks.

In the olden days a maintenance building may have been a decrepit barn, but as the nature of golf course maintenance became more sophisticated, so too the old barn gave way to a modern facility. At many golf courses this building has become known as the "Turf Care Center." The new term was an attempt to upgrade the status of the place where we work. It was much like a facelift with words, to gain acceptance as an important element in the framework of the golfing operation. The name Turf Care Center is often displayed on the side of the building or on a prominent sign, so that both golfers and passersby can easily see and become familiar with the new name and the new image.

The maintenance compound often includes more than just one building. Pesticides, fertilizers, and other materials are usually stored separately. Sometimes the compound includes living quarters for greens staff, and there is always space for mechanical repairs and a place to wash off equipment. If at all possible the maintenance compound should also include a large turf nursery and perhaps even a tree nursery. The entire area may exceed more than 2 acres. It should be functional and architecturally appealing, or it will need to be screened from the golfers by extensive plantings of trees and shrubbery. Ideally, the maintenance compound is attractive and draws attention to the important work that is being carried out within the compound and beyond. The

Turf Care Center makes a statement: a clean, well-organized facility that leads to superior golf course conditioning.

EQUIPMENT STORAGE

Seldom is a storage building big enough to hold all the golf course equipment and machinery. When space is insufficient, there is no choice but to store some items outside, exposed to the elements. Tractor-drawn implements such as tillers, graders, wagons, trailers, and large rotary mowers can be stored outside for extended periods. Ultimately, to preserve the equipment, arrangements should be made to have a roof over all implements. Many maintenance areas include an out-of-the-way place for castoffs and relics. Unless these items are well hidden, they detract from the overall appearance of the Turf Care Center.

THE SHOP

The shop is where the mechanic makes repairs and performs maintenance on all equipment. It is like a big garage, where equipment can be raised and lowered; a place full of drills and grinding wheels with air compressors and washup solutions. There are workbenches and tool chests and bins full of parts. Vises and jacks, crowbars and sledges, saws, hammers, and wrenches, all can be found in the shop at precisely the spot where the mechanic can always find them. Such a place can easily become messy and disorganized, and it takes a dedicated mechanic with the encouragement of the superintendent to maintain a shop that is clean and tidy.

Not only are mowers and machines washed every day, they are often polished when time permits and made to look like new. Many golf course operations now lease all their equipment on a two- or three-year basis. This policy makes for sparkling machinery that not only looks good but rarely breaks down. Many superintendents take great pride in the cleanliness of their places of work, and there often is a healthy competition among superintendents in a certain area as to who can provide the cleanest facility. It always includes a shiny floor, organized benches, clear windows, and spotless washrooms

The area where mowers are sharpened is often kept separate from the mechanics' shop, because of inherent dust problems. The same problem arises when painting or spray painting is done in the mechanics' shop. For both operations, special arrangements must be made that include adequate ventilation. Local building codes, which differ from one municipality to the next, must be consulted and adhered to.

Carpentry work is associated with sawing, planing, and sanding. All of these operations are dusty and messy and should be done in an area that can be sepa-

*Washing off mowers after use is a standard maintenance practice.
Recycling the wastewater is equally common.*

rated from the rest of the maintenance building. Provisions must be made for proper ventilation. It is difficult to be a golf course superintendent and not have some knowledge of carpentry work. Apart from repairs to benches, tables, signs, and markers, there will be signs to build or shelters to repair, and bridges and railings to construct. Almost always there is a crew member on the greens staff with special aptitude for carpentry. Such a person should be encouraged and placed in charge of the woodworking details.

CLEANUP AREA

When the workers return from their tasks on the golf course, there needs to be a place where the mowers and all other equipment can be cleaned and washed. Until recently a washup area consisted of a large cement pad with a catch basin in the center. Clippings and all other residue were washed down the drain. We have become conscious of the effects that such methods may have on the environment. Clippings and bits of soil or traces of pesticide and fertilizer residues make for an undesirable mixture.

Fully aware that the accumulation of such residues can hardly be beneficial and more than likely detrimental, prudent superintendents have installed a pre-washup station, equipped with forced air. Air hoses are used to blow away all loose material that has gathered on the mowers during a day's work. Only then are the mowers washed off. Using forced air as an intermediary step drastically reduces the amount of solids in the washup water. At contemporary facilities wastewater is recycled and never discharged into drains or streams.

After the machinery has been washed, it should be dried and put away once the fuel tanks have been topped. There should always be time to clean and wash machinery, even if it means overtime. No one likes to start the next morning with a dirty machine. There may not be time for polishing and shining, but perhaps a rainy day will come along, and instead of sending workers home, consider keeping them around to shine the machines.

FUEL STORAGE

Strict rules and regulations in most municipalities now govern how fuel must be stored. In some places double-walled tanks are sufficient. Many times tanks must be stored on a cement spill pad that can take care of leakage. All tanks are covered with a roof for protection from sun and rain. Walls are left open to provide ventilation. Steel posts filled with cement, strategically placed, protect the tanks from being bumped accidentally.

PESTICIDE STORAGE

Self-contained storage units that meet all the requirements of government ordinances are now available. Although such a building is functional and serves a useful purpose, it is seldom a thing of beauty. Some superintendents may wish to construct their own buildings that can be functional, blend in architecturally with the rest of the buildings, and be in compliance with prevalent building codes.

A pesticide storage building should be ventilated 24 hours a day so that noxious vapors can be whisked away. It should be heated in the winter so that liquids won't freeze. The floor should be enveloped in cement or some other leakproof material. In case there is a spill, the liquids will be contained. The pesticide building should be kept under lock and key at all times.

The contents of the building must be kept on file and should be available to anyone who needs to see them. It is prudent to keep inventories at low levels in case of a mishap. A month's supply is in most instances quite sufficient. In spite of all the precautions, the air inside a building where pesticides are stored smells disagreeable and is probably not good for one's health. Therefore, always wear a face mask inside a pesticide building.

Drying room for work clothes. Much appreciated by workers toiling in the rain at the Seymour Golf Club, Vancouver, British Columbia.

WORKERS' LUNCHROOM AND LOCKER ROOM

On a cool day, when there is frost in the air, the staff room needs to be cozy and warm for the workers to have their coffee and eat their lunch. Such a room is a second home for members of the greens staff, a place where they change, eat, drink, and talk to their companions. There should be a place to shower and wash, especially for those who have been applying hazardous materials.

A staff room needs to be equipped with plenty of full-size lockers and with spacious tables and sturdy chairs. There should be a refrigerator, a stove, a long counter with a microwave, a toaster, and a hot plate. There should be a coffee-pot or a teakettle and cold drinks for when the weather turns warm. One should always remember the need for hardworking people to eat well and in comfort. The human engine needs plenty of fuel to perform all day.

Who should clean the staff room, the lunchroom, the shop, and the wash-rooms? In large operations one person is frequently assigned this duty on a full- or part-time basis. Smaller operations often have several of the junior staff

Storing maintenance materials at the Turf-Care Center.

take turns. The lunchroom should be cleaned and swept immediately after lunch every day. The washrooms and the floors may need sweeping and washing more than once a day. The entire maintenance area should look presentable at all times, especially the washrooms and the eating area. Cleanliness benefits all the workers whose home away from home is the Turf Care Center. It is not unusual for visitors to drop in unexpectedly, and no one wants to be embarrassed and feel a need to apologize.

THE MATERIAL STORAGE YARD

Every golf course uses a variety of materials such as sand, topsoil, gravel, wood chips, and the like. For ease of handling, these substances must be kept separate, and inventive superintendents have designed a series of bins made with sturdy walls. Since many of the materials are delivered by dump trucks that have to back into the bins, their minimum width is at least 12 feet or 4 meters. Loaders then scooped up the materials and dump them into maintenance vehicles. If the walls that separate the bins and form the back wall are flimsy, they will soon collapse. Therefore, the walls need to be constructed with heavy timbers or even large solid cement blocks that won't break or collapse. The walls must also be sufficiently high to ensure that materials do not spill into adjacent bins. Some superintendents insist on covering the storage area with a roof so that the materials will stay dry and are always ready to apply.

There is a tendency on the part of many superintendents to stockpile vast quantities of fertilizer in the belief that savings can be realized by buying in large quantities. No doubt the price per ton or per bag of fertilizer declines as the quantity increases. Be aware that spillage does occur when fertilizer is stored for long periods. Another hazard is that fertilizer may absorb moisture from the air, even in sealed bags. This process hardens the fertilizer and makes it impossible to apply. Thus, the initial savings in bulk buying can be negated very quickly after long-time storage. The best policy is to practice moderation and limit supplies to immediate needs.

Grass seed, like fertilizer, comes in bags on pallets, and spillage of some seed is almost inevitable. Not only spilled seed but also seed in bags attracts varmint such as mice and even rats. Therefore, large quantities of seed for overseeding or new seeding should be used soon after delivery. Timing the delivery of seed is important. Smaller quantities of seed can be stored in sealed metal containers that are varmintproof. In a pinch, individual bags of seed can be hung on wires attached to the rafters to avoid rodent infestation. Low temperatures for prolonged periods during the winter does not significantly affect the viability of grass seed.

THE OFFICE

The office may be just a desk with a telephone in the lunchroom, or it can be an air-conditioned room with several desks for the superintendent, the assistant, and a secretary, who may manage the office. No matter how small the operation, there is a need for some degree of record keeping, and if office equipment such as computers and calculators is used, a dust-free and ventilated environment must be provided. Although secretaries are commonplace at many golf course operations, the advent of the computer has forced many superintendents to become proficient in the use of a keyboard. In some cases a computer may have been thrust upon the superintendent when a new irrigation system was installed. A record of all operations needs to be maintained, and the days of the handwritten journal are as distant in the past as a greens mower without an engine.

ESSENTIAL RECORDS

- An inventory of all equipment and machinery must be maintained and updated yearly. It is essential that all serial numbers be recorded, as well as the year and cost of acquisition. Consider also estimating the replacement cost.

- The mechanic should record all repairs to equipment and keep an accurate inventory of parts.
- Fertilizer and pesticide applications should be recorded in great detail, such as the rate and method of application and the prevailing weather conditions. Also maintain a current inventory of all materials.
- A daily journal of all activities that are performed by the green staff should be kept current. It is easy to fall behind in recording the daily events, and it is often a good idea to assign this task to a trainee or a student to do before or after work.
- Maintain daily time sheets for every employee, and calculate the number of hours that are devoted to the various tasks and projects. Employee information should be maintained, and performance evaluations need to be recorded at least twice yearly.
- Many superintendents now maintain budget information on spreadsheets. Frequently, purchases and the resulting invoices are recorded at the Turf Care Center, making it possible for the superintendent to provide current budget information on a timely basis instead of waiting for monthly reports from the club's office.

Although software packages are available that are specifically designed for golf course use, the information can easily be stored in the file programs of most any computer. The tendency is, however, to standardized record keeping, which makes it easy to compare individual operations to national averages. It is essential, no matter what system is used, that backup copies are made on a regular basis. To lose essential information because of computer breakdown can be devastating.

In addition to record keeping, the office at the Turf Care Center normally produces monthly reports and updates on the maintenance program. Such reports and memoranda are presented at the regular meetings of the green committee. It is not unusual for the superintendent to take minutes at the greens meetings, and these should also be filed for future reference. Contributions to the golf club newsletter are generated in the maintenance office, and so are letters and all other correspondence.

MEETING ROOM

Ideally, there is a room in the maintenance building sufficiently large to accommodate the entire crew. The purpose of this room is for the superintendent to address the troops before they set out in the morning. Such a room should be well lit and provided with many chairs for all the greens staff and visitors while the superintendent or the assistant speaks. There should be a blackboard or a white board for writing and making sketches. Unless the crew is excessively large, there is no need for a sound system. A room that can be darkened is a bonus since it can be used to show slides and training videos on rainy days.

It is customary for the superintendent or a designate to address the greens staff prior to the day's beginning. Work assignments are announced for the entire day, and as a result of this meeting everyone on the greens crew will know exactly what to do as well as what everyone else on the team is doing. During this briefing there is an opportunity to single out individual staff members who have done extraordinarily good work and praise their efforts in front of their peers. Special events that will take place on the golf course, and their implications, should be mentioned. Golfers' comments received by the superintendent are passed on to the workers to boost morale and raise their spirits. At the same time, criticism of course conditions should also be shared with the crew.

When there is an opportunity, introduce visiting superintendents, traveling agronomists, and club officials to the assembled staff. It makes everyone feel important and part of the team.

ADMINISTRATION

The modern superintendent certainly has become much more of an administrator than our predecessors ever would have thought possible. We must avoid the danger of becoming bogged down in the office and losing sight of our primary function on the golf course—that is, to grow grass for golfers. Superintendents should be visible as they direct their troops. They should communicate with the golfers and listen to their comments. When golfers raise a problem, avoid giving lengthy technical explanations that all too often sound like excuses. Similarly, it is prudent to listen to the workers and, after a period of reflection, explore the problem and take appropriate action. Rarely should one act impulsively, because decisions made in haste are often regretted at a later date.

Superintendents need to become better managers of time so that they can balance the time allotted to all their responsibilities. They should improve their communication skills, not just with their golfers and workers, but also with their fellow superintendents. They need to embrace the technology of the twenty-first century that provides opportunities to communicate instantly with colleagues, not only on the North American continent, but all over the world where golf is played.

21

Greenkeeping Common Sense

You may have the best of academic credentials. You may have been tutored by a well-known mentor. You know all about pesticides, trace elements, and surfactants. You attend all the conferences and seminars that your busy schedule permits. You are respected by your committees and admired by your staff. You are a master at the lectern and skillful with your pen or the keyboard. You have reached the pinnacle of your profession and are the envy of your peers. But if you lack greenkeeping common sense, the most important ingredient of your professional persona is missing. With just a smidgen of such common sense, you will avoid the pitfalls and make it over the hurdles of everyday greenkeeping. With a whole lot more of it, your professional life will be joyful and your career extended to a ripe age.

Greenkeeping common sense is the knowledge passed on from boss to apprentice and from father to son for at least a hundred years or more. Much of what was true in the beginning is still true today, and much of what we do today is based on how we did it yesterday. Technology may have changed, but the fundamentals of greenkeeping have remained the same.

*Greenkeeping Common Sense** has been condensed into a series of aphorisms that are easy to remember because the message is so crystal clear. The following are some of the best-known ones:

- Greenkeeping is mostly housekeeping! Never mind your college degree; here, in a nutshell, is the essence of our occupation. Think of your mother hovering over your shoulder as you make your rounds on the course and you will never again pass by a piece of trash. Pick it up and

---

*Greenkeeping Common Sense is the title of a booklet written by Gertrude Farley in 1927. She was the first secretary of the National Association of Greenkeepers of America (NAGA).

put it away. Many superintendents have always been very successful housekeepers and are paid handsomely for it, especially when they succeed a messy predecessor. There may be a valid reason for some strange disease that's attacking your grass, but there is never an excuse for a messy golf course.

- Plan your work and work the plan. Make a list of projects to do, and post it in the staff room for everyone to see. Your workers will feel part of the plan and joyfully cross off every job that has been completed. As they work the list, they will remind themselves not to postpone until tomorrow what can be done today.

- Don't let the little things escape your attention. If left undone, they will come back to haunt you. These words can be attributed to Colonel Morley, the founder of our great superintendents' association, who wrote them almost a century ago—and they are still true today. More superintendents lose their jobs by forgetting the little things than for any other reason.

- More grass is lost on Sunday afternoons than any other day of the week. Remember that one the next time you plan to take the family to the beach. Grass does not take a holiday. It needs attention even on the Lord's Day.

- Never experiment on the 1st or the 18th green. If the inevitable disasters happen on the 1st green, your golfers will get a bad first impression. If they happen on the 18th green, the same golfers will retain a bad impression.

- Not all greens are equal. Some greens are more important than others. The putting green is often the first that golfers, visitors, and guests see on your course. Their impression of your operation will be based on that first glimpse of the putting green.

- You can't get a clean shave with a dull razor! Words from the philosopher-superintendent Leo Feser who lived and worked many years ago. Leo knew the importance of cutting a green perfectly. All other work is of secondary importance compared to cutting grass perfectly. Leo kept his mowers Gillete-sharp, and so should we.

- Smell your grass! Just as you stop and smell the roses, you should stop and smell your grass. Get down on your hands and knees, pick a little tuft, hold it up to the sun, and then bring it to your nose. For maximum effect, do it on the 18th green, with golfers watching from the clubhouse veranda. This is no joke. Your nostrils may be far sharper than a lens in a microscope. An old-timer once told me that if your grass smells like fish, get ready to spray.

- Don't be afraid to make mistakes. Your critics will be disarmed if you readily admit to having made a mistake. Just the same, try not to make the same mistake more than twice.

- Cover up most of your mistakes with sod, leaves, and branches. But remember there is nothing more spectacular than a grandiose mistake. A young man, a novice greenkeeper, burned all 18 of his greens with a bad chemical mix. He survived that disaster and is a highly regarded and successful superintendent today.

- If a job can't wait, just go ahead and do it. Sometimes it is better to beg for forgiveness rather than ask for permission. Procrastinators lose their jobs much more often than the doers of the world.
- Golf was never meant to be played in a swamp. In fact, golfers don't like wet feet and neither does the grass. If there are a lot of ball marks on your greens, don't blame the golfers for being negligent. More than likely it means you are watering too much.
- One rotten apple spoils the entire basket. When you wake up in the middle of the night and the first thing that comes to mind is an employee who is not performing, it's time to take action. Don't wait another day. Fire that person. Life is too short. You should not be fretting over your workers when you need sleep. Remove that rotten apple from your basket and do it now!
- When it comes to golf, you will remember the company you keep far longer than your score and the condition of the course. Therefore, choose your friends carefully and be less critical of the course you play, unless it is your own. Your most memorable golf games will often be played on obscure and poorly conditioned courses. But if you don't play the game at all, you will lack passion when it comes to greenkeeping.

During the initial euphoria of a new position, perhaps your first job, applying these truisms will help you succeed. You may even develop some of your own to guide you to perfection. But as the years progress, you may fall into a rut and your professional life will be a routine instead of an enthusiastic journey. With advancing age your memory will start to slip, bit by bit. Then is the time to refresh your memory and once more study *Greenkeeping Common Sense*. It will help to keep you on the straight and narrow and guide you to a happy retirement.

SEVEN DEADLY SINS

Superintendents rarely lose their jobs for reasons of professional inadequacies. More often than not, the reason for dismissal is a clash of personalities, a failure to communicate, or promises to perform that are not kept. In all instances the person involved may possess excellent greenkeeping skills, but lack basic abilities that are necessary to get along in life and to excel. Our mandate in this work is to deal primarily with the art and science of greenkeeping. All other endeavors are best left to experts in those particular fields.

There are seven deadly sins that golf course superintendents and green-

*Scalping grass is not only unsightly but injurious to the health of plants.
Scalping grass is one of the Deadly Sins of greenkeeping.*

keepers must not commit at any cost. They are sins against the integrity of the profession. They are sins of ignorance, of neglect, and of omission. Any one of the following sins reflects badly on the professional image of the person in charge:

1. *Fertilizer burns, anywhere on the course.* Accidents can and do happen, but there is rarely an excuse anymore for burning turf with fertilizer. Modern fertilizers contain mostly slow-release-type nitrogen, but that is no reason for failing to try these products in the nursery or in the rough first. Be completely confident that the material you are applying will not mark the greens or the tees or burn the fairways. To be totally safe, it is always best to water all fertilizers in thoroughly.
2. *Greens mower out of adjustment.* Possibly the cutting cylinder is not touching the bed knife, and the quality of cut is very poor. More often, one side of the mower cuts lower than the other. On triplex mowers it frequently happens that not all mowers cut at the same height. In all instances the result is a poorly cut green that does not putt very well.
3. *Scalped hole plugs on the green.* Dead plugs on a green can spoil the ap-

pearance of an otherwise perfect putting green. Dead plugs result when the hole changer does his or her work improperly and becomes careless. The old hole must be filled perfectly level with the surrounding putting surface. If the plug is too high, it will be scalped by the greens mower and turn brown. When the plug sinks below the putting surface, the indent will deflect putts. Sometimes a fresh plug will dry out and turn brown because of wilt. Smart hole changers carry along a water bottle to give a squirt to stressed-out plugs.

4. *A greens mower cutting into the apron.* Cutting into the apron is an ugly mistake that should not be tolerated at a professionally managed golf course. More than likely it happens on the cleanup pass, when an operator becomes careless and moves too quickly. At times it happens when a novice operator does not lift the mower in time and cuts into the apron.

5. *Letting new sod die.* Fresh sod from a nursery, newly laid, is the culmination of a construction job well done. The shapes and the alterations have been carried out to perfection. The new sod, rolled and staked and marked as Ground under Repair (GUR), is the icing on the cake. Three days later it is brown and dead for lack of water because someone just forgot. Such advertising of a greenkeeper's incompetence is definitely a deadly sin.

6. *Killing a green with kindness.* It happens when topdressing, especially sand, is matted in on a hot afternoon with the green under drought stress. Invariably this results in the death of the turf. It can also happen when a green is aerated under similar conditions. Applying phytotoxic sprays such as Diazinon and liquid fertilizers, all mixed together, will surely kill even the healthiest green.

7. *A messy golf course* strewn with napkins, paper cups, and beer cans. There may be an excuse for brown grass; there is never an excuse for a messy, untidy golf course. Good greenkeeping equals good housekeeping. The superintendent should always set the example when it comes to housekeeping. Stop and pick up the litter. Collect it in your cart and dispose of it in the waste containers. Show the golfers and the workers that cleanliness is next to godliness. Remember also that invariably a messy maintenance building is indicative of conditions on the golf course. It is almost impossible to maintain a clean golf course from a dirty old barn. A messy golf course is possibly the worst deadly sin, because it is totally preventable.

Some superintendents have posted the deadly sins on the bulletin board in the Turf Care Center for everyone to see. Employees are reminded every day about the deadly sins. They check on their co-workers, and if someone commits a deadly sin, they'll pounce on that worker.

THE SEVEN VENIAL SINS

Besides the seven deadly sins there are seven venial sins. These are sins of a less serious nature, but sins just the same, and they should be avoided:

1. Smelly ball washers are all too common, even on some of the finest golf courses. While it is practically impossible to check all the ball washers all the time, a program should be in place to thoroughly clean the ball washers. Soap and water will do just fine.

2. Dirty putting cups ruin the look of an otherwise perfect green. After sinking a putt, retrieving the ball from a filthy cup is a most unpleasant experience. One does not need to be squeamish to resent sticking a hand into a dirty hole. The cup changer, in his or her daily routine, should carry along a moist sponge and use it to wipe off the inside of the cup. In addition, all cups should be changed several times during a golfing season. For special events a squeaky clean cup is mandatory.

3. Golfers take pride in their golf course and like to do their part in keeping it in fine shape. We must give them that opportunity, and we do it by placing divot boxes on the tees, especially the tees of the par 3 holes. While many golfers for whatever reason do not make use of the divot mix, many more do. To find an empty divot box on a tee is a black mark against the greenkeeper.

4. Golfers will blame anything for their poor scores, including mistakes committed by the greenkeeper. High on their list is a set of imperfectly adjusted tee blocks. It seems that when tee blocks are not set up straight for the middle of the fairway, the superintendent gets blamed for a hook or a slice. On par 3 holes, golfers miss the green because the markers are pointing the wrong way. Superintendents should scrutinize the work of their greens staff frequently. A daily routine tends to become monotonous, and mistakes are often the result.

5. All too often when a mechanical bunker raker leaves the sand trap, the operator forgets to wipe out the tracks. The result is an ugly pile of sand mixed with debris and at times dragged onto the turf. This venial sin borders on being a deadly sin. In addition to erasing the tracks, operators should also make sure that there are a sufficient number of rakes in each bunker. No rakes in the bunker is an unforgivable oversight; so are rakes with broken handles and missing teeth.

6. Torn flags are unsightly. It is best to start the new season with new flags and change them at least once more during the season. Keep additional flags on hand in case some are vandalized. A complete set of flagsticks, pins, and tee markers should always be on hand for emergencies. Thieves in the night have been known to steal all of those items. Be prepared.

7. Long grass around the bases of trees is an advertisement of incompetence. Long grass never looks more sloppy than when it is allowed to grow in profusion around trees, signs, and fence posts. Such lack of trimming is unforgivable even on the lowest of the low-budget courses. Time must be found to correct this untidiness. It can be done by occasional applications of Roundup, a grass killer, or simply by regular trimming. The latter is the most expensive method but probably the most appealing.

The seven deadly sins are serious omissions that must not be allowed to last or to recur on any golf course. Once a deadly sin has been committed, it usually takes some time to take corrective actions. Venial sins, on the other hand, can be quickly corrected. The lists of sins should be prominently displayed in the maintenance building for everyone to see. Members of the greens staff and the assistant should measure their course against all 14 sins committed against the art of greenkeeping.

THE SUPER SUPERS

In our travels all over the world and in visits with colleagues from many different countries, we have noticed that some superintendents stand head and shoulders above all the rest. These individuals possess special qualities that make them stand out. We have studied these individuals and prepared a list of the characteristics that all invariably have in common. These are the Super Supers and the following are their earmarks:

- The best superintendents in the world are invariably great greenkeepers. They can grow grass where there was none before. Their greens are strong and not anemic. There is grass on their tees, and their fairways are healthy.
- They are knowledgeable and well educated and remain that way by constantly expanding their wealth of know-how and information.
- They maintain the best possible golf courses within the limits of their budgets. They don't gripe about the lack of funds, but instead find ways of getting the job done anyway.
- They are environmentalists. They love the animal and plant life on their golf courses and do everything in their power to enhance and promote it. They share the concerns of their fellow citizens and use pesticides only as a last resort.
- They are dedicated and hard workers, always up early in the morning and on the job till the last employee leaves, and frequently come back

in the evening or late at night. They work hard and play when there is time. They play golf respectably.

- They have an excellent staff, knowledgeable and well trained, who work with the superintendent, not for the superintendent.
- They are enthusiastic about their work, and they inspire their assistants to follow in their footsteps. They encourage all to excel at whatever they are doing.
- They are effective communicators. They instruct their staff by both the written and the spoken word. They make information available to their golfers regularly, and inform through newsletters and at meetings. They patiently listen to golfer complaints and they respond to letters and always return phone calls and e-mail messages.
- They look the part and they exhibit a professional image. They wear jackets when it is appropriate, and they look distinguished and neatly dressed at all times.
- The Super Supers are active professionally. They serve in their professional associations. They attend meetings, conferences, and seminars. They stand up and speak when called upon.

22

Job Descriptions

GOLF COURSE SUPERINTENDENT

Function

A superintendent's primary function is to maintain the golf course at a level that satisfies the golfers and to keep all expenses within the limits of an operating budget. A golf course superintendent is first and foremost a greenkeeper, who can grow grass where there was none before and who can prepare a playing surface that meets the demands of the game. A superintendent is proficient at managing people and machinery and in getting the job done effectively. Above all, a superintendent is aware that the land that constitutes the golf course is a living habitat for all creatures and that it must be conserved for future generations.

Qualifications

The credentials of a superintendent are a combination of academic knowledge, technical training, and practical experience. Whereas there are some very successful superintendents with less than a high school diploma, it is now generally agreed that a postsecondary diploma from an accredited turfgrass school is a minimum requirement. There are many superintendents who have bachelor's and master's degrees in turfgrass science. Specific technical training is learned in seminars and specialized short courses. Experience is garnered under the tutelage of an established master in the art of greenkeeping. Such practical experience is passed on from old-timer to novice and often includes secrets that can be learned only on the job.

Areas of Responsibility

Highest on the list of responsibilities is the golf course, as the top priority in a superintendent's daily duties. The greens must be visually checked, as well as the tees and the fairways. Diseases, insect pests, and weeds must be kept under control. The grass must be cut regularly and to the satisfaction of the golfers, the bunkers raked, and the markers and pins changed in such a manner as to provide a pleasurable golfing experience.

With the heat of summer come the many pests that attack the grass. A superintendent needs to be vigilant to ensure the survival of the turf. During the busy golfing season, greenkeeping is a daylong occupation that rarely knows time off. Golf course maintenance is a service industry that requires a commitment on the part of the superintendent to serve and satisfy the customers.

In addition to the golf course, many superintendents look after the clubhouse grounds, swimming pools, and tennis courts. At the end of a busy day, there are administrative duties such as record keeping and report writing, chores that need to be taken care of. There are meetings to attend with the manager and the golf professional, as well as the green committee. The superintendent also has to deal with commercial suppliers of materials and equipment.

Deploying a large number of workers efficiently is essential to get the work done. The greens staff is hired very carefully, trained thoroughly, and their performance checked repeatedly. The work for the staff must be scheduled to keep everyone busy all the time. Some responsibilities can and should be delegated to the assistant. Golf course workers, under the direction of the superintendent and the assistant, must be well motivated, work diligently, and be trained to be considerate to the golfers. Workers who do not measure up to the accepted standards must be dealt with promptly and effectively.

Recently the superintendent's position has taken on an extra dimension: to present an image in the community of being a friend and a steward of the environment. Present-day superintendents demonstrate through their actions that they care about the land they have been entrusted with. They are, in essence, and at all times, the ultimate conservationists.

The superintendent presents a congenial image, neatly dressed and groomed, and is always willing to answer questions and to share knowledge in a professional manner. A superintendent is a somewhat competent golfer who plays regularly and fraternizes with neighboring colleagues.

Specific Skills That Are Required

A superintendent should know how to operate all machinery and equipment in the maintenance building and be capable of teaching this skill to others. A thorough knowledge of pesticides and fertilizers is essential. Being familiar with the irrigation system is paramount, since grass will not survive without water.

A thorough understanding of the needs of the golfers and the demands of the game is essential. A superintendent should know the rules of golf as they pertain to the maintenance of the course. A superintendent should play golf regularly and have an established handicap.

In addition to being a competent greenkeeper, a superintendent needs to possess administrative skills to deal with the business aspects of golf course management. From time to time a golf course superintendent is expected to address meetings and to present reports and budgets. The contemporary superintendent understands and knows how to use computers.

Professional Development

No one can operate in a vacuum, and least of all a superintendent in today's rapidly changing world of golf. Superintendents must belong to and participate in regional, national, and international professional associations. Attendance at seminars, conferences, and field days at universities where turfgrass research is conducted is essential. A superintendent should visit with colleagues to compare maintenance practices and to play golf.

A superintendent needs to attend refresher courses in turfgrass management and constantly learn new computer skills. In their formative years, superintendents should attend a Dale Carnegie course or belong to the Toastmasters organization. Participation in community groups is highly recommended.

ASSISTANT GOLF COURSE SUPERINTENDENT

Function

The function of an assistant golf course superintendent is to assist the superintendent in all areas of responsibility with regard to the maintenance of the golf course. The assistant should at all times function as an extra set of eyes, ears, and legs for the superintendent. The ultimate objective of both the superintendent and the assistant is to provide the best possible playing conditions within the limits of the operating budget.

Education

- A postsecondary degree in turfgrass science or a related field or, at a minimum, a diploma in turfgrass maintenance from an accredited institution
- A valid pesticide license, where applicable
- Attendance at a human relations course such as a Dale Carnegie program or membership in the Toastmasters organization

- Membership in professional associations
- Continuing education by attendance at turfgrass conferences and seminars
- A valid operator's license (if applicable) for chain saws, string trimmers, and other such tools

Areas of Expertise

- Total familiarity with the operation of the pump house and the irrigation system. Ability to troubleshoot and repair all parts of the system.
- Total familiarity with the chemicals and fertilizers used in turfgrass maintenance, knowledge of rates of application and calibration of sprayers, etc.
- Recognition of the correct mower settings and mowing patterns, ability to make adjustments to cutting heights and cutting quality.
- Ability to pick the right person for the job, to select suitable people for particular jobs, and to motivate the staff.
- Knowledge of the game of golf and the rules of golf, and ability to play golf reasonably well.
- Ability to write reports and attend meetings at intervals. Confident and conversant with all areas of golf.
- Ability to handle expertly most pieces of equipment required for maintenance.
- In conduct and deportment, should at all times reflect the image the greens staff is expected to project.

Responsibilities

- The hiring and firing of the greens staff is the primary responsibility of the superintendent. The assistant may be involved in the preliminary screening of new staff and reports on the performance of new staff to the superintendent.
- The assistant arrives at work well before the majority of the greens staff, not only to set an example, but also to take care of early emergencies.
- The assistant meets with the superintendent to plan the work for the day.
- Work assignments and daily tasks are handed out by the assistant and the superintendent to individual members of the greens staff, most often in a joint session.
- The assistant and the mechanic help with getting machinery started and getting work going expediently.
- When not involved in an actual project, the assistant will go out on the golf course and check on the performance of the crew as well as the condition of the course and the turf.

- The assistant will help the crew members and, by example, show how the work needs to be done to perfection.
- The assistant trains new crew members in the operation of machinery and various other tasks on the golf course.
- The assistant, with the superintendent, helps organize the crew in such a manner that all workers are busy and that the work gets done efficiently.
- The assistant never hesitates to participate physically in the work on the course.
- While working with the crew, the assistant keeps an eye on the grass, checks for disease, weeds, insects, and any other imperfections, and reports all findings to the superintendent.
- The assistant should converse intelligently with golfers and members on and off the course.
- The assistant should habitually check on inventories to ensure that materials and supplies are available when needed.
- The assistant must possess some business acumen and computer literacy in order to carry out various office tasks related to budgeting and accounts payable. Specifically, the assistant should be able to work with spreadsheet and word processing programs.

GOLF COURSE MECHANIC

Qualifications

In addition to several years of work experience, the golf course mechanic should be:

- Licensed,
- Certified via training programs, or
- Possess a diploma in mechanics from a recognized institution.

Continuing education by attendance at seminars, workshops, or training programs is mandatory. The golf club should provide the mechanic with his or her own set of tools, and the mechanic must have a valid driver's license.

Expertise

The golf course mechanic should be competent in the following fields:

- Small engine repairs
- Tractor engine repairs (gas and diesel)

- Hydraulics
- Welding
- Electronics
- Grinding and sharpening of reels and bed knives and operation of most equipment required for golf course maintenance

Responsibilities

The mechanic is responsible for:

- Preventative maintenance, repairs, and setup of all equipment and licensed vehicles used by the crew at the Turf Care Center
- Maintaining an adequate inventory of parts and supplies
- Keeping the shop in a clean and respectable condition
- Overseeing the assistant mechanic

The mechanic reports directly to the superintendent or to the assistant superintendent. Some overtime may be necessary in addition to the normal 40-hour workweek.

GOLF COURSE SPRAY TECHNICIAN

Function

The spray technician works under the supervision of the superintendent and the assistant. The main areas of responsibility are the application of pesticides and scouting for pest problems. The spray technician also participates in regular maintenance duties when time permits.

Education

The spray technician should have a strong background in disease identification, insect technology, weed identification, and nutrient deficiencies as they apply to turfgrass maintenance.

- The spray technician must either be working toward or already have a postsecondary education (degree or diploma) from a reputable institution.
- A valid Pesticide Applicator's License is a necessity.

- Continuing education by attendance at seminars and conferences related to spraying and/or pest control for golf courses is also mandatory.

Areas of Expertise

- Broad knowledge in the identification and life cycle of the diseases, weeds, and insects that invade fine turf
- Familiarity with pesticides and their phytotoxic characteristics
- Operation and calibration of all equipment used for spraying and fertilizing
- Knowledge of pesticides and fertilizers and their mode of action, and residual effects

Responsibilities

- A total commitment to safety precautions and measures related to pesticides and spraying, not only for oneself, but for others.
- Regularly checking the golf course for pest- and nutrition-related problems, and reporting all findings to the superintendent or the assistant.
- All spraying and fertilizer operations on the golf course under the direction of the superintendent or assistant superintendent.
- Filing accurate reports and records of all operations, which include application rates, spreader settings, weather conditions, pest symptoms, and quantities of materials used.
- Keeping an up-to-date and accurate inventory of all pesticides and fertilizers, and reporting any shortfall to the superintendent or the assistant.
- Performing all spray operations in a completely safe manner, preferably ahead of the golfers.
- At times, becoming involved in the application of wetting agents, biostimulants, and growth regulators.

IRRIGATION SPECIALIST

Function

The irrigation specialist works under the supervision of the superintendent and the assistant. The prime responsibility is the operation and repair of, and at times, making additions to, the irrigation system. The objective of the irrigation specialist is to ensure that the system is totally functional any time irrigation is needed.

Education

- Must be either working toward or already have a postsecondary education (degree or diploma) from a reputable school related to turfgrass maintenance
- Sufficient on-the-job training to troubleshoot, repair, and operate all parts of the irrigation system
- Continuing education by attendance at seminars and conferences related to golf course irrigation

Areas of Expertise

- Basic knowledge of hydraulics relating to volume, pressure, and flow of water
- Knowledge of soil/water relationships and turfgrass water requirements
- Total familiarity with the pumping stations as related to golf course irrigation
- Ability to repair and operate all types of sprinkler heads, piping networks, and control systems
- Basic knowledge of design and installation of irrigation systems
- Knowledge of electronics and computers required to operate and repair modern irrigation system components
- Ability to recognize dead or dying turf caused by wilt

Responsibilities

The irrigation specialist is responsible for:

- Ensuring that the irrigation system is totally functional when it is needed
- Troubleshooting and repairing all parts of the system as needed
- Checking the turf for drought stress symptoms, taking immediate remedial actions
- Making recommendations to the superintendent on the programming and scheduling of nightly irrigation
- Adding and/or changing the design of the current system when required to do so by the superintendent
- Ensuring that all heads are not only turning on, but functioning properly and distributing water evenly

- Ensuring that all heads and repaired areas are level with the surrounding turf so they do not interfere with golf

GARDENER

Function

The gardener works under the supervision of the superintendent and the assistant. The gardener is responsible for the maintenance of the flower beds, clubhouse lawns, parking lots, and halfway house. Being a gardener is a very important position since people's first impressions are made when arriving at the clubhouse.

Education

- A postsecondary education (degree or diploma) from a reputable school related to horticulture
- A valid pesticide license and other applicable permits
- Continuing education by attendance at horticulture-related seminars and conferences

Areas of Expertise

- Broad knowledge of annuals, perennials, shrubs, trees, and other woody plants, including size, shape, time of flowering, seasonal colors, hardiness, and planting locations
- Familiarity with common weeds, diseases, and insects
- Operation of equipment necessary to prepare/maintain flower beds and lawns
- Operation and programming of irrigation controllers
- Knowledge of pesticides and fertilizers pertaining to landscape plants

Responsibilities

- In discussion with the superintendent, determining the annuals and perennials required for the flower beds
- Keeping the clubhouse clean and tidy, especially when plants are dormant
- Preparing the beds for planting of annuals

Fall

- Removing annuals killed by frosts
- Cleaning up the beds and preparing them for spring flowering bulb plantings
- Planting of spring flowering bulbs
- Final winterizing of flower beds

GENERAL GREENS WORKER

Function

A general greens worker works under the supervision of the superintendent, the assistant superintendent, or any other designated person. The greens worker is responsible for the maintenance of the golf course grounds, which includes the cutting of various areas as well as topdressing, aerifying, divoting, and any other general maintenance work that may be required.

Education

- A general greens worker should have some high school education and a valid driver's license.
- It is necessary for the worker to be able to write brief messages and to follow written instructions.

Areas of Expertise

- Drive a maintenance vehicle.
- Drive a tractor.
- Operate several different types of mowers.
- Operate string trimmers.

Responsibilities

- Work proficiently under the direction of supervisors, and complete assigned tasks within given time limits.
- Work safely and take care of machinery and tools.
- At the conclusion of the work period, clean up tools and equipment.
- The occasional application of pesticides is part of the duties of a general greens worker.

Index

Aeration, 95–107
    machines for, 99, 101–102, 201, 205
    of fairways, 104–105
    of greens, 95
    of tees, 102–103
    of temporary greens, 17
    shatter core, 100
    timing of, 96–98
Aerial photos, 135
Ammonium nitrate, 78
Ammonium sulfate, 78
Annuals, 185–186
Aprons, 17, 33, 38, 69, 221
Artificial Turf, 23
Asphalt pathways, 164–165
Assistant GC superintendent, 194–195,
    227–229

Backpack sprayers, 109
Back yard putting greens, 22–23
Ball marks, 23
Ball washers, 122
Benches, 121
Bentgrass turf, 148
Bermuda turf, 145–147
Bluegrass turf, 36
Bonemeal, 77, 185
Brillion seeders, 148
Budgets, 199–206
    capital, 200
    operating, 200
Bulbs, flowering, 185
Bunker rakes
Bunkers, 51–65
    drainage of, 54–55
    edging, 64–65
    grass, 61
    pot, 57, 58
    raking, 61–64
    reason for , 51
    renovation, 56
    revetted, 58–60
    waste, 61–62

Catch basins, 140
Cement paths, 164
Clean-up area, 209
Clean-up pass, 4, 6, 10
Clippings
    diagnosis, 15
    disposal, 40, 170, 210
    distribution in basket, 7, 15, 16
Collars, 17, 33, 38, 69, 221
Compaction, 95–107
Composting, 40, 102, 103
Core disposal, 102–103
Course setup, 119–129
Cup puller, 126–129
Curbs on paths, 165
Cutting
    fairways, 33–42
    greens, 1–24
    rough, 43–49
    sod, 151–153
    tees, 26–29
Cyclone spreaders, 81,82, 148

Dew removal, 9, 10, 40
Divots, 92, 93
Dragging, 40,41
Drainage, 131–141
    bunkers, 139
    fairways, 139
    french drains, 139
    greens, 135–137
    roughs, 139
    surface, 131–134
    sub surface, 134, 135
    tees, 138

Fairways, 33–42
    aerating, 104–105
    area, 43
    cutting, 34, 36–40
    drainage, 139
    power carts on, 161
    top dressing, 90
    types of grass, 35

Fertilizers, 77–84
  application of, 81
  burning, 78,79
  for flower beds, 184
  liquid, 80
  records, 214
  for seeding, 149
  synthetic, 79
Fescue, 47, 145
Filter cloth, 54–56
Flags and flagsticks, 119–129
Flowers, 184–186
Flymo mower, 90
Forward tees, 29
French drains, 139
Fuel Storage, 210
Fungi, 114

Garden, 183–187
Ginkgo tree, 174
Golf carts, 157–156
Gravel, 140, 165
Grass, 1–236
Greenhouse, 187
Greenkeeping, 217–219
Greens, 1–24
  backyard, 22–23
  double, 21–22
  fast, 17–18
  sand, 22
  slow, 19
  temporary, 20–21
Greens workers, 234
Ground Under Repair (GUR), 169–171

Hazards, 167–169
Hazard stakes, 167–171
Holes
  changing, 125–129
  placement, 123–125
  cutter, 126
Hollow tyne coring, 98–99
Hydraulic spills, 12–15
Hydroject, 100–101

Impact hole cutters, 127
Integrated Pest Management IPM, 115
Interceptor drains, 135
Iron, 80–81
Irrigation, 67–76
  leak repair, 72–74
  localized Dry Spot (LDS), 70–71
  over watering, 68

sprinklers, 67–68
systems, 71–72
water source, 75–76
winterizing, 74–75

Kikuyu grass, 35
Kitty litter, 12

Ladies day, 120
Landscaping, 183–187
Leasing, 200
Levelawn, 103, 134

Maintenance facility, 207–215
Material storage yard, 212
Mechanics, 229–230
Meeting room, 214–215
Minitines, 100
Mowers
  cleanup, 209
  flymo, 90
  history, 3
  riding, 1–4, 10, 34
  sharpening 1–2
  triplex, 4, 33–35
  walk behind, 6
Mulching, 148

Naturalized rough, 47–49
Nitrogen, 78–79

Obstructions, 171
Office, 213
Out-of-bounds, 168–169
Overlap, 3–5

Paths, 157–166
Pattern cutting, 34
Paving stones, 165
Pea gravel, 140
Perennials, 185–186
Permanent markers, 122
Pesticides, 109 117
  on backyard greens, 23
  rate of application, 110–111
  records, 214
  regulations, 112
  safety, 109–117
  spray technician, 230
  storage, 210
Phosphorous, 77–79
Photo areas, 186
Ph, 83

Pindicator flags, 124
Plugs, 126
Poa annua, 22, 35, 96, 100, 160
Poa trivialis, 146
Potassium, 78
Power carts, 161–166
Pumphouse, 74
Putting greens, 1–23

Record keeping, 213–214
Revetting bunkers, 58–60
Riding greensmowers, 3–5, 10,
Rollers, 17, 152–155
Roughs, 43–49
Rules of golf, 167–172
Ryegrass, 144, 146

Safety issues, 112
Sales agents, 196
Sand, 51–65, 86
Seeding, 143–150
    application, 145, 148
    the first cut, 149–150
    germination, 144
    hydroseeding, 150
    overseeding, 145
    rates, 145–146
    sizes, 144
    soil temperatures, 144
Shop buildings, 207–209
Shrubs, 183–184
Signs, 122, 161
Sins
    Deadly, 219–221
    Venial, 222–223
Sodding, 14–15, 132, 151–153
Sodding knife, 73, 203
Soil sampling, 82
Spiking, 105–106
Spraying, 109–117
    calibration, 110–111
    equipment, 110
    technicians, 230–231
    timing, 113–114
Spreaders, 81, 202
Sprigging, 153–154
Sprinklers, 67–68
Staff Members, 189–197
    appearance, 194
    breaks, 191
    golfing, 195
    hiring and firing, 192–193
    lunchroom, 211

performance review, 195–196
    records, 214
    staff meetings, 214–215
    training, 194
Stairs, 31
Steel mats, 88
Stimpmeter, 17–18
Stockings, 138
String trimmers, 46–47
'Sunday afternoon disease', 116
Superintendents, 215
    cart decisions, 161–162
    appearance, 191
    job description, 225–227
    special qualities 223
    staff management, 190–191
Syringing, 69, 149

Tees, 25–31
    area, 26
    aeration, 102
    cutting, 25–31
    draining, 138
    edging, 28
    first, 26
    forward, 29
    furniture, 121–122
    markers, 119–121
    permanent markers, 123
    practice range, 29
    repairing, 30–31
    rectangular, 27
    topdressing, 89
    traffic, 159
Teflon tape, 73
Temperature for seeding, 144
Thermal blankets, 144
Tile drainage, 54,135–137
Tools, 201–205
Topdressing, 85–93
    after aeration
    application of, 87–88
    equipment for, 89, 91
    on fairways, 90–91
    material, 85
    mixes, 87
    of sand, 86
    on sod, 91
    on tees, 89
    thickness, 86
Tractors, 202, 204
Traffic, 157–166
Training, 194

Trees, 173–182
  leaves, 180
  nursery, 176
  maintenance, 179
  planting program, 175–178
  selection, 174
  spade, 178
Trenching, 136
Triplex mowers, 4, 33, 37
Triplex ring, 10–11
Turf Care Center, 207–215
Turf doctor, 203

Urea formaldehyde, 79

Verticutting, 106–107
Vertidrain, 101–102

Walk-behind mower, 6
Washroom, 158
Water, 67–76
Whipping, 9
Wildflowers, 47–49
Winterizing, 74–75

About the Authors

Michael Bavier grew up in the small Minnesota town of Wilmar. He developed his love for golf as a caddie at the Wilmar Golf Club and later worked on the grounds crew while attending high school. After graduating from Pennsylvania State College, he did his internship under Warren Bidwell at the Olympia Fields Golf Club in Illinois.

In 1964 he began serving his country as a proud member of the U.S. Marines. Later he became Assistant Superintendent at the Oak Ridge Country Club in Hopkins, Minnesota, and soon after served as Superintendent for four years at the Calumet Country Club in Homewood, Illinois. For the past 37 years he has been Superintendent at the Inverness Golf Club near Chicago.

Michael has always been active professionally, serving as director, secretary, and president of the Mid West Golf Course Superintendents Association. In 1981 he was elected President of the Golf Course Superintendents Association of America (GCSAA). One of his proudest moments came when the GCSAA honored him with the Distinguished Service Award.

To this day he is active in the Musser Foundation, an organization that raises money for students in their final year of a doctorate program in a turf-related field. Together with his friend and colleague Gordon Witteveen, he is a frequent speaker on the Turf Conference Tour both in North America and overseas, often presenting "The Magic of Greenkeeping" seminar to wide-ranging audiences.

Gordon Witteveen was born in the Netherlands and attended the Ontario Agricultural College in Guelph, Ontario. During summer vacations he developed a love for golf while working at the Noranda Mines Golf Club in the province of Quebec. Upon graduation from college, he became Superintendent at the Highland Country Club near London, Ontario, and after three years moved on to Toronto as Superintendent at the former Northwood Country Club for 12 years. In 1973 he became Superintendent at the 45-hole Board of Trade course in the village of Woodbridge near Toronto, from where he retired in 1999. Presently, Gordon and his wife, Marilyn, own and operate a 11-hole golf course near Brantford, Ontario.

Gordon Witteveen helped start the Canadian Golf Superintendents Association in 1965 and served as that association's first secretary. He initiated *The Green Master* magazine and served as its editor for five years. In 1970 he was

President of the Canadian group. He has also served on the Board of Directors of GCSAA.

Gordon is well known for his many presentations at turfgrass meetings all over the world. The best known is "25 Years of Mistakes." In addition to *Practical Golf Course Maintenance,* he wrote *A Century of Greenkeeping* for the Ontario Superintendents Association and was the co-author of *Keepers of the Green* for the GCSAA. He writes a monthly commentary for *Turfnet* magazine and is a past Leo Feser Award winner of *Golf Course Management* magazine. In 2004, Witteveen received the Distinguished Service Award from the GCSAA.

Michael Bavier

Gordon Witteveen

Harris County Public Library, Houston, TX